PROBLEMS OF ETHNICITY IN THE NORTH-EAST INDIA

Other books from Asha Bharati

- Illegal Migration From Bangladesh
- India and Central Asia : Classical to Contemporary Periods

About the Editor

B.B. Kumar, (b.1941), M.Sc. (Chemistry), M.Sc. (Anthropology), M.A. (Hindi), Ph.D. (Anthropology), former Principal, Sao Chang Government College, Tuensang (Nagaland) and Science College, Kohima, was member, Executive Council, Academic Council, University Court, College Development Council, Examination Committee, School Board of Physical Sciences and other numerous Committees of the North-Eastern Hill University, Shillong (India). He was Chairman, Hindi Board of Studies, and member, Board of Studies, of 'Science for Rural Development', Gandhigram Rural University, Tamil Nadu. He remained associated with a large number of NGOs as President, Vice-President, Secretary and member. He was founder Secretary of Nagaland Bhasha Parishad and Thinkers Forum, Nagaland and Governing Body member of the Nagaland Peace Centre, the organization founded by Jai Prakash Narayan. Presently, he is Secretary, Astha Bharati, New Delhi, and member, Governing Body of India Central Asia Foundation, New Delhi.

Dr. Kumar has written/edited/co-authored 136 books and more than 100 papers. Presently, he is editing Quarterly journals, *Dialogue* (English) and *Chintan-Srijan* (Hindi), both published from Delhi.

PROBLEMS OF
ETHNICITY IN THE NORTH-EAST INDIA

Editor
Dr. B.B. Kumar

Published for
ASTHA BHARATI, DELHI
By
CONCEPT PUBLISHING COMPANY, NEW DELHI-110059

Cataloging in Publication Data—DK
Courtesy: D.K. Agencies (P) Ltd. <docinfo@dkagencies.com>

Seminar on Problems of Ethnicity in the North-East India (2006 : New Delhi, India)
Problems of ethnicity in the North-east India / editor, B.B. Kumar.
p. cm.
Papers presented at the Seminar on Problems of Ethnicity in the North-East India, held at New Delhi during 6-7 July 2006.
Includes bibliographical references.
Includes index.
ISBN-13: 9788180694646
ISBN-10: 818069464X

1. Ethnicity—Political aspects—India, Northeastern— Congresses. 2. Insurgency—India, Northeastern— Congresses. 3. Ethnic conflict—India, Northeastern— Congresses. I. Kumar, B. B. (Braj Bihari), 1941- II. Title.

DDC 305.800 954 1 22

ISBN : 13-978-81-8069-464-6
ISBN : 10-81-8069-464-X

First Published 2007

Published and Printed by
Ashok Kumar Mittal
Concept Publishing Company
A/15-16, Commercial Block, Mohan Garden
New Delhi-110059 (India)

Phones : 25351460, 25351794
Fax : 091-11-25357103
Email : publishing@conceptpub.com

Preface

During over hundred years of inter-face with the British colonial rule in the North-East India divisive trends among various groups on basis of territory, religion, etc., were encouraged and sharpened. The elite driven ethnicity and identity formation got impetus after the creation of Nagaland due to the benefits flowing with it. It led to an obsession with one's ethnicity and connected demands for territorial and political protection and identifications. Result was recognition of such sentiments in formation of a number of states like Nagaland, Mizoram, Meghalaya, Manipur and a host of Autonomous District Councils.

However, the appetite for ethnicity related demands, even new formations, has not declined. Such demands are rooted in a sense of security related to one's land and people. It has, however, led to conflicting demands, overlapping claims and even resort to passage of arms to reinforce one's claims. A stage has reached where neighbours do not communicate with each other and have hostile relations resulting in mutual suspicious and even bloodshed.

The North-East had the state of Assam and the Princely states of Manipur and Tripura when the freedom dawned on August 15, 1947. Today, the region has seven states of Assam, Arunachal Pradesh, Manipur, Meghalaya, Mizoram, Nagaland and Tripura. We had only four Autonomous District Councils in Assam under Sixth Schedule of the Constitution. Today, we have more than a dozen of the ADCs and Tribal Councils in the region. Autonomy demands started in the Naga Hills district of Assam. And the Naga National Council was the only insurgent outfit in the region. Nagas got their state in 1963. The problem did not end. Nagaland was replicated elsewhere; the insurgent outfits have multiplied. The problem of ethnicity in the region defies solution. The North-East continues to suffer from insurgency and ethnic problem of various dimensions. Astha Bharati, Delhi, organized a seminar on

"Problems of Ethnicity in the North-East India" in July 2006 to deliberate on the same. The senior educationists, administrators, journalists and others, including former Vice-Chancellors, former M.P., University Professors, former Home Secretary, former Governors, former Police Chiefs, editors, etc., presented papers and deliberated on various aspects of the problem. The book is the collection of their scholarly papers.

The publication of the book was necessitated by the need of sharing the informations imparted and ideas generated on a larger scale. Important suggestions have emerged during the deliberations in the seminar, which are also included in the 'Statement of the Seminar' annexed in the book. We hope that the book may be useful for the readers. I take this opportunity to thank Dr. Jayanta Madhab, Professor Mrinal Miri, Shri J.N. Roy, treasurer, Astha Bharati and the members of the organization for making the seminar success. I thank Shri B.P. Singh, who gave valedictory address and all the scholar participants, who presented papers. I also thank the publisher, Shri Ashok Kumar Mittal of the Concept Publishing Company, for speedily undertaking the publication of the book. Shekhar Singh Negi typed many papers included in this book. I thank him for the same.

— Editor

Contents

Part V

Perspective on Ethnic Issues

Part VI

Issues of Identity and Governance

THE CONTRIBUTORS

Professor A.C. Sinha, former Dean, School of Social Sciences, North Eastern Hill University, Shillong.

Dr. B.B. Kumar, Editor, Quarterly Dialogue & Chintan-Srijan.

Dr. B.D. Sharma, IAS (Retd.), former Vice-Chancellor, North Eastern Hill University, former Chairman, SC&ST Commission; is well-known scholar and social activist.

E.N. Rammohan IPS (Retd.), former DGP BSF; former Advisor to the Governor of Manipur; member, National Security Advisory Board. He is from Assam Cadre and has extensive experience of North-East; is an expert on security issues.

Professor Mrinal Miri, former Vice-Chancellor, North-Eastern Hill University, Shillong (Meghalaya).

H.N. Das, IAS (Retd.), former Chief Secretary, Assam (1990-1995), was the Chairman of the Committee on Fiscal Reforms.

N. Changkakoti, IPS (Retd.), former Director General of Police, Assam; former Chief Vigilance Commissioner, Assam.

Dr. Nani G. Mahanta, Coordinator, Peace and Conflict Studies and Human Rights, Gauhati University, Assam.

Professor Niru Hazarika, Professor of Political Science, Gauhati University, Assam.

O.N. Shrivastava, former Governor of Nagaland and Manipur. He has worked in North-East for long and has extensive experience of the region.

Pradip Phanjoubam, Editor, Imphal Free Press, Manipur.

Ms. Patricia Mukhim, an eminent Journalist and Social activist from Meghalaya.

Subir Bhaumik, BBC's Eastern India Correspondent and author of "Insurgent Crossfire : North-East India"; Queen Elizabeth Fellow, Oxford University (1989-90), has presented more than thirty papers at regional, national and international seminars, has written for compendiums and journals on a regular basis. He has recently completed a book on North-East India to be published by the Penguins. He made a presentation before the World Commission on Dams seeking the decommissioning of the Dumbur Hydel Project in 2002.

Professor Udayon Misra, Head, English Department, Dibrugarh University, Assam.

PART I

Understanding North-East

1 Two Views of the North-East

Mrinal Miri

1. We can say that for the North-east there is a view from inside and a view from outside. Both these views may be nuanced in a variety of ways. But it may be instructive to present them in their unqualified starkness. The view from outside sees the region as a relatively unitary entity, delimited by India's boundaries with other countries such as China, Bangladesh and Myanmar, inhabited by vaguely differentiated "tribal" people who seem "racially distinct" from Indians elsewhere. The view from inside is one of extreme diversity: of tribes, communities, languages, religions, customs, traditions and histories. This diversity in the insider's eye — or at least its perceived enormity — is, one might venture to suggest, of very recent origin. One might even further venture to suggest that there might be a contrast between this viewpoint of diversity and a view likely to be fostered by a close attention to the historical, cultural, spatial and economic closeness within the region. This would be in consonance with the view, held by some, that this closeness is the deeper truth of the region which is now masked by splintered, fragmented face. One thing that can lead to this deeper truth is a close, careful attention to the vast number of languages spoken in the region — their many meeting points, their mythical resources, and the intricate network of resemblances that is their common inheritance. Unfortunately, our linguistic

research so far does not bear much evidence of this kind of close attention. It is clear, however, that this kind of covert closeness within the region is quite the opposite of the outsider's unitary view of it.

2. But, whether or not this kind of closeness is a matter of historical fact, it is at the same time extremely important that separateness and difference are acknowledged with utmost seriousness. It is the recognition of separateness and difference that makes some of the things that are crucial to our being human possible, e.g. love and justice. The possibility of human love requires an autonomous other who is separate and distinct from one. One can of course love supposedly non-autonomous beings, such as infants and mentally incapacitated people. Or inanimate creatures such as tress, sceneries, works of art, books and so on. But human love, at its most fulfilling, requires reciprocity, and reciprocity is something that comes from the separate and different other. Also, while there is certainly such a thing as being just to oneself, the idea of justice is firmly embedded in the recognition of demands that others make on one — in modern language, in the recognition of the *rights* of others.

But an exclusive engagement with the ideas of separateness and difference — think of some of the current tensions within the region — is also responsible for some very crucial errors that humans have made. Let me say a word about one of these errors. A natural ally of an unqualified commitment to separateness and difference is the egocentric view of the world — the view from within the complex of one's own acknowledged and unacknowledged interests; the view from within one's culture; the view from within the framework of one's ideology. The egocentric view of the world has a natural propensity to lead to what might be called the egocentric predicament. The predicament arises when the egocentric view forces out all other views. The egocentric predicament is responsible for some of the most vicious distortions of human reality that human kind has seen — religious fanaticisms, racial hatreds, horrible repressions in the name of ideologies, linguistic exclusivisms and so on.

3. The egocentric view is somewhat unavoidable in much the same way was what I see now is determined by *my* location in space and time, and, as such, is different from what everyone else in this room sees, although in a global sense we all see the "same" things. There are necessarily as many view-points as there are pairs of eyes to see from. But the egocentric predicament is certainly avoidable. The egocentric view does not rule out the possibility of other egocentric views; nor does it rule out the possibility of overcoming egocentricity in the light of the possibility of other kinds of views. It is the possibility of overcoming egocentricity that is truly distinctive of humanity.

4. Now let us look at the insider's view of the north-east — a multiplicity of human collectivities each claiming an overriding identity centred on tribal allegiances; linguistic affiliations, community loyalties and so on. The problem of course is that all these markers of overriding identity are fluid and unstable — and in the last fifty years or so we have seen a proliferation of these identities each promoting and attempting to sustain an egocentric view of the world. So we have an incredible multiplicity of egocentricities arrayed against each other: the Assamese against the Bodos and the Mishings and the Karbis; the Karbis against the Dimasas; the Nagas against the Meiteis; the Tangkhuls against the Aos and the Angamis; the Khasis against Garos and so on. I am not touching here Arunachal Pradesh at all which also has the potential of proliferating exclusive identities.

5. The ethnic — for want of a better word — egocentricity frequently collapses into what I have called the egocentric predicament and very often the only relief from this predicament is violence. What has led to this proliferation

of identities? One simple but telling answer to this question is "despair" — a state of helplessness that makes one recede into an illusory shell of inviolability. Paradoxically, but truly, the smaller the shell the more the feeling of inviolability.

6. There is of course no doubt at all that the peripheral status given to the north-east in national life has had much to do with the despair and helplessness I have talked about. The threat of a possible militaristic solution does not help matters. But we have blamed others enough. We must look into ourselves and see if it is possible for us by our own effort to confront our own sense of inadequacy. The first step: look beyond our own egocentric views and take the views of others seriously. Not just the serious stance we adopt at negotiating tables. To take another's point of view seriously is to take all the elements that go into its making seriously — its historical situatedness, the particular articulation that it receives, its cultural specificities, the knowledge that it bases itself on, i.e. its "truths" and "falsehoods" (e.g. the ULFA's "truths" and "falsehoods"), its "rights" and "wrongs", its hopes and aspirations, its loves and hates and the places it accords to views other than itself. Of course, many of these elements are unclear and inarticulate to the owner of the point of view itself. Try asking ULFA what it is to be "free" and "liberated". It is by paying serious attention to one another, by seriously listening to one another and responding to the other that a basis of friendship can be established — the beginning of a process of emerging from our tiny "security" shells and achieving a degree of mutuality.

7. Perhaps the initial step is the coming together of the economies of the north-east. It won't be an exaggeration to say that the economies of the north-east are more or less isolated units — the only link they seem to have is their near total dependence on the economy of the mainland, notwithstanding the efforts of the North-East Council, unit

has its strengths and weaknesses. Our economic self-confidence will come from a reciprocal enhancement of our strengths and a similar overcoming of our weaknesses. Our self-confidence will receive a further boost when we have achieved a degree of mutuality with the economy of the mainland.

8. But the coming together of the economies is only the first step. Much more important is for the points of view to meet and converse with one another informed by a common purpose and a common sympathy. Recovery of the old sense of mutuality which in all probability predated the process of fragmentation; at one level a rich, many sided historical understanding of ourselves — an insight into the deep threads cultural manifestations, e.g. music, dance, folklores; knowledges about human well-being (health), plants, animals, rivers, mountains and so on.

9. If what I have envisaged has any realistic chance, then its eventuality would seem to evoke a vision of the north-east somewhat similar to the present outsider's vision of the north-east — a unitary, singular entity. But, as you will easily see, the two visions are poles apart. The outsider's vision of unity is abstract, empty of content, devoid of insights, based on ignorance. The vision that I have envisaged is complex, not that of a unitary entity. It is that of an entity that derives its sustenance and energy from a mutuality of respect and reciprocity — the complex recognition of a separateness based on the successful overcoming of the barriers of egocentricity.

2 North-East : More a Lack of Understanding

O.N. Shrivastava

1. I landed in the North-East (NE), for the first time, in January 1964, did 9 postings in all — at least one in each of the seven States, spread over a period of 20 years — briefest being 4 months in Tripura as Advisor to the Governor — longest 6 years in Nagaland and Manipur as Governor. In 1964, there was just one under-ground group led by Mr. Phizo — only two districts effected — violence sporadic — UGs possessed just 200 assorted weapons — mostly of Second World War vintage. In 2000, when I finally left the North-East — the number of UG groups had risen to 50 + with assorted fire power of 2-3000. Just about 10 districts free from violence. How did this mess up come about — notwithstanding that the political leaders and the bureaucrats who handled the area appeared well meaning? Did the treatment envisaged, i.e. coercive measures, AFSPA included — prove counter productive? Or did too much publicity by the GOI/Prime Minister to the "offer of talks with all and sundry if they gave up violence" made people/groups believe " that violence pays — the more violent one became greater would be the length of the red carpet which Delhi would lay for you ?" Was it that the two — pronged strategy of coercive measures coupled with largesse's — Statehood to each and everyone with special safeguards included, was ill-conceived or ill-timed?
2. Those from the North-East would remember that in September 1997 an important Seminar was held in Guwahati University

attended by intellectuals — leaders of the main stream political parties and UG sympathizers. The seminar deliberated mainly "Restructuring of the Federal-State relations." It rejected out of hand concepts like "mainstreaming" and "periphery" concepts that were held sacred by the Centre over a period of time. The Seminar favoured "equal partnership in the Union for the North-East" with aspirations revolving round a concept that envisaged partnership of a type in which the Centre would keep just 4-5 subjects like defence, foreign affairs, communication and currency, with rest going to States. In the Seminar, Shri P.K. Mahanta was of the opinion that "strong States would go to make a strong Centre".

3. It has earlier been stated that the sit in the North-East has witnessed a serious down turn in the past 50 years. It would, therefore, be useful to examine some accusations as also counter — accusations related to this down turn.

(a) According to the Central Governments — army included, the State Governments, the Civil, its rampant corruption — misutilization of funds as "the mess created by the Civil" are the main reasons for the spread of insurgencies and lawlessness — resulting in denial of economic development, consequent denial of employment opportunities — resulting frustration in the minds of youth ending up in a feeling that there was no advantage in being a part of India. But if corruption-maladministration, abandoning of responsibility by the politicians and the 'Civil' — the Army being required to clean up the mess were to be the reasons — there were prolonged spells of PR in these Sates (32 times till 1995) — lasting for years — no political meddling — honest administrationa — no misutilisation of funds, then all insurgencies would have vanished. But the fact remains that each insurgency has a different motivating force. Similarly, almost all States barring Nagaland were quiet for almost 20 years after Independence accepting Indian democracy? Then what happened that prompted groups in these Sates to take up arms? Independent opinion in the North-East — volunteered in confidence, blames Delhi for the neglect of this Region — for its imperialistic style of functioning — step-motherly treatment — resulting in denial of econ development — consequent unemployment — ending up in prolife-ration of the ranks of the undergrounds. Is this a valid argument?

(b) Many in Delhi, on the basis of personal experience assert that the North-Easterners, exceptions notwithstanding, do not feel to be a part of India. The North-Easterners perennially complain of being treated as foreigners in our cities.

(c) It is generally acknowledged, that Independence and the creation of East Pakistan did result in snapping of vital road and rail links from and to this Region, ending in an explainable development differential of about 25 years *vis-a-vis* other Sates. However, there can be no explanation for North-East remaining, noticeably, 40 years behind.

4. My personal experience of 20 years in this Region has convinced me that there is a lack of understanding in Delhi of :

(i) The interplay of historical forces both at subterranean and overt levels and therefore, of the deeper nuances of the sit itself;

(ii) Of the aspirations, expectations and now more importantly the fears of the people, and

(iii) Of the activities of foreign intelligence agencies/ neighbouring countries in this Region.

This has resulted in even good decisions/pronouncements turning counter-productive. Reluctance on the part of Central Service officers — unlike their IFAS counterparts — to dig themselves in this Region and work in this area, coupled with hesitation on the part of Central officers to frequently tour this area, over prolonged spells, to rub shoulders with people in general to know what irked them, has complicated decision making giving rise to a set of region experts, (without any depth in their understanding of the area) acquiring ascendancy — who appear determined to simplify problems — no end.

5. Reluctance to meet grievance at first sign and an irrepressible urge to push problems under the carpet, till they were ready to explode has also complicated problems. Even thereafter reactions have just been *ad hoc*. Politicians too have sometimes misutilised the ferment to further own agendas, but after all they are politicians. It would however be wrong to blame politicians for most of the insurgencies, as is generally made out. More politicians have lost their lives at the hands of the UGs in this Region. And, finally, excessive reliance on use of force/army has not helped much. On the contrary it has led to weakening of Rule of law — of the Police and judicial set ups — so vital for democracy. States like Assam, Tripura and Manipur used to have effective police set ups till Army was called in for dealing with insurgencies resulting in marginalization/sidelining not only of police but also of Judiciary.
6. Economic amelioration could have become a bulwark. But that too did not take place. Poverty, unemployment and hunger still remain basic issues.
7. It needs to be realized that North-East is top diverse, too sensitive a mix of religions, ethnicities and races, has a very complicated history, long tradition of internal tensions, fuelled by ethnic and religious differences, which have been exploited, from time to time, by politicians for furthering their own agendas. The area sits on a cultural fracture with people having greater similarities/affinities with regions in the East. The neighbouring countries have either been supportive — providing sanctuaries, or have been or ignoring the presence of — or even instigating our malcontents. Myanmar as a neighbour has never tried to stop the lucrative trade/profession of heroin smuggling and gun running. Presence of Bangladeshis has remained a potential destabilizing factor leading to formation of too many armies and organizations supporting

Bangladeshis and Muslims. Lucrative trade of smuggling, from heroin to weapons, has generated in this Region sizable black money. People involved in these trades are influential and have acquired a vested interest in violence and conflict. Foreign agencies too are up to their own games. And our policy planners and officers have neither time nor interest to go into the machinations/ manipulations of these groups which are time consuming.

8. Today the people of this Region :
   (i) Are fed up with continuing violence and want peace/ development.
   (ii) Are generally not against the Nation though coercive measures can force them into making a common cause with the undergrounds.
   (iii) Delhi's failure in being able to identify people/ organizations standing solidly with the Nation has made such people/groups suspect with the undergrounds. To make matters worse they are also at the receiving end of SF action in some places.
   (iv) Politicians are generally not with the UGs as is generally made out. If taken in confidence they can help in winning the UGs to Governments side.
   (v) People have started believing that they are being subjected to different laws/Constitution than their counterparts in other States. They would have been happier if Pandit Nehru's assurance given to the Nagas in 1952, that they were being asked to share a Constitution that would give them powers to govern their areas in their own volition without any let or hindrance from outside, was implemented in letter and spirit.
   (vi) A hard core in each of these States, for varying reasons, continues to encourage and work in support of armed struggle.
   (vii) Leadership of many of the UG groups, enjoys the support in some cases, are instigated by neighbouring

Countries, in some case by the ISI and some foreign countries.

(viii) Lack of understanding of what moves the people of this Region has remained the main drawback in decision-making with blanket/*ad hoc* approaches making matters worse.

PART II

Ethnicity and Insurgency in the Region

3 Ethnicity and Insurgency in India's North-East

B.B. Kumar

Background

When the freedom dawned, the North-East region of the country had the State of Assam and two Princely States of Manipur and Tripura. It was then widely known as Assam. The phrase 'North-East' got wide currency only after the reorganization of the region and liberation of Bangladesh. Today, we have seven states in the North-East, if we exclude Sikkim, which joined the North-East Council recently, and is separated from the rest of the region by the North Bengal districts.

The Sixth Schedule of the Constitution made provisions for the tribal Autonomy in the Hill districts of Assam in the form of Autonomous District Councils (ADCs). Initially, there were only four Autonomous District Councils (ADCs) in the entire region. Today, Mizoram, which was only a district of Assam and had an Autonomous District Council, completed the journey from a district through the Union Territory status to the Statehood, has four ADCs within it for Chakmas, Lakhers, Pawis and the Hmars. The Brus (Reangs) are even now continuing their autonomy demand in Mizoram.

Prior to 1947, there was hardly any forum in the North-East demanding secession or autonomy, except Naga National Council (NNC). Mizo Union was for keeping Mizo Hills as a district of Assam in India. Even Naga National Council resolved in 1946 to keep Naga Hills as a district in Assam within India. Initially, Phizo was forced to leave Naga National Council and moderate voice continued to be heard from NNC platform. Later on he became the leader of the outfit and NNC became the platform for demanding autonomy for the Nagas.

Initially, the NNC (and its creation Nagaland Federal Government, NFG) in Nagaland and the Communist outfit of Hijam Irabot Singh in Manipur were the only insurgent outfits in the North-East; today there number, including the dormant and withered away ones, may exceed a hundred. The list of the terrorist outfits given in 'Annexure I' of this paper is in noway exhaustive.

Historical Background

The Britishers sowed the seeds of separateness and secessionism in the region. Their **policy of gradual segregation** of the tribals and non-tribals, hills and the plains; segregation of the tribal population by introduction of the "Inner Line Regulation", creation of "non-regulated", "backward" and "excluded" areas/tracts was able to **break centuries of historical, cultural, social and religious continuum and connectedness**. The **colonial theories/myths — the myth of race, core-fringe conflict, isolation — colonial mis-interpretation of history and culture** further deepened the impact. The **lies of exploitation and hegemony** increased the suspicion of the segregated population. Like rest of India, **colonial education and left ideology** — as in Manipur — weakened nationalist feeling. **Non-participation in freedom movement in many areas** due to segregation was an added factor. Over and above, there was a colonial design, such as the Coupland Plan to separate the hills of India and Myanmar, and to make it a Crown colony.

Historically, the insurgency in Nagaland developed in above-mentioned colonial background. The British came in contact of the Nagas after their occupation of upper Assam and Cachar. The Naga inhabited areas were gradually and reluctantly incorporated in Assam. The Naga turbulence was gradually controlled and Deputy Commissioner of the Naga Hills districts was able to win over the Nagas. The Naga Club was established in Kohima with some employees of the Deputy Commissioner's office, a few village chiefs and some others in 1918. Its members submitted a memorandum to the Simon Commission. Out of 20 signatories of the same, 15 were from the Angami tribe, two Kacha Nagas and one each from the Sema, Lotha, Rengma and Kuki tribes. Workwise, one was head interpretor, 8 interpretors, one peshkar, three masters/teachers, one doctor, one potdar, one treasurer, one sub-overseer, two clerks and one Chaprasi. The Lotha and Ao Tribal Councils were established in 1923 and 1928 respectively. The Naga Hills District Tribal Council (NHDTC) was formed in April 1945 under the guidance of the Deputy Commissioner, C.R. Pawsey, who was knighted and awarded M.C. later on. This very organization was renamed Naga Nationalist Council (NNC) which spearheaded Naga insurgency under the leadership of Angami Zapu Phizo in mid-1950s.

The NNC made a demand of the right of self-determination for the Nagas based on the following:

(i) Ethnic distinctiveness,
(ii) Distinct social life, way of living, laws and customs, etc.,
(iii) Different religion: Christianity and Animism.

While Phizo demanded separation of Nagaland from India, started rebellion; the moderate Nagas demanded the formation of Union Territory merging Naga Hills district of Assam and Tuensang Division of the then NEFA; and then a fullfledged state within Indian Union. The Naga Hills Tuensang Area (NHTA, a Union Territory) was given to the Nagas in 1957 as desired by the 'First Naga People's Convention'. There were two more Naga People's Conventions, which wanted fullfledged Statehood. Nagaland, the 16th State of the Indian Union was inaugurated by the then President of India, Dr. Radhakrishnan on 1st December, 1963. Parallel to the above, the activities of Phizo continued. He was instrumental in the creation of underground 'Federal Government of Nagaland' and 'Naga Army'. **Nagaland developed as the epicentre of insurgency in the North-East. Ethnicity linked problem slowly spread throughout North-East region.**

Origin of Insurgency in the North-East

As stated above, the insurgency originated in the Naga Hills district of Assam. NNC was the outfit and Phizo, the leader of the insurgent activities. **The inept handling of the Naga insurgency resulted into the proliferation of insurgent activities in the entire region** and the number of insurgent outfits continued to increase.

Growth of Insurgency in the North-East

The formation of Nagaland sent unhealthy signals throughout the North-East region, leading to destabilization of Assam state and the Assamese society. It adversely affected Manipur's situation also. The reasons of the same are:

- **Economic and demographic viability criteria was waved** for the creation of Nagaland State.
- The expenditure for the development and maintenance of the state machinery was given from the Consolidated Fund of India. **The new State was not given the burden to mobilize resources.**
- The huge flow of funds after Statehood created **resource-rich area in Nagaland and resource-poor areas in its neighbourhood** in Assam and Manipur.
- **Big states were replicated in Nagaland** creating unprecedented avenues for appointments and promotions for the educated lot.
- The Naga Hills district of Assam had five Assembly constituencies; the **new State had 52, and then 60. Majority of the MLAs managed to become ministers.**
- The above-mentioned **scenario was tempting for others.** Following **two unhealthy signals emerged** in the North-East:

  — that the social distancing pays,
  — that the violence pays.

These signals were never effectively countered. Others also

wanted all that the Nagas got by following their path. Laldenga and Mizo National Front followed Phizo and NNC; followed the path of secessionist insurgency; **Mizoram State** was created. Laldenga and MNF were the role models for Bijoy Kumar Hrankhawl and **Tripura** Upajati Juva Samiti. There was upsurge of ethnic identity claims resulting into social distancing leading to the demands for secession or autonomy.

- The **Manipuris** were psychologically hurt. They had ancient kingdom were to be satisfied with UT status; Nagas had State. The demand of greater Nagalim has further aggravated the problem in Manipur.

The net result is that the insurgency continued to grow; number of insurgent outfits has almost touched three digit mark; the society and the state is destabilized.

The insurgency in Nagaland persists; Nagas link flow of funds from Delhi and insurgency; they want to be superior to other states status-wise. Udayon Misra has observed: "Every government in Nagaland since the State was formed, has had some **stake in having the insurgency continue.** Among other things, the insurgency has always been a convenient lever to secure greater benefits from the Centre." (Udayon Misra, *The Periphert Strikes Back*, Shimla, Indian Institute of Advanced Study, 2000, p. 55).

The Nagas have psychological problem also; they **want to be superior to others** status-wise. Otherwise, greater autonomy is not going to benefit common Nagas. Many view it as **a step forward towards the ultimate aim of secession.**

Kinds of Insurgent Outfits

There are three kinds of insurgent outfits in the North-East region depending on their demands. They are (i) **secessionist outfits,** (ii) **outfits demanding separate state within India,** and (iii) **those demanding Autonomous District Councils (ADCs).** All most all the insurgent outfits in the North-East region, starting with NNC, based their secessionist demands on **separate ethnic identity assertion**.

Insurgent outfits, such as: ULFA, NSCN, UNLF, Revolutionary People's Front (political wing of People's Liberation Army) and many others aim at secession from India. Hynniewtrep National Liberation Council, HNLC wants to transform Meghalaya into a state exclusively for the Khasis. Achik National Volunteers Council, ANVC and Garo National Council, GNC want a state exclusively for the Garos. Many organizations, such as Bru National Liberation Front, BNLF demand autonomy within Mizoram under the provisions of the 6th Schedule of the Constitution. Most of the secessionist outfits have armed wings.

ATTF demands separate tribal homeland. The demands of the outfits like ALMA, Hyniewtrep Volunteer Council (HVC), Hmar People's Convention (HPC) come within the Constitution of India. Kuki National Assembly (1947; Kuki Inpi) was revived in 1992 to provide relief to Kukis during Kukis-Naga conflict. The Kuki National Organization (1992), and its armed wing, KNA, aim at having a Kuki state within Myanmar. The aim of Kuki National Front, KNF is to get Kukiland within India. Its armed cadres were trained by Kachin Independence Army of Myanmar (KIA) and it has link with ULFA.

Separatist/Secessionist Ideology

The separatist/secessionist ideologies in the North-East are of the following type :

(i) Ethnic,
(ii) Ideological/leftist/Communist, and
(iii) Religious.

Many insurgent outfits combine the above-mentioned ethnic traits. The NNC combined ethnic (Naga ethnicity) and religious (Christian); the NSCN combined Naga ethnicity, Christianity and Socialism/Scientific Socialism/Communism. ULFA combines ethnic and Communist/Scientific Socialism factors and has religious linkages through ISI and Bangladesh intelligence. Most of the Manipuri outfits claim separation/secession on ethnic (Pan-Mongolian/Mongolian/Meithei) and Communist ideological ground. The first two secessionist groups in the region, NNC under Phizo; and Revolutionary Nationalist Party (and its armed wing, Manipur Red Guards) under Hijam Irabot Singh emphasised on Ethnicity. The latter was also a Communist outfit.

People's Revolutionary Party of Kangleipak (PREPAK), United National Liberation Front (UNLF), Kangleipak Communist Party (KCP), People's Liberation Army (of Manipur; PLA), All Tripura People's Liberation Organization (ATPLO), Tripura National Volunteers (TNV) combined ethnic identity with Scientific Socialism/Socialism/Communism. Ethnic extremism in the North-East was started by Phizo. Manipur has old history of left extremism; Irabot Singh was a communist. But the secessionist left extremism got boosted up due to the activities of PLA under Biseshwar Singh. He combined left-extremism with anti-Mayang (anti-outsider) and pan-Mongoloid sentiments. NSCN and National Liberation Front of Tripura (NLFT) under the leadership of Bishwamohan Debbarma promoted Christian terrorism. NSCN and NLFT worked for forcible conversion to Christianity. These outfits were responsible for the religious oppression of the Hindus and Buddhists in Arunachal Pradesh and Tripura respectively. Jamatiya Hoda and its leaders, to a large extent, were able to control NLFT run religious terrorism. NSCN's religious terrorism continued unabated.

An Insight into Naga Ethnicity/Naga Identity

An understanding of the Naga ethnicity and identity formation is necessary so that to understand the insurgency related proliferation problem in the region.

As mentioned above, Phizo based his autonomy demand on distinct Naga social life, ethnicity, way of living, laws and customs. In reality, it is difficult to distinguish the Nagas from the other communities of the region in one hand and their homogeneity on the other. Hutton wrote:

> "If not impossible, it is exceedingly difficult to propound any test by which a Naga tribe can be distinguished from other Assam or Burma tribes, which are not Nagas."[1]

The intra-Naga heterogeneity, on the other hand, is unimaginable. Hutton further writes about the features of the Angami Nagas:

> "It would be impossible to give any general description of the type of the Angami features, as it varies from village to village and even from house to house to remarkable degree. The flattened nose and slightly oblique eye of a decidedly Mongolian type may be seen side by side with a straightness of eyes and nose that might be purely Aryan."[2]

W.C. Smith has listed **14 traits** of the Tibeto-Burmans — head-hunting, dormitory for the young men, house on piles, disposal of the dead on platforms, tribal marriage customs, betel chewing, aversion to milk, lack of political organization, double sylinder forge, loin-loom, hexagonal shields, residence in hilly regions and jhum cultivation. **These are not the common markers for the Nagas.** Anthony Smith, in his definition of the ethnic community, enumerates the marker of ethnic community as "a named human population with a myth of common ancestory, shared memories and cultural elements, link to a historic territory or homeland; and a measure of solidarity."[3] The language, race, religion and colour are the markers, according to Ghai.[4] It needs mention that the **Nagas do not have common myth of origin and migration. They lack common language, identical social and cultural elements and all the Naga markers enumerated above. To talk of the common memory of the Naga tribes is absurd**, as they **did not know even the names of the tribes** except for the few and had the memory of only the mutual feud and enmity only 17 years before voicing of their autonomy demands in 1929. The deplorable state of the knowledge of the signatories of the Simon Commission memorandum about the Nagas comes to light from the following quote from the memorandum:

> "Our country within the administered area consists of more than eight tribes, quite different from one another with different languages which cannot be understood by each

> other, and there are more Tribes outside the administrated area which are not known at present. We have no unity among us and it is really the British Government that is holding us together now."

It is clear from the above that Nagas lack ethnic and socio-cultural identity, as is the case with some other tribes/groups also, and as such **any anthropological basis of Naga identity is a fluid one as different communities constantly come in and out of it. At one time, even, Kacharis, Kukis, Abors[5], Karbis, Nepalis,[6] Khamtis and Singphos[7] were included in the list of the Nagas, whereas Manipuri Nagas, including Muivah's own tribe, Tangkhul was excluded from the same.[8] Today Muivah is continuing his ethnic cleansing drive against the Kukis forgetting the fact that one of the Kukis signed Simon Commission Memorandum as a Naga.**

Phizo propagated that Nagaland had never been a part of India, that only the British conquered it. Therefore, with the lapse of the suzerainty, the Nagas *ipso facto* became independent. **The truth is that various tribes of the Nagas remained under the Ahom[9], Meithei[10] and the Kachari kings. The Eastern Nagas remained under Singhpho Chiefs.** These facts cannot be ignored and therefore, it is difficult to understand the "**unique history**" of the Nagas claimed by Muivah.

Anals, Lamkhangs and Monsangs belong to Kuki-Chin group and use Kuki-Chin languages as mother-tongues. Now they claim Naga identity.[11] **Muivah is indulging in forced identity formation** not only by ethnic and communist terrorism, but also by religious terrorism by forced conversion to Christianity. NSCN-IM has the slogan of 'Nagaland for Christ'. The eastern Nagas of Mynmar have closer affiliations with the Kachins; NSCN-IM had to forcibly establish themselves among them in some of the areas as in Kesan Chanlam, and convert them to Christianity. The book of **Bertil Lintner,** *Land of Zade*, which points out these facts, is reportedly banned by Muivah.[12] The tribes of Tirap and Arunachal Pradesh are being forcibly converted in similar way to Christianity.[13]

There always existed historical, cultural, social and religious

'connectedness' between the hills and the plains of the North-East region of the country. The British worked to break the same by isolating the hills and plains of the region by segregation of different communities and the sub-regions. They introduced 'Inner Line regulation', created 'non-regulated; 'backward' and 'excluded areas/tracts: prevented freedom movement to penetrate and get strengthened. The British wanted to separate the hills of North-East India and Myanmar and create a **separate 'Crown Colony'**. Their plan, known as **Coupland plan,** could not succeed, as the freedom came too early. However, the over all impact of the colonial British functionaries on selected tribal intelligentsia was responsible for sowing the seeds of separatism in the North-East.

The British gave twist to the interpretation of the history and culture of the region. The **myth of race, hypothesis of core-fringe conflict; myths of isolation, hegemony of and exploitation had no basis.** But their overall impact created suspicion in the mind of one section of our people for the others. A grudge that tribes were neglected, that they were exploited by their neighbours in the plains, were completely baseless colonial fabrications, which created divisive mind-set. The impact of these colonial theories and myths and the colonial education, weakening of the traditions and the traditional values were responsible for creating mercenaries out of half-educated ones not only in NE region but in the entire country.

Factors responsible for Strengthening Insurgency

Some of the factors responsible for unrestricted growth and strengthening of insurgency/insurgent outfits are given below:

Insurgency-Politician Nexus

It is well-known fact that many insurgent secessionist outfits in the North-East, especially in Assam, Manipur, Mizoram, Tripura and Nagaland could grow and get strong due to insurgent-politician nexus. **ULFA "was able to become a large outfit primarily due to the tacit support provided by the first AGP regime** under Prafulla Kumar Mahanta". The outfit was running a parallel government in Assam during that period.[14] This was described as "One of the classic example of culpable inaction on the part of the

State Government" by Assam's former Governor D.D. Thakur.[15] Mr. B.P. Chaliha, the then Chief Minister of Assam and a shrewd politician, ignoring the serious implications for national unity and security, **released Laldenga** from jail in 1963, taking him to be potential ally for neutralizing the growing influence of the Mizo Union in the Mizo Hills district. Laldenga continued his anti-national activities and the nation paid the price for the short-sighted party politics of Mr. Chaliha[16].

Lt. Gen. V.K. Nayar (Retd.), the Governor of Manipur and acting Governor of Nagaland accused S.C. **Jamir of patronizing NSCN-K.**[17] Gen. Nayyar in his special report to the President of India wrote about S.C. Jamir:

> "With Shri Jamir supporting NSCN (K), tribal alignments with Aos, Konyaks, Phoms firmly with NSCN (K), and Semas, Angamis and other Southern Tribes against him and NSCN (I) have already fermented."[18]

NSCN (IM) has increased its influence internally. This process was helped considerably by the defeat of the Congress (I) led Jamir government in the last elections. It is alleged that with the **connivance of the then NDA government at the Centre**, which gave the NSCN-IM cadres free hand to intimidate and influence the results. It allowed the NSCN-IM to drive out the moderate leadership from the Naga HOHO and other civil society establishments. This short-sighted strategy has given the secessionist NSCN-IM a clout beyond its support base, mainly based on fear.

Gen. Nayar also wrote about Rishang Keishing in his report :

> "NSCN (I) and its sympathizers and collaborators over the past few months have surreptitiously revived and propagated successfully the old theme of South Nagaland by exploiting the sentiment of Naga identity and interest. In this, Shri **Rishang Keishing**, Dy. Chief Minister, Marung Makunga, Minister of State and A.S. Arthur, ex-MLA (all of Congress-I) have **played a dubious role** with the help

> of over-ground front organizations of United Naga Council, Tangkhul Long and tribal youth and student organizations (.) A combination of Naga sentiment, threat and Kuki baiting have been effectively employed to dominate Naga inhabited areas of four of the five hill districts of Ukhrul, Chandel, Senapati and Tamenglong (.) In real terms it is domination of NSCN (I) and Tangkhuls" (.)[19]

In Manipur, "almost **every party are busy cultivating underground groups** to be one-up on their political adversaries as also to strengthen their bargaining position *vis-à-vis* the Central Government, while **paying lip-service to their nationalistic credentials. Constitutional perversity and political bickerings have crossed new limits. Political opportunism has led to erosion and breakdown of democratic institutions.**[20] It is alleged that some political leaders of Manipur maintained close links with secessionist terrorist outfits like PLA and NSCN.[21] **Evidences are not lacking about the complex web of collusion between substantially criminalized terrorist outfits and various political parties of Manipur.** At least five ministers of Nipamacha Singh government, as per a Union Ministry of Home Affairs Report, had direct links with terrorists of the NSCN-K, PLA, UNLF, KYKL (Kanglei Yawol Kunna Lup and ZRA (Zomi Revolutionary Army).[22] Parliament was informed about the **receipts of Rs. three lakhs by UNLF from former Manipur Chief Minister** Nipamacha Singh and former Speaker Chandramani Singh of Manipur Legislative Assembly.[23] Two Kuki National Front terrorists were arrested at the official residence of the then Transport Minister of Manipur, Haokholet Kipgen by the security force personnel on November 28, 2000. This led Central Government to announce an investigation into clandestine alliance between the politicians and terrorist outfits.[24]

In Tripura, the seed of insurgency was sown by the Communist Party of India (CPI) under the leadership of Dashrath Deb during 1948-51 as a part of the larger movement to 'liberate India from its then ruling classes.' The political parties — **Congress and CPI/CPM — have developed stable nexus over the years**

after independence. The insurgent outfits target the civilian population during elections as a part of their strategy to help their patron political parties. Out of the two most criminalized terrorist outfits, "the **NLFT is said to have close link with the Congress** (I) while the **ATTF is aligned with the ruling left front.**"[25] Here it needs mention that it goes to the credit of the electorate of Tripura as elsewhere in the country, that they go and cast their votes inspite of the threat of the terrorist outfits, who act as **vote-mercenaries**. It is alleged that the terrorists in spired mass killings during elections helped the formation of alternative ministries in Tripura.

Pre-poll violence was witnessed in Tripura during December 1982, before January 1983 Assembly elections. Violence unleashed on non-tribals before 1988 elections by the TNV, under the leadership of Bijoy Kumar Hrankhawl, took the toll of more than hundred lives, and **turned the poll-eve atmosphere in favour of Congress, as alleged**. The Congress-TUJS coalition government was formed and Hrangkhawl came overground. The CPI-M, then supported the formation of All Tripura Tribal Force (ATTF) so that to keep away the Congress from the Tripura Tribal Area Autonomous Tribal Council, (TTAADC). **ATTF continued to kill selectively the leaders of Congress** and TUJS during the rule of Congress-TUJS coalition and brief President's rule period. The killings before April 1993 elections resulted into the Left Front's victory in the elections. A section of the ATTF, under the leadership of Lalit Debbarma, surrendered. Another factions continued insurgent activities under the leadership of Ranajit Debbarma so that to reap the benefits of insurgency-politics nexus.[26] It is alleged that NLFT sponsored a political Front, the Indigenous People' Front of Tripura (IPFT) before April 30 and May 3, 2000 elections of TTAADC. The NLFT selectively killed 78 activists and leaders of the CPI-M after the notifications of the elections and 111 after the election. The NLFT backed IPFT came to power by winning 18 seats out of 30 for which the elections were held.[27]

The degenerate politics of the Congress and the CPI-M in Tripura is solely responsible for the continuance of the

insurgency in that tiny state. The NLFT and ATTF are highly criminalized gangs. Though there are over thirty terrorist outfits in Tripura, the most powerful among them are NLFT and ATTF only. The others are either just rag-tag criminal gangs or are dormant.[28] The terrorist outfits of Tripura have transformed **abduction into a lucrative industry.** Tripura accounts for 70 per cent of the abductions of the North-Eastern region.

Arunachal Pradesh suffers mostly due to spill over of the terrorist activities of the NSCN-IM and NSCN-K. The state is not free from terrorism-politics nexus. I Wanglat, MLA demanded CBI or judicial enquiry in June 2000 to ascertain abetting and sponsoring of insurgency in Tirap and Changlang districts. He further demanded that the political leaders found guilty should be arrested and asked to relinquish office.[29] Former Chief Minister Gegong Apang alleged on April 6, 2001 that some ministers and MLAs were harbouring and abetting insurgents in the State, and had direct links with NSCN-K, and NSCN-IM in Tirap and Changlang.[30] NSCN-K, with sizeable presence in Tirap and Changlang districts of Arunachal Pradesh had established a reciprocal relationship with Chief Minister Mukut Mithi's Arunachal Congress.[31] As stated earlier, ULFA received unchallenged political patronage in Assam, which made the outfit most powerful. The attitude of the first AGP government towards the outfit may be judged from the fact that Bhrigu Kumar Phukan, the then Home Minister described ULFA as being 'from among us'.[32]

Insurgency-Bureaucracy Links

The reports of the collusion of government servants, including the senior IAS officers with the insurgent outfits comes to light from time to time. It was alleged that S.K. Tiwari, Commissioner, General Administration Department, Assam and P. Verma, Secretary, Transport maintained direct links with ULFA. It was reported that Verma even met the ULFA General Secretary, Golap Barua and foreign secretary, Raju Barua, before their arrest in Calcutta. The former was carrying an identity card issued to him by Verma.[33] H.N. Das, Chief Secretary, Assam wrote to the Ministry of Home

Affairs (MHA) to take action against Chandra Das, Commissioner, Panchayat and Rural Development, and Food and Civil Supply, Education Commissioner, Prafulla Kumar Sarma and Revenue Commissioner, P.C. Misra for their alleged involvement and direct connection with the ULFA.[34] There may be many reasons for such deviant behaviour of the administrative officers. It may be due to fear or due to acting on taking a cue from their over-conciliating political bosses. But a large number of the officers remained firm and did not yield to the threat/terror and many such officers were killed.

Collusion with Bureaucracy

In Manipur, many officers resisting terrorist demands were shot. The Director Tourism, an IAS officer, did not agree to pay ransom, and was shot. The Registrar of Cooperatives was abducted and severely injured for not paying ransom. The Director of Education also suffered. The Divisional Engineer, telephones did not waive the bills of two PCOs operated by NSCN-IM and PLA, and was killed. The Chief Engineer, Loktak Project was killed by KYKL insurgents on January 12, 2000. As reported, his security was withdrawn on an unwritten order to the Director General of Police.[35]

In Manipur, the militant outfits were successful in subverting the Public distribution system through their linkages with the politicians. The tankers of kerosene oil, petrol, and diesel were diverted from the dealers and sold in the black market by all militant groups. In many cases contracts were procured by unqualified members of militant groups at gunpoint. Only 50 per cent of the work is executed, but Executive Engineers and their seniors are forced to enter full execution of the work in the measurement book and to make full payment for the half executed work. Half of sum goes to the caufers of the militant group. Such extortions continue in all other departments and in other states also.[36] Diverted rice from the Public Distribution System were partly supplied to the underground camps; partly supplied to the black-markets. The PLA and UNLF sold rice and kerosene oil at very low rates in the villages around their camps in Churachandpur and Chandel districts and thus aquired a 'Robin Hood' image. The people in Imphal were getting a litre or two per month per family against the quota of five, whereas the villagers were hardly getting any.[37]

Initially, the **politicians started siphoning or large-scale diversion of development funds in collusion with spineless bureaucrats. After that the insurgent outfits intervened and started taking a major share of the deals. The non-governmental organizations (NGOs) of Manipur, mostly run by the politicians on the names of their hanger-on, use only a trickle of the funds, approximately five per cent, for the real work**, such as the housing for the rural poor, watershed projects. Rest of the money received by the NGOs from the Central Government as grants is siphoned out.[38] In such a case, these schemes also came under the extensive network of extortion enriching the terrorist coffers. The situation worsened most during the People's Front government in Manipur of 2000, when the 'nexus between the PLA and the UNLF with the politicians reached its peak.'[39]

Many Central leaders have warned the State Governments of the NE region in the past against payments of the development funds to the insurgents. Venkiah Naidu, Union Rural Development Minister, during the meeting of the Rural Development Ministers of the region at Shillong on June 14, 2001, warned that "the centre would stop disbursing rural development funds to those States, where a bulk of the funds go to the coffers of the extremist outfits."[40] Such warnings have been given to the NGOs also.

> Partisan dealing of the Central Agencies with the insurgent outfits was also reported by the Governor, Gen. V.K. Nayar. It, to a large extent, contributed in escalation of divisive politics of Manipur (Nayar, V.K., p. 101).

Insurgent-Police Collusion

Some cases of the collusion between the insurgent groups and the police have also been reported from time to time. The Nagaland Armed Police lost 96 weapons and large quantities of ammunition during July 1995 during two raids by NSCN-IM at Peren and Ranga

Pahar. It was possible due to collusion between the local police and the insurgents, according to the Army sources. Lt. Gen. O.P. Kaushik of the Eastern Command of the Army, in a Press Conference in Calcutta in July 1995, **accused the local police, State Government officials and politicians for their collusion with the underground groups.**[41]

In Assam there were cases of desertion from the service, collusion and illegal arms sale to the ULFA by policemen. Two policemen disappeared with their arms and the ULFA insurgents, they were guarding, and joined ULFA camps. Chief Minster Saikia issued a statement after this incident that 500 police constables recruited in Assam during AGP regime between 1985 and 1987 had ULFA links and four of them were actually being trained in ULFA camps in the Kachin state in Myanmar.[42] It was reported that higher police department officials were in possession of a good number of documents, reports and video-cassettes revealing the intensity of the nexus. As reported, policemen participated in valleyball matches with ULFA cadres, attended *shraddha* ceremony of slain ULFA insurgents; and imparted martial art training to their cadres in Upper Assam (*Patriot*, New Delhi, August 24, 2001). There was media report of the sale of arms to the ULFA from an armory in Sibsagar district by two constables in September 1992.[43] The nexus included some higher police officers also. It was reported that ULFA received prior information about army raid during operation Bajrang from a top IB officer, having cordial relation with the outfit.[44]

The Media Support

Media coverage in India does not provide in-depth objective information about insurgent outfits and their activities. In many cases, we find coverage sympathetic to the insurgents. A large section of our intellectuals and mediamen share the ideology with the ultra-left communist terrorists. Many share the confusions of the ethnic insurgents. Unfortunately, our mediamen have scant understanding of the North-East. Many of them create havoc when they attempt at doctrinairing on behalf of the terrorists. Parag Kumar one such journalist. He was the editor of the Assamese journal *Budhwar*. He was regarded as one of the finest theoreticians of ULFA. Weekly *Budhwar* acted as a front for the ULFA. ULFA's Publicity Secretary answered queries and explained the policies of the outfit in almost every issue of the weekly. Das wrote a booklet *Swadhinatar Prastab*, in which he emphasised that the Assamese have always been ethnically different from the rest of India. According to him, the Assamese are closer to their 'Mongolian brothers' than to the Indo-Aryan ones. Assamese 'socio-cultural ethos' are different from those of the Indians. Das brings the case of well-known Vaishnavite saint, Sankaradeva and writes that **being a fish-eater, Sankaradeva was not a part of the 'Indian socio-cultural ethos'.** Das did not know that all categories of Indians, including the Brahmins from Bengal and Mithila to Konkan coast, eat fish. Parag Kumar Das and the supporters of secessionist insurgency like him base their anti-national arguments on unverified simplistic and selective facts ignoring the commonality of pan-Indian socio-cultural traits and over emphasizing the differences. Two journalists of Assam, Rajib Bora of *Sentinel* and Manjit Mahanta of *Ajir Asom* were accused by the Government and arrested on November 25 and 26, 1991 for running errand for the ULFA serving as low-level couriers, using their office telephones to send and receive message, type, photocopy and distribute ULFA's statements among other journalists, etc.[45] Many newspapers of Assam, published from Guwahati and other districts, used to publish ULFA Press Release without changing even a word. When there was mass surrender of the ULFA cadres in 1992, then the editor of *Ami*, an Assamese journal wrote: "ULFA did not drop from the sky, nor is ULFA a wild animal. ULFA is our child. (The members of) ULFA are our brothers, they are our kin. (We must understand) why they have chosen the path of the jungle."[46] **These amply illustrate the emotional attachment of a section of the Press towards ULFA** and the latter's sway over the media. The insurgents in other states also use the media for their benefit in more or less the same way.

It will be **over-simplification to say that the press in general**

supports terrorist/insurgent outfits in the North-East. There are many in the media who do not toe to the line of thinking of the latter; are pressurized by them and work under severe strain. **Many in the media have deep understanding of the region and its problems;** its links with the country in socio-cultural-historical continuum frame. India is neither an 'imaginary state' for them, nor the 'nation' and 'nationalism' is anathema. **They are not enchanted and romanticized by the 'revolutionary' image of the ULFA, NSCN, RNP, PREPAK, TNV, KCP and the like. But the task of the media is difficult. Media men are threatened and even killed. The 'messengers are in peril' as Patricia Mukhim asserts.** She rightly says: "North-East India is afflicted by two very pernicious forces both of which want to either gobble up media space or to gag the media. The former demand that their statements be reported verbatim. The latter want media to look the other way while they commit a crime. Both are difficult propositions for any media person worth his salt."[47] Recently four journalists of Assam received warnings from ULFA for their truthful reporting and analysis. We are happy and proud to have such journalists who continue to face such challenges.

As always happens whenever the country tries to reach at some sort of understanding with, be it Pakistan, USA, NSCN-IM or ULFA, planted stories appear in the media, advising New Delhi to be either more flexible, show more commitment, or to reject any proposal outright. The media, thus creates haziness and confusion, fails to play positive role.

Support from Human Rights Organizations and NGOs to the Insurgents

The insurgents of North-East, and elsewhere also, receive overt or covert support from a large number of 'Human Rights Organizations' and the organizations of the civil society. The open support and sympathy of Human Rights activists, Naga Students Federation and many NGOs for the Naga insurgents is well-known fact. As reported, the Centre was "contemplating suspension of all funds to Manipur based NGOs, as several of them act in collusion with the terrorists."[48]

Support from Foreign Human Rights Groups/NGOs

NSCN and other terrorist/insurgent outfits continue to get external support.[49] NSCN-IM has simultaneously expanded its activities outside India. While India failed to send representatives and NGOs to Unrepresented Nations and Peoples Organization at Hague, and at the same time contest the entry of NSCN-IM as a member of the same, the outfit got an opportunity to propagate its cause in international forums and was able to open avenues for arms and ammunition in SE Asia, Europe and America. Flemish support group for indigenous people (KWIA) also made a 'Declaration on Nagaland', committed itself to "the inherent right of the Naga people to self-determination and independence."

Many fronts of the insurgent outfits, such as UK based Assam Watch, an alleged front of ULFA, work in UK and other countries. It needs mention that the Assam Watch sponsored ULFA's chairman Arabinda Rajkhowa and its general secretary Anup Chetia to attend a meeting of the UN Sub-Commission's Working Group on Indigenous people held in July 1997 at Geneva; they fled only after the Interpol issued Red Corner Alert notice against them. Organizations and the individuals attend the meetings of the United Nations Working Group of Indigenous People (UNWGIP) and discuss internal matter of India.

External Help

The reports of the help received by various insurgent outfits from foreign agencies and Governments pour in from time to time. These outfits receive fund, arms, arms training, and shelter; their leaders are provided with fake passports and visas to enable them to travel in different countries. These outfits received help from China, Pakistan and Bangladesh, Pakistan's ISI and Bangladesh Directorate of Forces Intelligence (DGFI) from time to time. Camps of various insurgent groups are safely sheltered in Bangladesh. Such camps were located in Myanmar, and for some years even in Bhutan. There have been allegations of NSCN's link even with al-Qaeda. Kachin Independent Organization (KIO) and Kachin Independent Army (KIA) under Bransen in Myitkyina in Northern Myanmar used to provide arms and training to various outfits on payment. Its link with NSCN was established in 1985. The People's Liberation Army of Manipur has also link with the KIO. ULFA joined later on in 1985. Training facilities for ULFA cadres was arranged by ISI in the camps of Hizb-e-Islami of Gulbuddin Hekmatyar. ISI and DGFI facilitated the arms procurement for Indian insurgent outfits from South-East Asian arms market.

Networking between the Insurgent Outfits

The NSCN-IM increased its strength by the establishment of new insurgent organizations and networking with the old and the new. It helped in the formation of NDFB (National Democratic Front of Bodoland), BLT (Bodo Liberation Tigers; formerly, Bodo Liberation Tiger Force), KNV (Karbi National Volunteers), DHD (Dima Halim Daoga), ANVC (Achik National Voluneer Council) and NLFT (National Liberation Front of Tripura). The NSCN-IM sells arms to these outfits and provides arms training to their cadre. It receives 60:40 shares from the collections out of extortions, kidnappings, taxes, bank robberies.

United Liberation Front of Assam (ULFA) also received arms and training from the NSCN. The former helped in the formation of Kamtapur Liberation Organization (KLO). ULFA's condition to the Rajbongshi leadership and to All Kamtapur Students Union (AKSU) to provide arms training was that they form a secessionist outfit. As a result of their agreement, Kamtapur Liberation Organization (KLO) was formed. It provided arms and arms training to the cadres of the outfit, and used to receive share from the collections out of extortions, kidnappings by the KLO or during their joint operations. ULFA cultivated its links with like-minded other outfits also. Bijoy Kumar Hrangkhawl and his outfits continued to receive help and training from Mizo National Front.

Other Factors: There are many other **factors, which strengthen the insurgent/terrorist outfits,** especially during the formative days. Some of them are:

(i) **Robinhood image of the terrorist outfits:** Many insurgent groups acquire Robinhood image and become popular among the masses. ULFA's steps against corruption, drug-trafficking, illegal trade in rhino horns, molestation of women, prostitution and private tuition, etc. gave them popular legitimacy and strength. Manipuri outfits distributed rice and K. oil on cheaper rates among the villagers around their camps. This, however, does not continue for long as the masses become tired due to prolonged violence and extortion or due to some unpopular act of the outfit. ULFA's Robinhood image was broken after Sanjoy Ghosh's killing.[50]

(ii) There is **lack of proper perspective among the politicians**; they seldom look at the problem from long-term perspective. Governments/politicians allow terrorist organizations to consolidate; start peace process when the outfits need time to reorganize. The former often ignored growth of anti-national secessionist forces. The weaknesses in handling terrorism give them strength.[51]

(iii) **Non-percolation of development benefits** leads to alienation among the masses. The masses, at a time start believing that the insurgents may bring positive change.

(iv) **Simplistic approach of tackling insurgency through show of force; taking it only as law and order problem;** talking in terms of deployment of army/para-military forces/modernization of arms only exhibits our lack of understanding of the problem. Then failure of the approach leads to panic response.

(v) **Weak intellectual front; inability to fight intellectual war** strengthens insurgent cause as people start believing the myths and the propaganda of the insurgents.

(vi) Cases of **security forces remaining unalert even after timely warning,** as happened during attack on Oinam camp in Manipur, has come to light. Recently, the seizure of 73 gigabytes of classified defence information carefully stored in 40 CDs and two laptops from I. Mani Singh, a "deputy intelligence officer" of the PLA, an insurgent outfit of Manipur, points towards our **flopped security net** and

> the militants going high tech. This is an equally disturbing feature of our lapse.[52]

Faction Fights

A permanent trait of the insurgent outfits of the North-East is factionalism. This trait is even more prominent among Maoist and Islamist insurgents. The main reason of factionalism in the insurgent outfits is the personality clash and dictatorial/intolerant attitude of the insurgent leaders. Sakhrie was mercilessly butchered by Phizo when he differed from him. After NNC accepted Indian sovereignty and signed Shillong accord, in 1975, a splinter group of NNC named Nationalist Socialist Council of Nagaland (NSCN) was formed in 1980. The NSCN split in 1988 into two factions; one led by Isaak Swu and T. Muivah, and the other by S.S. Khaplang. NNC was also divided into two factions after the death of Phizo. In Manipur, both PLA and PREPAK were formed by one time members of UNLF. PREPAK has two factions led by Salam Nabachandra **alias** Khomba and Meriaba respectively. The two factions of KCP are led by Yendrembam Ibohanbi, the president of the United outfit, and by Mutum Ibopishak. A group of UNLF is led by Oken Singh. In Manipur, only PLA did not suffer from factionalism and split. A very large section of ULFA has surrendered to the Government and is presently known as SULFA. The Bodo insurgent outfits also could not remain free from this malady. The split and factionalism was seen in the insurgent outfits of Tripura also. ATTF and DHD split into Hindu and Christian factions. In many cases there is split on tribal lines.[53]

A very sad aspect of the factionalism among insurgent outfits is the internecine clash in which thousands of persons have lost their lives. The fratricidal war between NSCN-IM and NSCN-K continue unabated. A large number of Bodos have lost their lives in the fratricidal war between the BLT and NDFB.[54]

Weaknesses of the Indian Insurgent Outfits

Certain weaknesses are inherent in Indian insurgent/terrorist outfits. Their leadership is dictatorial; the ethos are non-democratic. The military wing often dominates over the political wing. As reported about ULFA, "the individual member at the lower rungs has hardly any right to express his opinion". The organization often throttles inner party democracy; violence is used in order to settled 'personal scores'.[55] Lion's share of coffers is operated by the leaders of ULFA without the knowledge of its cadres. The topmost rebel leaders lead lavish lifestyle, which has earned them disrepute and the title of "silver screen' rebels'.[56] It is pertinent to quote Sanjoy Hazarika in this case. He writes :

> "The Assamese widened the description of guerrilla warfare in this region: from jungle camps and in uncertain income from villages — in the form of taxes levied by the Nagas and Mizos — the rebel movement soared to the five star culture".[57] Money laundering by ULFA leaders has been a well-known fact.[58] They have invested huge money in the industry in Bangladesh.

The other outfits, especially the NSCN-IM, is second to none in the traits mentioned above. Muivah and other insurgent leaders do not tolerate dissent, live lavishly. It is reported that the NSCN leaders have purchased property in Shillong.[59]

Lumpenisation of all the insurgent outfits is a well-known phenomenon due to the willing acceptance/recruitment of the criminals in their ranks. This is true in case of bigger outfits like ULFA also.[60]

The unprincipled about-turn stand of the ULFA on the issue of 'Illegal Migration from Bangladesh' is not viewed favourably by Assamese civil society. In reality, an Ulfa leader staying in Bangladesh is viewed as the "Enemy's Friend'. Paresh Baruah, C-in-C of ULFA, who has 12 safe addresses in Dhaka, is known by 'friendly' names Kamaruj Zaman Khan and **Zaman Bhai.** Zaman Bhai is compelled to give his wife and two children also 'friendly' Bangladeshi names. None is convinced in Assam, and in the rest of the country, that ULFA leader's aim is to create sovereign 'Xonar Asom'. In reality, his aim and that of his host,[61] Bangladesh to create 'Greater Bangladesh' converge. In reality, the people understand the rhetoric whether of an insurgent outfit or of a political party. AGP wanted to form government with Assam United Democratic Front (AUDF), whose whole agenda is to safeguard, nourish and expand the domain of illegal Bangladeshis and retention of the provisions of IMDT Act. The voting pattern changed during last Assam Assembly elections after AGP's rhetoric. AGP wanted to form government with AUDF, whose whole agenda is to safeguard, nourish and expand the domain of illegal Bangladeshis and retention of he provisions of IMDT Act.

The people know that **insurgency in the North-East is anti-people;** it facilitates corruption; helps politicians, bureaucrats, government suppliers, criminals, extortionists in pocketing government funds; keeps perpetual resource crunch and does not allow the poorest of the poor from getting the benefits of development. The insurgents promote cleavage among communities; deepen faultlines. People want, but do not oppose the insurgents due to fear of gun.

Ethnic clash in many parts of North-East region has assumed worrisome proportion. This has taken the form of ethnic cleansing in many areas such as in Manipur due to NSCN's action against the Kukis and anti-Santhal violence in Bodo areas. The clashes between the Karbis and Kacharis in Karbi-Anglong district, Kacharis and Hmars in North-Cachar Hills district of Assam, Mizos and Brus (Reangs) in Mizoram and many more used to cause concern and worry. NSCN-IM's attempt towards ethnic cleansing of the Kukis started when the former's interest of monopolizing the benefits of illicit trade through Moreh route came in clash with that of the Kukis (Marwah 294-95). This led the chain of developments resulting into arming of Kukis and insurgency among Paites of Churachandpur district of Manipur.

Funding of Insurgent Outfits: Sources of the Funding of the insurgent are bank-robberies, extortion, pilferage of government funds, smuggling, drug trafficking, and other criminal activities.

Demise of India: ULFA's Hope: ULFA's hope of Swadhin Assam rests on the demise of India. This is in conformity with the thinking of the Islamist insurgents also.

Conflict Resolution

There have been many attempts towards conflict resolution in the region in the past. It included official conflict resolution and the civil society driven attempts for the same. The talk of the Central Government with the NSCN-IM is going on for some years. In Assam, the People's Consultative Group (PCG) initiative has brought fruit; Central Government and ULFA may talk directly and resolve the problem. However, caution is necessary as the **insurgent outfits of the North-East are not known for honoring the agreements,** be it the understanding with Naga moderate leaders leading to NHTA or Nagaland State formation or the Shillong Accord with the NNC, 'Memorandum of Understanding' (MoU) signed with the outfits in Tripura and in many other places. **The signing of MoU and surrenders lead us nowhere as a splinter group of the insurgents often revives the issue, gathers strength and the problem continues. As the tired Governments gradually concede their demands, the insurgents/outfits slowly move towards their goal.**

In Assam, while at one hand PCG was trying to bring the Centre and ULFA together for direct talks, the spurt in violence by ULFA continues. Attempts are going on to get some ULFA leaders released from jail to facilitate talks. Such attempts failed earlier to bring result, as a released leader went to Dhaka not to return back. NSCN-IM, in all these years of ceasefire, continues to indulge in mobilizing arms and resources, recruiting cadres, extortion and violent activities. Its extortion activities continued even in Assam and bank dacoity in collusion with another terrorist outfit outside Nagaland. It was reported that NSCN-IM mobilized foreign trained cadres with sophisticated arms to prevent eviction of illegally settled persons in Assam. This outfit does not want any other outfit or civil society body to talk on behalf of the Nagas. It wants to be their only representative in the talks with Government of India. Thus the outfit's attitude and its impossible demands, such as that of 'Greater Nagaland', are the greatest hurdles for the peace process. There is no doubt that even if there is an agreement with the NSCN-IM, the peace will not return as other non-participating outfits have the capacity to prolong insurgency.

It is felt that patience, mutual dialogue and understanding are the key factors to resolve such disputes and problems. Threats and actual use of force to reinforce one's claims are not only destructive but are becoming increasingly counter-productive. Every protagonist, it is felt, must weigh his or her options and explore possibilities of dialogue and conciliation. To expect the Central and the State Governments alone to resolve it is becoming increasingly impractical. Besides, any effort to hurry the process by force of arms is no longer acceptable. With patience and mutual restraint with passage of time solutions can be found.

It needs mention that some recent positive developments in the region generate hope. Although the chauvinist voice, prompted by the fear of gun, continues to be heard in Assam, the Assamese auto-critiquing has blunted its edge. Moreover, the Assamese have very strong under-current of nationalist feeling. This was amply demonstrated during Kargil War, when ULFA was thrown to the margin after its appeal to support Pakistan. In Nagaland, Sema Hoho has raised its voice against NSCN-IM inspired violence and then asked the outfit to apologise. In a parallel development, Chakhesang Students Union, Chakhesang Baptist Church Council, Chakhesang Mothers Association and Chakhesang Youth Front jointly urged the Government of Nagaland to send ultras back to designated camps. The Naga urge for peace combined with the courage to counter violence is a happy development.

Ethnicity-related problems need multi-dimensional/multi-stage tackling, including tackling on intellectual and human rights fronts. **While peace efforts should be allowed and facilitated with utmost sincerity, the Governments — Central and the States — should ensure** that the terms of cease-fire agreements are strictly adhered to and none falls prey to insurgents' bullets.

It is high time that the Central Government (i) formulates proper policy regarding the ethnicity and insurgency related problems; (ii) learns to say **'no'** to the impossible demands of the insurgents, e.g., the demands of inclusion of parts of Assam where not even two per cent Nagas reside; (iii) ensures proper utilization of the funds flowing to the states; and (iv) initiating positive changes in the system of education with the help of the State Governments, UGC and the Central Universities of the region.

The State Governments should ensure (i) the stoppage of extortions and pilferage of the public funds; (ii) gradual assumption of their duty of mobilization of local resources; sharing the financial burden more and more; (iii) gradual reduction in their dependence on army and paramilitary forces for the maintenance of law and order in the state.

It is essential to answer every myth and lie; counter every wrong signal — emanating even from the governments' wrong actions; as discussed earlier — and every propaganda of the insurgents and the media supporting them. There is need of an all out frontal intellectual war with a view to eliminating confusion and haziness of ideas. The conscientious citizens, the civil society forums and the media should play a positive role.

The political parties and the civil society in the North-East should ensure that (i) the State Governments properly deliver; (ii) blame game — blaming Delhi for every local failure, as for example, the failure of the State Governments to pay salaries of their oversized workforce on the name of Centre's 'lack of concern' — stops; (iii) local and intra-regional conflicts, as far as possible, are resolved peacefully and democratically with local/regional initiative, (iv) ethnic cleansing is stopped; (v) inter-tribal and inter-communal hatred is discouraged.

The combined strength of the police force of the states of the region is large. They should play greater and effective role in controlling insurgency and violence so that need for and dependence on army and paramilitary forces is reduced to the minimum.

The Centre and the States should see that the problems related to ethnicity, insurgency and illegal migration is speedily solved. Growth of infrastructure in the region needs to be prioritized.

NOTES

1. Hutton, *The Angami Nagas*, p. 4.
2. *Ibid*, p. 24.
3. Anthony D. Smith, *Nationalism in the Twentieth Century*, Martin Robertson Oxford, 1979, p. viii.

4. Ghai, *Autonomy and Ethnicity*, p. 4; quoted by Sushil K. Pillai, Lt. Gen. (Retd.) in '*Ethnicity, autonomy and Governance, Faultline*, Vol. 10, p. 31.
5. Dalton, *Descriptive Ethnology of Bengal.*
6. Faultline, Vol. 14, p. 73.
7. ·Charles Chasie, *The Naga Imbroglio*, p. 19.
8. *Faultline*, p. 73.
9. Gait, *The History of Assam*, p. 308, Hutton, *The Angami Nagas*, p. 13; J.P. Mills, *The Ao Nagas*, p.5, *The Lotha Nagas*, p.1.
10. The Nagas of Manipur were under Meithei kings before the advent of the British.
11. See '*Linguistic Survey of India; Faultline*, Vol. 10, p.27.
12. Kishadale, 1990 has been reportedly banned as it has pointed out the fact. *Faultline*, Vol. 3, pp. 43-45.
13. *Tehelka*, Special report, July 10, 2004.
14. H.N. Das, *Insurgency and Development, The Assam Experiment, Faultline*, Vol. 10, Ed. KPS Gill & Ajai Sahni, New Delhi (2002), p. 69.
15. *Ibid.*
16. Ved Marwah, *Uncivil Wars*, New Delhi, (1995) p. 234.
17. *Ibid*, p. 282.
18. Lt. General V.K. Nayar, (Retd.), *Low Intensity Conflicts in India*, New Delhi (2000), p. 199.
19. *Ibid*, p. 195.
20. Marwah, op. cit., p. 298.
21. Marwah, p. 294.
22. Ajai Sahni, *Survey of Conflicts and Resolution in India's North-East, Faultlines*, Vol. 12, p. 65.
23. *Ibid*, p. 65; Parliament on April 25, 2001; *Statesman*, New Delhi, April 26, 2001.
24. "*Manipur Minister-ultra outfit nexus, MHA requested to look into charges*: CM", *Assam Tribune*, December 2, 2000.
25. Sahni, op. cit, p. 93.
26. Praveen Kumar, *Tripura: Beyond the Insurgency Politics Nexus, Faultline*, Vol. 14, p. 117.
27. *Ibid*, p. 118.
28. Ajai Sahni, op. cit., p; 93.
29. *"CBI or judicial probe into Tirap insurgency demanded"*, *Nenanews*, June 22, July 6, 2000.
30. Ajai Sahni, p. 105.
31. PV Ramana, '*Networking the North-east: Partners in Terror, Faultline*, Vol. 11, p. 117.

32. Sanjoy Hazarika, *Strangers of the Mist*, p. 184.
33. *Steps against three IAS officers likely, The North-east Observer,* Guwahati, November 11, 1992.
34. *Ibid.*
35. E.N. Rammohan, *Manipur : A Degenerated Insurgency; Faultlines,* Vol. 11, pp. 11-12.
36. *Ibid*, pp. 12-13.
37. E.N. Rammohan, *Blue Print for Counter-insergency in Manipur, Faultline,* Vol. 12, pp. 8-9.
38. *Ibid,* p. 9.
39. *Ibid.*
40. *Sentinel*, June 15, 2001.
41. Marwah, op. cit., p. 285.
42. *Hindu*, August 23, 1991.
43. Sentinel, Guwahati, September 2, 1992.
44. Bibhu Prasad Routray, *The 'Revolution' comes full circle; Faultline,* Vol. 13, pp. 126-27.
45. *"Press under Freedom in Assam"*, *Hindu*, December 28, 1991; referred by Bibhu Prasad Routray, op. cit., pp. 127-28.
46. Quoted in Sanjib Barua, *Indian against itself: Assam and the politics of nationality,* New Delhi, OUP, 1999, p. 149.
47. Patricia Mukhim, *Messengers in Peril, Dialogue,* Vol. 7, No. 3; January-March 2006, pp. 18-19.
48. Ajai Sahni, *Survey of Conflict and Resolution in India's North-east, Faultline,* Vol. 12, p. 66.
49. Marwah, *Uncivil War,* pp. 227-29.
50. Gill 12/26; 13/126, Marwah/289 ii.
51. Marwah pp. 23, 170-75.
52. *Sentinel*, June 28, 2006.
53. *Faultline*, Vol. 11, pp. 144-45, Vol.12 p. 76; Marwah, op. cit., p. 282.
54. Ajai Sahni, op. cit., pp. 54-55.
55. *Faultline*, Vol. 13, p. 101.
56. *Ibid.*
57. Sanjoy Hazarika, *Strangers in the Mist, Tales of War and Peace from India's Northeast,* New Delhi, Viking, 1994, p. 175.
58. *Faultline*, Vol. 7, p. 36.
59. Marwah, op. cit., p. 284.
60. Ajai Sahni, op. cit., p. 52.
61. *The Sentinel, Editorial,* 16 June, 2006.

Other Books used but not Referred in the paper (All by Dr. B.B. Kumar)

Tension and Conflict in North-East India,
Small States Syndrom in India,
Trends of British Annexation in North-East India,
Naga Identity,
Reorganization of North-East India.

Annexure -1

Insurgent Outfits in the North-East

Umbrella Organizations

Some insurgent outfits of the North-East combined and formed umbrella organizations from time to time. Some such organizations are the following:

Indo-Burma Revolutionary Front (IBRF): comprising UNLF, NSCN-K, ULFA, KNO (Kuki National Army); formed on May 22, 1990. It is not active now.
United National Liberation Front of Seven Sisters (UNLFSS), Self Defence United Front of South-East Himalayan Region (SDUFSEHR).
United Liberation Force of Seven Sisters (ULFSS) was formed under aegis of NSCN-K with ULFA, DHD, UPDS, ADF (Arunachal Dragon Force), PLA, RDF (Revolutionary Democratic Front in July 2001 to oppose greater Nagaland.
Manipur People's Liberation Front (MPLF) consists of PLA, PREPAK, UNLS, which are Meitei outfits.
Sanmilita Janagoshthiya Sangram Samiti (SJSS): outfit co-ordinates non-Bodo organizations; it is non-secessionist umbrella outfit.

Nagaland

Naga National Council/Federal Government of Nagaland/ Naga Army, NNC/FGN/NA: NNC: The NNC, under the leadership of Phizo, started secessionist insurgency in Nagaland: it set up Federal Government of Nagaland and the Naga Army. The outfit accepted Indian Sovereignty after Shillong Accord signed on November 11, 1975. The NNC became gradually ineffective after the Nagaland State formation and elections, and especially after the Shillong Accord. Earlier a faction of the outfit formed by the Semas surrendered with the arms. There was a split in the NNC after the death of Phizo; the two factions were led by Ms. Adino, the daughter of Phizo and the other by his follower Khodao Yanthan, a Lotha Naga. Yanthan faction merged with NSCN-IM during 1996-97 winter.

National Socialist Council of Nagaland (NSCN): About 140 NNC activists under the leadership of Issak Chisi Swu, Thuingaleng Muivah and S.S. Khaplang repudiated Shillong Accord and formed NSCN in 1980 and pursued their secessionist insurgent activities. The NSCN also split into Issak-Muivah and Khaplang factions in 1988.

Assam

United Liberation Front of Assam (ULFA) was formed on April 7, 1979 at Rong-ghar, Sibsagar in Assam a few months earlier than the commencement of anti-foreigners movement in Assam in July that year led by all Assam Students Union (AASU) and All Assam Gana Sangram Parishad (AAGSP). Its leaders were Paresh Barua (Chief of Staff), Arabinda Rajkhowa (Chairman), Anup Chetia (General Secretary) and Pradeep Gogoi (Vice-President). The declared goal of the outfit was secession of Assam from India. Initially, the outfit operated in close co-ordination with the Agitationists. However, after the Assam Accord in August 1985 and the formation of the Asom Gana Parishad (AGP) by the leaders of AASU-AAGSP, and its entry into the electoral politics, ULFA distanced itself from the AGP.

All Bodo Students Union (ABSU): established in 1967, became active in late 1980s; it demanded statehood under the leadership of Upendranath Brahma.

Bodo Volunteer Force (BVF): the armed wing of ABSU; laid down arms to facilitate creation of Bodoland Autonomous Council (BAC) in February 1993.

Bodo Liberation Tigers (BLT): a section of BVF did not accept "Bodo Accord", formed **Bodo Liberation Tiger Force (BLTF)** in 1996, which was later named as Bodo Liberation Force (BLT); it had ceasefire agreement with Government of India on March 29, 2000 for the establishment of Bodoland Territorial Council (BTC).

National Democratic Front of Bodoland (NDFB), established in 1988; initiated 'guerrilla war'; established as **Bodo Security Force (BSF)** earlier in the same year under the leadership of Ranjan Daimari; it aims at establishment of "independent Bodo nation" north of Brahmaputra river. It has networking and 'working arrangement' with NSCN-IM.

Dimasa National Security Force (DNSF) ceased to exist after mass surrender in 1995.

Dima Halim Daoga (DHD)/Dima Halong Daoga was formed with the objective of establishing Dimaraji/Dimaland for the Dimasa Kachari tribe out of Assam comprising of North Cachar Hills and the adjoining areas; it was formed by Jewel Garlosa, 'Commander-in-Chief' of the DNSF, who did not surrender. It was headed by Bejoy Nandung, its 'Commander-in-Chief' till his arrest on July 3, 1999.

Karbi National Volunteer (KNV) : an outfit of the Karbis of the Karbi Anglong district of Assam.

Kamtapur Liberation Organization (KLO): formed by Koch-Rajbongshi tribes in 1995 with the objective of the formation of Kamtapur state comprising of the Goalpara, Dhubri, Kokrajhar and Bongaigaon districts of Assam and six North Bengal districts. Tushar Das *alias* Jiban Singha is the 'Chairman'; other leaders include Hiten Rai, Ravi Rajbongshi, Rahul Rai and Kajal Rai.

Some other insurgent groups: (out of about three dozen listed in Assam) are:

United People's Democratic Solidarity (UPDS); an umbrella outfit of DHD, KNV and Muslim United Liberation Tigers of Assam (MULTA).

Some splinter groups/not so active outfits are :

People's United Liberation Force (PULF)

Rabha National Security Force (RNSF)

Tiva National Revolutionary Force (TNRF): set up in 1996 with the aim of setting up 'independent Tiwa Land' and to fight against the perceived 'systematic exploitation and repression of the Tiwa community by the Indian state machinery. Its leader is Bhogeshwar Bordoloi.

All Assam Koch-Rajbongshi Students Union (AAKRSU)

Birsa Commando Force (BCF) demands to include separate Adivasi state and Scheduled Caste status for the Santhals, Mundas, Oraons and other tea-garden tribes of Assam.

Adivasi Security Force (ASF)

Bengali Tiger Force (BTF)

Gorkha Tiger Force (GTF)

Muslim outfits (out of some 15 outfits reported):

Muslim United Liberation Front (MULFA): has come out with the demand for a separate state comprising of five Muslim majority districts of Assam.

Islamic Liberation Tiger Force (ILTF)

Muslim Liberation Militia of Assam (MLMA)

Minority Volunteer Force (MVF)

Manipur: out of some 35 outfits about 18 insurgent groups are presently active in Manipur.

Meitei/Valley-based organization of Manipur are:

Revolutionary Nationalist Party (RNP) established by the Communist leader Hijam Irabot Singh in 1953. Irabot Singh also formed **Manipur Red Guards** for waging war for 'liberation of Manipur'.

United National Liberation Front (UNLF) was formed under the leadership of Samarendra Singh on November 24, 1964 with the objective of Manipur's independence and establishment of a 'socialist society' in Manipur.

Revolutionary Government of Manipur (RGM) was formed

by a breakaway faction of the UNLF under the leadership of Oinam Sudhir Kumar Singh in December 1968 as a government-in-exile with headquarters at Sylhet in East Pakistan/Bangladesh with the objective of 'liberating Manipur through armed struggle'.

People's Liberation Army (PLA) was founded by N. Bisheswar Singh in September 1978. He had Communist/leftist ideology; was reportedly trained in guerrilla warfare in China. His objective was to organize a revolutionary front covering North-East; to unite all nationalities to liberate Manipur.

People's Revolutionary Party of Kangleipak (PREPAK) was founded in 1977 under the leadership of R.K. Tulachandra with communist ideology; it demanded expulsion of mayangs (outsiders).

Kangleipak Communist Party (KCP) was founded in 1980 with the same objective as of PLA.

People's Liberation Army (PLA).

Kanglei Yaol Kanna Lup (Oken faction), KYKL(O)

Kanna Yaol Kanna Lup (Tonjamb faction) KYKL (T)

Kangleipak Liberation Organization, KLO

Ireipak Kanba Lup, IKL

People's Republican Army (PRA) : set up in early 1990 to work against Mayangs (outsiders) and for countering PLA; formed by PLA dissenter, Prakash.

People's United Liberation Front (PULF).

Revolutionary People's Front (RPF) : formed in 1989 as the political wing of PLA after its re-organization; it formed a government-in-exile in Sylhet (Bangladesh).

Revolutionary Joint Committee (RJC), umbrella organization/a united front of Meitei Terrorist organizations — PLA, PREPAK and KCP

Manipur People's Liberation Front (MPLF); umbrella platform of UNLF, PLA and PREPAK

Indo-Burma Revolutionary Front (IBRF): a pan-Mongoloid coalition of NSCN-K, ULFA, UNLF and KNO formed on May 22, 1990; its objective: to pursue 'common battle' against the 'totalising power' of the Indian state.

Manipur People's Revolutionary Front (MPRF);

Naga Insurgent Groups (operating in Manipur):
National Socialist Council of Nagaland (Issac-Muivah): NSCN-IM
National Socialist Council of Nagaland — Khaplang; NSCN-K
NNC-Adino/NFG

Kuki-Chin outfits:

Kuki National Front (KNF); formed on May 18, 1988 for establishing separate Kuki state within Indian Union and unification of all the scattered members of the tribe. It was set up under the leadership of Rancho Thangboi Kuki. About one thousand people, mostly of the Kuki tribe have lost their life in NSCN-IM, KNF clashes. Hundreds of members have received training in Kachin Independent Army (KIA) camps. Its factions are:

-Kuki National Front (Military Council), KNF (MC)
-Kuki National Council (President), KNF (P)
-Kuki National Front (Zogam), KNF(Z)

Kuki National Army, KNA
Kuki/Khongsai Revolutionary Army, KRA
Kuki Security Force, KSF
Hmar People's Convention (Democracy), HPC(D)
Hmar Revolutionary Front, HRF
Zomi Revolutionary Army, ZRA
Zomi Revolutionary/National Volunteers, ZRV/ZNV
Zomi Revolutionary Army, ZRA
United Kuki Liberation Front, UKLF
Kom-Rhem People's Convention, KPRC

Islamic Outfits:
North-East Minority Front, NEMF

PULF

Islamic National Front, INF
Islamic Revolutionary Front, IRF
United Islamic Liberation Army, UILA

Tripura

Tripura Ganamukti Parishad (TGP), formed in 1948, under the leadership of Biren Dutta, by Aghor debbarman, Dasarath Debbarman and Sudhanva Debbarman to wage an 'armed Communist struggle'.

Seng Krak (Clenched First), formed in 1947 by Balai Devbarman, Durjay Karta, Prabhat Ray, Bansi Thakur and others as a secret, militant tribal organization. It was banned in 1948 for the alleged violence against the refugees. Its impact on the tribals was insignificant; it remained dormant; revived in 1967, but could not become an effective organization.

Tripura Upajati Juba Samiti (Tripura Tribals Youth League), TUJS; an overground political organization with a militant wing, Tripura Sena (Tripura Army).

Tripura Sena: a force of armed volunteers raised by TUJS under the leadership of its assistant general secretary, Bijoy Kumar Hrangkhawl in 1970.

Amra Bangali (We are Bengali): a communal Bengali organization and a constituent outfit of **Anand Marg,** formed to counter militant activities of TUJS and other militant organizations.

Tripura National Volunteers (TNV); Hrangkhawl formed Tripura National Volunteers, TNV in December 1978. He engineered two riots in May 1979 and June 1980 in which about 1800 person died and thousands of houses were burnt down. TNV violence was retaliated by 'Amra Bangali'. Hrangkhawl was arrested in June 1980, after which he dissolved TNV and revived it again in August 1982. The insurgency re-started. TNV members surrendered after tripartite agreement and were rehabilitated.

Army of Tripura People's Liberation Organization (ATPLO): formed by disgruntled members of TNV after its dissolution by Hrangkhawl. It indulged in extortion in rural areas and existed till the surrender of Binanda Jamatiya and his faction in 1983.

ATPLO (Chuni Kaloi faction) formed in 1981 due to split in the outfit.

National Liberation Front of Tripura (NLFT): formed in 1989 with Dhananjoy Reang, erstwhile TNV Vice-president, TNV as President and other disgruntled TNV members.

Tripura Resurrection Army (TRA), formed by Dhananjoy Reang in 1994 after his expulsion from NLFT. The outfit surrendered en-masse to the Government in 1997.

NLFT-Bishwamohan Debbarma faction: There was difference between Christian members of the outfit and Hindu tribals due to their forcible conversion leading to split in the outfit in 2001. Bishwamohan Debbarman remained the president of the **Christian faction.**

NLFT-Nayanbashi Jamatiya faction: the Hindu faction formed after split in 2001.

Borok National Council of Tripura (BNCT): There was split in the NLFT in 2000 due to differences between Halam and Debbarma tribal members leading to the formation of BNCT under the leadership of Joshua Debbarm.

All Tripura Tribal Force (ATTF): The outfit was formed in 1990 by the disgruntled members of the TNV under the leadership of Lalit Debbarma and Ranjit Debbarma, who were not happy with the TNV surrender in 1988. Lalit Debbarma surrendered with 1633 members of the outfit on August 23, 1993 after signing a 'Memorandum of Settlement'. A faction led by Ranjit Debbarma did not surrender.

Republican People's Army (RPA): Changed name of **ATTF**.

Plungers and Rangers: changed name of NLFT!

United Bengal Liberation Front (UBLF): formed in 1999 with the objective of protecting Bengalis from the terrorist attacks.

Mizoram

Mizo National Front (MNF): 20-year old Mizo insurgency came to an end in 1986 after accord of the Central Government with the MNF under the leadership of Laldenga. Mizo Hills district became a Union Territory in 1972 and fullfledged Mizoram state in 1987 as a result of the accord.

Bru National Liberation Front (BNLF) demands Autonomous District Council under 6th Schedule of the Constitution within Mizoram for the Bru (Reang) people.

Hmar People's Convention (HPC): an insurgent outfit of the Hmar people. HPC led insurgency ended after agreement with Mizoram government.

Zomi Re-Unification Organization, ZRO.

Meghalaya

Hynniewtrep Achik Liberation Council (HALC) was the first militant outfit representing Hynniewtrep (Khasi and Jaintia) and the Garos (Achik) communities which was formed to fight against the outsiders (Dkhars).

Hynniewtrep National Liberation Council (HNLC) was formed in 1992 due to split in HALC due to inter-tribal antagonism between Khasi-Jaintias and the Garos of Meghalaya. It aims at transforming Meghalaya into a State exclusively for the Khasi tribe.

Achik Matgrik Liberation Army (AMLA) is the other insurgent outfit of the Garos formed after the split in HALC.

Achik National Volunteer Council (ANVC) formed in December 1995; demands the Achikland comprising of the three Garo districts of Meghalaya and adjoining areas of Assam. The Government of India banned it on November 16, 2000.

Garo National Council (GNC) demands the formation of Garo state consisting of the three Garo districts of Meghalaya.

Arunachal Pradesh

National Socialist Council of Nagaland (NSCN): The two NSCN factions have made forcible inroads in Arunachal, especially in Tirap and Changlang districts. The violence, extortion and forcible conversion by the two NSCN outfits have greatly disturbed the peace in Arunachal.

Arunachal Dragon Force (ADF) now known as '**East India Liberation Front (EILF)**, is formed by the surrendered terrorists belonging to the **United People's Volunteers of**

Arunachal Pradesh (UPVA). It aims at the protection of indigenous Arunachalis from the infiltrators and immigrants and formation of an 'independent homeland' for the Khamti tribe in the State. With an estimated cadre of 400, the outfit operates in the Lohit, Changlang and Dibang valley districts of Arunachal Pradesh.

Annexure -2

YEAR-WISE VIOLENCE SITUATION IN N.E. REGION DURING THE YEARS 2002 TO 2006 (UPTO 31.05.06)

Year	*Incidents*	*Terrorists Killed*	*Security Forces Killed*	*Civilians Killed*
2002	1312	571	147	454
2003	1332	523	90	494
2004	1234	404	110	414
2005	1332	405	70	393
(31.05.06)	(554)	(179)	(21)	(124)
2006 (upto 31.05.06)	518	172	27	109

Head	*Meghalaya*			*Arunachal Pradesh*			*Mizoram*		
	2004	*2005*	*2006*	*2004*	*2005*	*2006*	*2004*	*2005*	*2006*
Incidents	47	37 (16)	23	41	32 (06)	10	03	04 (03)	05
Terrorist Killed	22	23 (10)	09	35	16 (05)	03	03	0 (-)	0
SFs Killed	08	0 (-)	0	02	01 (-)	0	01	0 (-)	0
Civilians Killed	17	01 (01)	06	06	03 (-)	0	0	02 (02)	0

(Figures in brackets are upto 31.05.05)
Source: Compiled from various sources.

STATE-WISE SECURITY SITUATION DURING THE YEARS 2004, 2005 AND 2006 (UPTO 31.05.06)

Head	*Assam*			*Tripura*			*Nagaland*			*Manipur*		
	2004	2005	2006	2004	2005	2006	2004	2005	2006	2004	2005	2006
Incidents	267	398 (162)	137	212	115 (62)	30	186	192 (74)	106	478	554 (231)	207
Terrorist Killed	104	74 (33)	10	51	21 (14)	06	55	70 (34)	46	134	202 (83)	98
SFs Killed	17	07 (02)	08	46	11 (06)	05	0	01 (-)	0	36	50 (13)	14
Civilians Killed	194	173 (37)	46	67	28 (11)	05	42	28 (11)	13	88	158 (62)	39

(Figures in brackets are upto 31.05.05)

4 The Insurgent North-East

E.N. Rammohan

The Nationalist Socialist Council of Nagaland (Isaac-Muivah) NSCN (IM)

When the Shillong agreement was signed between the moderate group of the old Naga National Council and the Government of India in 1975, two leaders of the NNC, Isaac Swu, a Sema and Thuingaleng Muivah, a Thangkhul from Ukhrul in Manipur were in China with a group of cadres of the NNC. They refused to be a party to the Shillong accord. They teamed up with Kaphlang a Hemi Naga living in the Sagaing Division of Northern Burma and formed the NSCN splitting from the NNC. In Nagaland, the NNC had already split into a moderate and a diehard faction. The Naga tribes were not united. The die-hard faction teamed up with the NSCN. By 1985, the NSCN had made an arrangement for training their cadres and procuring weapons with the Kachin Independent Organization (KIO) and its armed wing the Kachin Independent Army (KIA) under Bransen in Myitkyina in Northern Burma. The Peoples Liberation Army of Manipur had also linked up with the KIO. The United Liberation Front (ULFA) of Assam joined the two in 1985 and they were also taken to the Kachin area for training. In 1988 differences between the Konyak Nagas and the Thangkhul Nagas that had been simmering for some time erupted into a fight and Thuingaleng Muivah and his Thangkhul Nagas had to hastily retreat from Burma to Ukhrul in Manipur. This was a permanent split. Thus, two groups came into being — NSCN (IM) and NSCN (K) never to reconcile. In 1990, the Government of India managed to persuade Bransen to disassociate the KIO from the Indian insurgent groups. Anticipating this, the ULFA leader Paresh Barua, had, after being refused by the Chinese Government, sent a team to Bangladesh to ask for sanctuary. The Bangladesh Directorate of Forces Intelligence (DGFI) gladly agreed to help and took the ULFA team to the Pakistan embassy and soon the team was on its way to Karachi and Peshawar for training in the camps of the Hizb-e-Islami of Gulbuddin Hekmatyar. This was in 1990-1991. Very soon, the NSCN (IM) joined the ULFA in Bangladesh and the Pakistan Inter Services Intelligence (ISI) had agreed to arrange supplies of arms for the Indian insurgent groups from the arms bazaar of Thailand to be brought by coastal steamer to Cox's Bazaar and thence carried overland through Burma, Manipur and then into Nagaland. The first such consignment was brought through this route in 1992. Probably, two more consignments were brought by this route in 1993 and 1994. In 1995, the Indian Army learning of a consignment being carried along this route by the NSCN (IM), ULFA and the National Democratic Front of Bodoland (NDFB), ambushed the column in conjunction with the Burmese army killing fifty eight cadres of the two groups and capturing as many arms. This was operation Golden Bird.

The NSCN (IM) changed the complexion of insurgency in the North-East. They looked around and began to link up with other insurgent groups in the area. In 1986 the MNF in Mizo Hills had signed a peace agreement with the Central Government and surrendered their arms. Within a few years, the Hmars, a sub-tribe of the Mizos, who lived in eastern Mizo Hills, Churachandpur district of Manipur and in Cachar and North Cachar Hills districts of Assam had taken arms against the Mizo Hills government, feeling that the Mizos had neglected them. The Nagas and Mizos were ancient enemies, but surprisingly, the Hmars accepted the proffered hand of friendship extended by the NSCN (IM). Very cleverly, the NSCN (IM) did not operate with the Hmars in Mizoram, but they did operate with them in Cachar and North Cachar Hills. Here they set up training camps for the Hmar Peoples Convention (HPC) as the insurgent group of the Hmars was called. The group normally operated in a section of ten cadres of whom eight were from the

NSCN, while two were from the HPC. Interestingly, the money extorted from the corrupt District Council officials of the North Cachar Hills District Council and from the tea garden managers of Cachar was also shared between the NSCN and the HPC in the same ratio.

In Manipur, and Nagaland, the NSCN (IM) were in full cry from 1992 after they got the first consignment of arms through the ISI channel. The largest collection of money by the NSCN (IM) was in these two states from extortion from trucks and buses plying between Dimapur and Imphal. All houses in the towns and villages of Nagaland and the Naga areas of Manipur had to pay house "tax" to the NSCN (IM). In addition, the NSCN (IM) extended a helping hand to three insurgent groups of their sworn enemies, the Meithei Kanglei Yawol Kanna Lup (KYKL), that had been carved out of disgruntled elements in the United National Liberation Front (UNLF), the Kangleipak Communist Party (KCP) and two Kuki groups that had broken off from factions of the Kuki National Organisation (KNO) created to fight the Nagas. These were the United Kuki Liberation Front (UKLF) in Chandel district of Manipur and the Kuki Revolutionary Army (KRA) operating in the Saikul valley. The money extorted in joint operations with the NSCN (IM) by these groups was again divided in the ratio 8:2. The KYKL operated in the Imphal valley and they had an elaborate extortion network. The NSCN (IM) benefited immensely with this collaboration. The UKLF was placed under the NSCN (IM) in Chandel district. In November 2000, a combined group of the NSCN (IM) and the UKLF got the Deputy Commissioner and his five Block Development Officers to cash five cheques totalling Rs. 44 lakhs of rural development funds sent by the Central Government by holding them at gunpoint in custody for three days and walking off with the money. When they heard this, the Home Ministry directed the Cease-Fire Monitoring Group (CFMG) to take it up with the NSCN (IM). When the central leadership of the NSCN (IM) asked the explanation of their unit at Chandel, they blindly replied that it was the UKLF that did this job! The NSCN (IM) also had a link with the Zhomi Reunification Army (ZRA) that operated in the southern areas of Churachandpur district.

In Mehgalaya, the NSCN (IM) established a relation with the two insurgent units that had come up there. These two units, the Hynniewtrep National Liberation Council (HNLC) and the Achik National Volunteer Council (ANVC) were basically nothing but criminal gangs set up to extort and rob money from the Marwari and other outside elements in that state. There was no basis whatsoever for an insurgency in this state. The agreement with these two groups gave sanctuary for the NSCN (IM) in Khasi Hills and Garo Hills and covert infiltration and exfiltration routes to and from Bangladesh besides a fat share of all the money robbed by these two groups.

In Assam, two tribal groups took to arms in the 1990s, the Dima Halem Daoga (DHD) in North Cachar Hills and the United Peoples Democratic Solidarity (UPDS) in Karbi Anglong. Both these hill districts had a District Council that received development funds directly. In both these districts, the politicians elected to the Disrict Councils misappropriated development funds and particularly in the North Cachar Hills, virtually no development took place in more than thirty years of the District Councils functioning. The NSCN (IM) was on hand to help these two small insurgent groups which armed and trained them. Here they had a specific design as in the case of helping the HPC. The NSCN (IM) wanted a foothold in these two districts as they planned to claim both districts for their expanded Nagaland.

The initial cause for the insurgency in the Naga Hills was the alienation created among a section of their leaders and a feeling that they were not like the plains Hindu or Muslim peoples. This sense of alienation was fostered by the proselytisation carried out by the British from the nineteenth century. This was compounded by the policy of the Central Government to flood the state, when it was created, with development funds followed up by sending a band of contractors that acquired the dubious name of the Delhi durbar who corrupted the politicians and bureaucrats of the state and brought back large percentage of the development funds sent to the state back to Delhi by carrying out development work and supplying stores on paper. Unhappily, the bureaucracy in conjunction with the politicians and the contractors/suppliers who controlled all essential commodities like rice, sugar, petrol, kerosene and later gas ensured from the beginning that all these supplies were diverted to the black-market from the railheads itself. As a result the states of Nagaland, Manipur, Mizoram, and Arunachal Pradesh has only known a black economy from inception.

The mistakes made by the Government of India when the Naga insurgency broke out exarcebated the situation in the Naga and Manipur hills in the late fifties and sixties. The Central Government enacted the Assam Disturbed Area Act in 1955 and the Armed Forces Special Powers Act in 1958 and deployed the Army to tackle the situation. The Police and the Judiciary were sidelined in the process and inevitably excesses occurred during operations. The policy measure of the Army to regroup the Naga villages also deeply alienated the people. This was a leaf picked from the Malayan insurgency. In Malaya the people regrouped were Chinese settlers in the Rubber plantations. They were living in temporary shanties. The Naga villages were ancient with sacred groves. The last major action of the Para Military Assam Rifles was the incident at Oinam village in Senapati district of Manipur. On 9 July, 1987, a group of the NSCN (IM) overran the Assam Rifles post at Oinam village killing a Junior Commissioned Officer and eight soldiers capturing 90 Self Loading Rifles, 27 Sten Guns, 10 Light Machine Guns, two Mortars and a large quantity of ammunition. In the reaction to the incident, the Army almost flattened Oinam village, killing14 persons, none of whom were cadres of the NSCN(IM). Oinam has passed into the legend of the Naga struggle for independence and songs are sung during memorial services for the innocent people who were killed there.

In 1997 a cease-fire was signed with the NSCN (IM) leaders and a Cease-Fire Monitoring Group (CFMG) was set up. Unfortunately, **the Government of India made two mistakes**. At the time of signing the cease-fire agreement, the NSCN (IM) had several camps in the Naga districts of Manipur. The cease-fire was signed for Nagaland only, but was unofficially extended to Manipur. Secondly, the **Government of Nagaland did nothing to enforce the conditions prescribed for the insurgent group.** The NSCN

(IM) had already established a **well-oiled extortion network** in Nagaland and Manipur. After the cease-fire, the **NSCN (IM) continued to extort money** from all businessmen and the people with impunity. The cease-fire is now eight years old. **During these eight years, the NSCN (IM) has flouted virtually all the conditions of the cease-fire with impunity and extorted crores of rupees that has enabled the group to set up offices in Bangkok, Manila, and Amsterdam. They have also brought in considerable number of weapons, purchasing them with the assistance of the ISI and the DGFI and bringing them by coastal steamer to Cox's Bazaar and then taking them overland via the Chittagong Hill Tracts (CHT), Mizoram, Manipur to Nagaland and then to Assam. Today the NSCN (IM) has about 5500 cadres and as many weapons.**

The NSCN (IM) has a list of unreasonable demands. They want a separate constitution, with complete autonomy of administration, with permission to retain their armed cadres as their army. They want a separate flag. They of course want the Government of India to finance their revenue and development expenditure. They obviously do not want inconvenient institutions like the Comptroller and Auditor General, the Income Tax Department and the Supreme Court.

The Nagas have no case whatsoever for a greater Nagland. Their claims on the North Cachar Hills and Karbi Anglong district and Tirap and Changlang districts of Arunachal Pradesh are not justified by demography. There can be no question of detaching the Naga majority districts of Manipur, as this was a country ruled by its kings for more than 2000 years with a well-defined boundary, before it was merged into India. There can be simply no question of granting any kind of autonomy to any state in India, be it Kashmir or Nagaland as this would open a Pandora's box and a hundred different groups in different parts of India would raise similar demands. Government of India can and should immediately create District Councils in all the five hill districts of Manipur and leave development to them in these five districts.

The social bodies in Nagaland like the Naga Ho Ho, the Naga Mothers body and the Baptist Church do not want the cease fire to be abrogated after eight long years. The Government of India has committed several grievous mistakes in the least eight years of the cease-fire. They have not enforced the conditions of the cease-fire. They have allowed the NSCN (IM) to openly extort money from the business community. Frankly the writ of the Government today runs only in the precincts of the Raj Bhavan in Kohima. The first step should be to firmly and gradually stop all extortion by detailing escorts and guards for the private sector. They should then ensure that all civil supplies are made available to the remotest village at the correct price. The people of Nagaland have not known what is the white market since its birth. The Government of India should then talk to the NSCN (K) and to the old NNC along with the NSCN (IM). They should confine all armed cadres of the NSCN (IM) in camps and see that all weapons are surrendered to the Government. They should then be taken back and issued to the Army or the Paramilitary forces. The cadres of the two NSCN groups should then be absorbed in the paramilitary forces of the country. If the NSCN (IM) do not agree, we should be ready to take them on again in a fresh round of jungle war. There is no doubt that we can call their bluff.

The Insurgent Groups of Manipur

The causes of the insurgency in Manipur are easily identifiable. There is a strong sense of alienation among the Meithei people. There is today a sizeable group of intellectuals among them who advocate separation from India. The Government's mistakes are also easily identifiable. The Central Government has from the time Manipur was made an Union Territory treated the state like a colony of India. The bureaucrats who went from Delhi in collusion with the Marwaries and other traders from India's mainland thoroughly corrupted the administration. Firstly, they saw to it that all civil supplies coming from the mainland was diverted at the railheads itself. The people of Manipur have not known a white economy since its absorption into India. In this process the local businessmen, bureaucrats and politicians also joined the bandwagon. Development money was swindled in crores. Since there was no real development, there was no generation of employment in industries, horticulture, and a hundred other ventures. There was only the Government for milking and it was bled dry by the unholy trio of the politicians, the bureaucrats and the traders. When the unemployed frustrated angry youngmen took to the gun, they added to the unholy trio in taking the largest share of the money diverted from development. Extortion has become pervasive in Manipur, particularly in the valley. All government servants contribute to different insurgent groups. The cashier or accountant of each department deducts the contribution and pays to the insurgent group. When the government offices are cordoned by the CRPF, the insurgents visit the heads of departments at their houses. The politicians pay the highest shares to the insurgent groups as they get the biggest cut of the development money.

The two biggest groups of the Meithei insurgents were the PLA and the PREPAK. They were at their peak in the late 1970s looting banks, attacking police stations and ambushing security patrols to get their weapons. The Army deployed in the valley, was able to break the back of these two groups after sustained operations capturing the chief of the PLA and killing many of their top leaders. Unfortunately the causes of the insurgency were not addressed and both the groups revived in the 1990s. The UNLF that was raised in 1964 as a social organisation now joined the PLA and the PREPAK. Two other groups that sprung up were the KCP and the KYKL. All these groups took advantage of two factors in Manipur that gave a distinct advantage to guerilla warfare. These were the lack of roads and a vast hinterland. Both these factors were in Chandel and Churachandpur districts. Both districts had a long unpoliced border with Burma. The border to a depth of 100 kilometres was thickly forested and without any roads. All the groups took full advantage of these two factors and established base camps deep inside this hinterland. Across the border in Burma from Chandel district was the Kebaw valley and the Somra tracts, while across the border from Churachandpur district was the Chin Hills. The Burmese government had very little presence in the Chin Hills and in the Somra tracts. Also, China after its economic liberalisation had set up an industrial base in the Kunming and Yunnan area. There were several arms factories set up in this industrial complex. Some of the insurgent groups in northern Burma that had surrendered to the Burmese army had been rehabilitated in drug cartels and as clandestine weapon dealers. The PLA, UNLF, PREPAK, KYKL and the KCP were able to purchase arms from these arms dealers. The UNLF has besides AK rifles, LMGs, rocket launchers and even some air defence guns. The PLA and the KYKL both had links with the NSCN (IM) and procured weapons from them through the ISI and the DGFI links from Bangladesh. The whole tract of several thousand hectares comprising Churachandpur and part of Tamenglong districts bounded by the Thangjing hills in the east, national highway 53 in the north, the Man Bahadur road in the west and the Burmese border in the south is a liberated area. In 2000, the BSF was given the task of clearing four sub-divisions in this rectangle of land that was occupied by the PLA and the UNLF for three years. These were the sub-divisions of Thinghat, Henglep, Thanglon and Parbung. All the four sub-divisions were cleared and the Indian flag flew over these four subdivisions again. Regrettably, the State Government did not cooperate and send the civil administration to re-establish their authority. In 2001 the BSF was withdrawn and the insurgents returned. In 2005, the Army was deployed extensively in both Chandel and Churachandpur districts. They have reoccupied the four sub-divisions and also cleared the area of south Chandel. The civil administration is yet to re-establish their presence in these areas.

Besides the Meithei groups, a Kuki group called the Kuki National Army (KNA) was set up in 1992 to fight against the NSCN (IM). The KNA has split up into at least five to six factions during the last fifteen years. Each group is a rag-tag band that supports a politician during elections and gains patronage from him for shares from the development funds. All these groups should be disarmed. Some of them are being used to fight against the Meithei groups — the UNLF and the PLA. This should be forthwith discontinued and all these rag-tag groups asked to disband. The cadres of these groups can be rehabilitated by absorbing them in the Paramilitary forces.

What is the answer for Manipur. The government has today a fine chance of retrieving the situation. It has to prepare a detailed plan to develop the hinterland in Manipur. With the Army in position, roads should be constructed connecting all villages to the nearest towns. The Border Roads should do this work. Each village should get a water supply system. Once this is done, experts from different fields, poultry, fisheries, horticulture, piggery, dairy farming, forestry, cultivation of orchids and medicinal plants should prepare detailed plans for the two districts. In each project the local people should be involved in the execution. Only the expert should be from outside. It should be possible to transform the two districts in a time frame of two to three years, after which the same plan should be implemented in Ukhrul, Senapati and Tamenglong districts. Development grants should be released in instalments for each project, ensuring that concurrent audits are done at each stage before releasing the next instalment. The audit parties should be detailed from states outside the north-east.

All convoys of civil supplies should be escorted by the CRPF from the road heads to the depots in Imphal and from there to the district HQs and thence to every single village. This will break the nexus between the trader, the bureaucrat, the politician and the insurgent in the state. This one measure will turn the people of the state against the insurgents.

As this plan is being executed, the valley must be divided into sectors and strongly policed by the Army or Paramilitary forces to prevent the insurgent groups from reorganising there. Secondly, a border road should be constructed along the Indo-Burma border in Arunachal Pradesh, Nagaland, Manipur and Mizoram and a string of border outposts constructed and manned by the Border Security Force.

The Insurgent Groups of Tripura

The insurgency in Tripura is due to one cause only, the domination of the tribal state by Bengali Hindus and Muslims after partition in

1947 and the second class treatment given to the tribal people by the caste Hindu Bengalis.

Tripura was a kingdom ruled by a tribal king of the Tripuri tribe that migrated into this hill state long before recorded history. The tribes of Tripura all migrated westwards from the headwaters of the Yangtse Kiang and the Hwang Ho along with other Tibeto Burman tribes like the Boro Cacharis of Assam and the Garos of Meghalaya. The tribes that migrated into the Tripura tracts were the Tripuri, Riang or Bru, Jamatia, Halam and Noatia. The Tripuri dominated the other tribes and ruled as the dominant Kingdom of Tripura till it was merged with the Indian Union in 1949.

Migration of Bengali Hindus and probably Muslims into Tripura started from the 14th century. The Tripuri kings encouraged migration and settlement of Bengali Hindus into Tripura to encourage their tribal people to take to wet cultivation. The Tripuri kings also encouraged the Bengali language to the exclusion of Kok Barok, and the other tribal dialects. The tribal percentage was reduced to 50 per cent by 1941. In 1951, just three years after partition, the tribals were reduced to 36.85 per cent. One other interesting factor is also the increasing percentage of conversion of the tribals into Christianity. The figure in 1947 was just 6151. It was 46,472 in 1991.

When a flood of refugees swamped Tripura in 1947, the Congress Party was seen to side with the Bengali Hindus. The Communist party of India (CPI) and later the Communist Party Marxist (CPM) sided with the tribals. The tribals formed the *Gana Mukti Parishad* (GMP) in 1948 to protect the civil rights and economic development of the tribals. The GMP organised a rally against smuggling of rice into East Pakistan. The resultant police suppression led to the creation of a guerilla wing in the GMP called the *Shanti Sena.* Khowai sub-division became a liberated area. The CPI joined the tribals in their struggle. The GMP became the tribal wing of the party after this.

In 1943, the tribal king had reserved an area of 1950 square miles for tribals and prohibiting transfer of land of tribals to non-tribals. The tidal wave of refugees was so much that the Regent queen dereserved 330 square miles. Worse still, even the reduced area could not be reserved for the tribals. Encroachment and illegal transfer of tribal lands continued. The Tripura land revenue and land reforms act was passed in 1960. This prohibited transfer of tribal land to non-tribals. The provision for restoration of alienated land was, however, passed only in January 1969 thus regularising land alienated even after the land reform act was passed for nine years. The Bengali lobby was still strong and the Congress party got firmly identified as anti-tribal and pro-Bengali.

In 1967 tribal leaders set up the Tripura *Upa Jati Samity* (TUJS). Paradoxically this group strengthened ties with the Congress. In 1979, the Foreigners agitation started in Assam and spread to Tripura. The Left Front supported the tribals. At this moment the Anand Marg stepped in and a number of attacks on CPM meetings took place. Tripura was polarised into two ethnic camps. In the clashes that ensued the police sided with the Bengali Hindus. The tribals killed 380 Bengali Hindus at Mandai. After this the CPM Government asked the Centre for an Autonomous District Council, which the Centre refused. The CPM then opened the Tripura Tribal Areas Autonomous District Council (TTAADC) under the seventh schedule. Meanwhile the TUJS under Bijoy Kumar Hrangkhawl had organised an armed wing and formed the Tripura National Volunteers (TNV). He went to the MNF across the Jampui ridge and linked up with them. He organised a guerilla war against the government from safe bases in the Chittagong Hill Tracts (CHT). He fought a desultory bush war with the government for about ten years. The TUJS had Congress links and this finally brought Hrankhawl overground in 1988. This deal which the Centre signed with Hrankhawl was a mistake because the problems of the tribals had not yet been solved. Several disgruntled leaders of the TNV reneged and formed two insurgent groups the National Liberation Front of Tripura (NLFT) led by Dhananjoy Reang and the All Tripura Tiger Force (ATTF) led by Lalit Debbarma and Ranjit Debbarma. The NLFT patronised by the Congress and the ATTF by the CPM, established bases in the hill ranges north of Tripura in Bangladesh and in the CHT in the south. Both groups extorted money from the *mahajans* in the towns in the valleys and also from the tea gardens. The decade from 1990 saw a proliferation in the activities of these two groups. The NLFT linked up with the NSCN (IM) and were trained by them. The ATTF did not link up with the NSCN (IM) but got sanctuary in Bangladesh helped by the DGFI who also helped them to procure weapons. The 1990s saw a spate of kidnapping for ransom and killing of innocent Bengali Hindus by gangs of the ATTF attacking the civilian supporters of the Congress and the NLFT attacking the supporters of the CPM.

By 2002, the Tripura Police was able to break the kidnapping/ransom nexus of both the main groups. The NLFT split into several factions and two of them surrendered by 2005. The ATTF severed its links with the CPM and is holding out in the CHT. It has linked up with the UNLF of Manipur and the ULFA of Assam.

Tripura has the cleanest of all governments in India. Corruption is not a cause of the insurgency. The TTAADC has however not been able to carry out sustainable development in the tribal areas. The interior areas still do not have roads connecting all the villages to the towns. Block Development Officers are not able to freely visit interior tribal areas and supervise development projects because of lack of security. They disburse grants in cash. This is frittered away by the tribals in the interiors. The BSF are thinly deployed on the borders and have not been able to prevent the gangs of the NLFT and the ATTF from infiltrating ambushing a convoy and returning to their bases in the CHT or in the north into Bangladesh.

The formula for finishing the insurgency in Tripura is as follows :

1. Divide the tribal areas into small development blocks.
2. Deploy sufficient force in a few adjacent selected blocks along the border.
3. Deploy a battalion of BSF in border outposts two kilometres apart along this stretch. Fence the border and also complete a border road behind the fence. This should seal the villages behind from access from across the border.
4. Construct roads linking the villages to the nearest town under complete security.

5. Construct a water supply scheme in each of the villages in this block.
6. Formulate a development plan for all the villages in this block pertaining to the possible schemes that would suit the village be it horticulture, agriculture, piggery, poultry, forestry, pisciculture, growing orchids etc. In each project the local people of the village must be involved and only the expert, should be brought from outside.
7. In each project security force should be deployed till the project comes to maturity and the produce escorted to the market in the towns. Each family should thus become self-sustaining.
8. The whole border should meanwhile be fenced and the border road completed.
9. Other blocks can then be taken up and the experiment repeated.
10. It will be seen that the quantum of security forces required is very high. Its optimum level should be maintained so that the insurgent groups cannot penetrate and extort money or ambush and attack the civilians of the block concerned.

In general all land alienated from the tribals should be returned to them. Tribals should administer the TTAADC areas as far as possible. They have been alienated. They should gradually be encouraged to lead the state in all fields.

The United Liberation Front of Assam, The National Democratic Front of Bodoland, Dima Halem Daoga, and the United Peoples Democratic Solidarity.

Assam has three races of people who migrated into its verdant Brahmaputra valley. The first were the Mongoloid peoples who migrated from the headwaters of the Hwang Ho and the Yangtze Kiang. One group went west from Burma and settled in the Brahmaputra valley and the hills to its north and south. The tribes who diversified in the valley were the Bodo Cacharis, Sonowal Cacharis, Dimasa Cacharis, Thengal Cacharis, Karbis, Lalungs or Tiwas, Chutiyas, Morans, Borahis, and Rabhas. Later the Austrics,

Aryans, and Dravidians came from the Gangetic valley. The caste Hindus and the Tribals do not seem to have had serious differences and the migratory groups settled down. The first Hindu kingdom that left copper plates ruled in Kamarupa. In the 12th century, the Ahoms, a group related to the Shans of Burma, migrated to Upper Assam and established their kingdom there. They ruled for 600 years till they were defeated by the Burmese king who also laid waste their beautiful country. The British East India Company came to the rescue and defeated the Burmese in 1826. When the British occupied Upper Assam, they found that the land was very sparsely populated. They also found that tea grew well there. By the end of the century, the British had spread tea gardens all over the foothills to the north and the south of the Brahmaputra valley.

They found that the indigenous population was not willing to work in the tea gardens, so they imported Adivasi tribals from South-eastern and Central India. Then they found that the indigenous population was not capable of growing surplus rice to feed the tea garden labour. In neighbouring East Bengal, the Bengali Muslim population was already running short of cultivable land. The British consciously encouraged immigration of Bengali Muslims from East Bengal districts. They came in hordes and settled in Goalpara, Kamrup, and Nowgong districts. By 1931, just thirty years after the migration had started more than ten million Bengali Muslim peasants had settled in the above three districts. C.S. Mullen the Census Commissioner of Assam recorded this. Later the government of Sir Saadullah again encouraged the Bengali Muslims to settle by de-reserving grazing reserves for them. There was a growing disillusionment among Assam's intellectuals and some voiced sentiments that Assam should be a separate country like Burma. The third group of people that was to play a significant role in alienating the people of Assam were the Marwaris whom the British brought to be their middlemen as Assam at that time had a barter economy. Within a short time of their arrival, the Marwari had opened shops in all tea gardens, diversified into the grain trade and by the time of independence had established a complete grip on the trade and commerce of Assam. The last group that the British brought was the Bengali Hindus from East and

West Bengal. They were brought to work as clerks in the tea gardens and the oil and coal industries that had developed in Upper Assam. Thus by the time of independence, the Bengali Muslim peasant was grabbing the land of the caste Hindu and the tribals, the Bengali babu was beating the Assamese babu in the job market, the Marwari had taken firm control of the grain and essential supplies, textiles and every other item of commerce. The alienation of the Assamese was already complete.

In the run up to independence, Assam was almost lost to Pakistan. The Congress leadership in Delhi did not object to Assam being included with Bengal in the boundary commission. It was Mahatma Gandhi who interceded on behalf of the Assam leaders and reversed this decision. Later after independence, the Assam Congress leaders were rebuffed by Nehru when they objected to more than three lakh Bengali Hindu refugees being sent to Assam. In 1957, the centre decided to construct a 3.3 million-ton refinery at Barauni by taking the crude from the oil fields in Assam by a 700-kilometre pipeline. There was a huge agitation, the first of its kind in India after independence. Ultimately a 0.65-ton mini refinery was conceded to Assam at Noonmati. This only confirmed the feeling that Assam was getting stepbrotherly treatment from Delhi.

In the sixties the Marwaris who controlled the grain trade created huge shortages in rice by smuggling out large quantities to East Pakistan. Hojai the rice bowl of Assam was not giving one kilogram of paddy to the state levy for years together. This boiled up into an anti-national agitation on 26 January, 1968 when the national flag was desecrated at Gauhati after the flag hoisting and mobs of students calling themselves the *Lachit sena* burnt Fancy Bazaar, the business centre of Gauhati and crores worth of property went up in smoke. Interestingly not a single person was injured. Once again the Centre planned to construct a refinery outside Assam. The students organised a huge agitation. The war cry in the agitation was — "*Tez deem Tel ni dim*"(We will give blood not oil). The centre relented and established the refinery at Bongaigaon. The conclusion was that the centre was trying to treat Assam like a colony.

Two issues had by now crystallised in Assam — the continually deteriorating economic situation and the continuing illegal migration from East Pakistan. The tea, oil and coal industries in Assam did not seem to improve the economy of the state. Most of the sales tax on tea was being paid to West Bengal as most of the HQs of the tea companies were at Calcutta. The royalty paid to Assam for its oil was a paltry Rs. 42 per tonne. The centre refused to raise the royalty. Most of the jobs in the Central Government departments and in the public sector in Assam were going to Bengalis and other outsiders. The feeling began to take ground among Assamese people that the Centre was continuing to treat Assam like a colony.

Throughout the fifties and the sixties, Bengali Muslim and Hindu immigration continued unabated mainly abetted by a venal bureaucracy. However, a sizeable number of immigrant Muslim and Hindu Bengalis were detected and deported. In the early seventies, the concept of committed bureaucracy that had been fostered by the party in power at Delhi brought about a sea change in the administration. The politicians of Assam and the Centre realised that the immigrant Bengali Muslim was an infallible vote bank and the bureaucracy when made to bend would willingly crawl. After this, detection and deportation of immigrant Bengali Muslims simply stopped in Assam. At this time the sitting member of the Lok Sabha in Mangaldoi constituency died in office and a bye-election was called. A large number of representations were sent to the Chief Election Commissioner (CEC) at Delhi that there were a number of foreigners in the electoral rolls of Mangaldoi constituency. The CEC had the matter enquired and made a press statement that the electoral rolls of Mangaldoi had to be revised before going for the by-poll. Just at that time the Janata Dal Government was toppled and a lame duck Prime Minister Charan Singh was installed with the Congress driving from behind. The Muslim lobby immediately petitioned the Congress that the polling in Mangaldoi should be conducted without revising the electoral rolls. The CEC humbly recanted and announced that the by-poll would be conducted in Mangaldoi on the basis of the 1976 electoral roll. By that time hundreds of petitions had been filed about foreigners in the electoral rolls of Mangaldoi. The reaction in Assam was electric and the All Assam Students Union (AASU) and the Assam Jatiyatabadi Yuba Chatra Parishad formed the Assam Gana Sangram Parishad and started the Foreigners movement on 6 November, 1979 with mass *satyagraha*. The movement snowballed with thousands of people courting arrest. Not since the 1942 civil disobedience movement had India seen such an agitation. The State administration came to a halt.

The Centre tried their best to woo the leaders of the movement. The issue was the question of the cut off year for detection of foreigners. The year was 1951 as per the Citizenship Act. In 1971 after the liberation of Bangladesh, during the Indira-Mujib talks, Mujibur Rehman had told our Prime Minister that he would not take back any citizens of East Pakistan who had migrated to India before 25 March, 1971, the date of formation of the Government of Bangladesh in exile in India. Our Prime Minister agreed to this. After this the Government of India was maintaining that the cut off year was 25 March, 1971 an illegal premise, as there was no legal basis for this. The people of Assam had a very strong case and the Government of India had no case at all. Despite their best efforts, the Assam Gana Sangram Parishad would not budge. The Foreigners Movement soon developed an extremist wing. After four years, the Government of India forced an election on the state in February 1983.

The people of Assam boycotted the election. The state went on a natural curfew from 2 February, 1983 till 21 February, 1983. In this span of 21 days, more than three thousand people died in ethnic clashes and in police firings. The elections were a farce, with hardly 20 polling booths being opened in most of the Assamese constituencies. In fact in more than a dozen Assamese constituencies the polling had to be countermanded. In several polling booths, the polling figures were 350 or 400 against an electoral roll of one lakh. The elections were patently illegal. Police had to open fire on mobs several hundreds strong opposing the election in dozens of places. Assam was divided on ethnic lines. The Centre allowed a Congress government to be formed on the basis of this illegal election. It was this terrible election that set the youth of Assam to join the insurgent path of ULFA to fight against the injustice meted out to them by the Centre. A group of young men from the villages of Jheraigaon and Lakwa in upper Assam had met at the Ranghar in Nazira in 1979 to discuss the problems of illegal migration in Assam. Now they decided that they had no alternative but to take to the gun. They went to Dimapur and met the leaders of the NSCN there, who warmly welcomed them. By the end of the year the first cadres of the United Liberation Front of Assam were being sent to the NSCN camp in Burma for training. To add insult to injury, the Home Ministry legislated an Act — the Illegal Migrants Determination by Tribunal Act (IMDT) in 1983 after the terrible elections. The Foreigners Act was kept in abeyance and the IMDT was substituted for it in Assam. This was absurd. How could there be two acts for the same offence? Under the IMDT Act the onus was on the accused to prove that he was an Indian citizen, while under the Foreigners Act it was for the accused to prove that he was an Indian citizen. The act was patently illegal and unconstitutional.

The Congress government was in position till they were asked to step down by the Centre in 1985. Till then the ULFA was not seen in action. During the elections of 1985, there was no sign of the ULFA cadres influencing the election campaign or the polls later. It is only after the Assam Gana Parishad (AGP) formed the government that the ULFA started their insurgent activities. This was the first mistake of the insurgent group and of course of the AGP government. With the tacit backing of the State Government, the ULFA did not have the police behind their backs. They were thus not blooded like all insurgent groups. They did not have to attack police stations, or armed police camps to snatch weapons. They only robbed two banks in their march forward. Later they found that extortion was a much easier way to collect funds for purchasing arms and rations for their cadres. The AGP government neutered the police. ULFA made their main base camp in Lakhipathar Reserve Forest near Digboi police station. No directions were given to the police to encircle and attack the base camp of the ULFA. By this time the ULFA leaders had linked up with the Kachin

Independent Army (KIA) in northern Burma and their cadres were being trained there. Very soon the ULFA coffers were bulging. This led to the second big mistake of this insurgent group. Like in many insurgencies, besides highly committed rural youth, lumpen elements from the urban areas also joined the ULFA. Many lumpen elements became second level leaders. Large sums of money extorted were not deposited in the central treasury of the organisation. This cancer of corruption was to be the nemesis of this insurgent group. There was a pall of fear over Assam from 1985 to 1990, when the Centre declared President's rule and deployed the army in Assam. The Army operations were one sided. There was hardly a single ambush on the army. The ULFA had not been blooded like the Naga underground army or the Mizo National Front (MNF). But they had the support of the people. This helped them to elude capture and for almost nine months, not a single first line leader was captured.

The AGP government had a very fine chance of taking the state forward when they formed the government in 1985. They were fresh, new to politics and government and they had the chance of a lifetime to take Assam away from the festering corruption of the previous Congress government. Regrettably they threw away this chance to make history and became as corrupt as their predecessor government.

The counter-insurgency operations were proceeding well under Presidents rule. When the elections were called prematurely after just five months of Presidents rule, the whole picture changed. The Chief Minister directed that all surrenders should be made before him. He allowed every single important ULFA leader who surrendered before him to keep his weapon. He organised them into a mafia that continued to extort money from the business community, this time with the police being made to look the other way. The people of Assam was now at their wits end, with the ULFA extorting money from the people, and the SULFA as the surrendered ULFA were called also extorting money from the people with the police looking the other way.

By now the ULFA had been denied sanctuary by the KIA and

they perforce had to go to Bangladesh for help. The ULFA cadres were welcomed by the Bangladesh Directorate General Forces Intelligence (DGFI) and the Pakistan ISI in Dacca. Very soon ULFA cadres were going to Peshawar for training and the ISI had arranged to bring arms for them and the NSCN (IM) from Thailand. The ULFA had to pay a price for this. One of the main causes for the insurgency was the illegal immigration from Bangladesh to Assam that was being colluded by the Congress government. Now the ULFA was taking sanctuary in the same Bangladesh. The organisation lost a good deal of support from the people of Assam on this issue. This reached a turning point during the Kargil war when ULFA asked the people of Assam to support Pakistan in this war. The call came when an emotional funeral was being given to Captain Jintu Gogoi a young Assamese army officer who was killed in Kargil. ULFA lost a great measure of support on this issue too. Later a number of children were killed in Dhemaji by a bomb detonated by ULFA cadres. Today the ULFA has very little support from the people of Assam.

In 1990, a group of Bodo young men set up an insurgent group called the Bodo Security Force (BdSF) in Udalguri sub-division of Assam. The leader was a young Bodo postgraduate student of the North-Eastern Hill University, Shillong. He had earlier studied in the Union Christian College Barapani, a Baptist college. Several Naga leaders of the NSCN had also studied in this college. The majority of the cadres of the BdSF were Christians. Their demand was for a separate country for the Bodo people of Assam. In 1991, the ULFA had a meeting with the BdSF leaders across the border in Bhutan where the BdSF had set up three camps and it was decided that the ULFA would also set up camps there. Within a couple of years, the ULFA had shifted its Council and General HQs to Bhutan. The ULFA leaders took the BdSF leaders to Bangladesh and both groups brought the arms they purchased through the ISI to their camps in Bhutan. The BdSF changed its name to the National Democratic Front for Bodoland (NDFB). Unlike the ULFA, the NDFB was a very disciplined organisation and its cadres were very honest and all money extorted from tea gardens and businessmen were deposited in their GHQ. Both the ULFA and the NDFB kept good relations with the Bhutan Government officials by investing money with their business ventures. With continual pressure from the Government of India, the Bhutan government finally directed the ULFA and the NDFB to leave their country. When they did not listen, the Bhutan army attacked their camps and both the ULFA and the NDFB lost all their weapons in their camps. Several cadres of both groups were arrested. The ULFA regrouped in Burma with Kaphlang, but the NDFB was badly hit. Shortly after, they sued for peace and talks started between the Government of India and the NDFB.

Two other small insurgent groups that came up in Assam were the Dima Halam Daoga (DHD) in the North Cachar Hills and the United Peoples Democratic Solidarity (UPDS) in Karbi Anglong. Both these insurgent groups came up at the instigation of the NSCN (IM). In North Cachar Hills the District Council was a thoroughly corrupt body and eight families swiped all the development money since inception. The district was still very undeveloped after forty years and the Dimasas took to the gun. The story in Karbi Anglong district was also similar. Both groups are now talking to the government and there is a cease-fire on.

The insurgencies of Assam are very easy to solve. Ever since independence, the trade in essential supplies is in the hands of the Marwaris in the state. They divert 90 per cent of all foodgrains brought into the North-East into the black market from the railhead itself. The first step is to deploy CRPF at the railheads and see that all civil supplies are taken to the depots from the railheads. From there they should be carried with CRPF escorts to the wholesalers and retailers. Clean officers should be posted in the Food Corporation of India and in the state supply departments.

Both the AGP and the Congress governments have been very corrupt. Both these governments completely swindled development money sent to the state from 1991 till 2001. Today the state is on the verge of financial bankruptcy. Assam has had no green revolution. It has only one or two small weirs worth the name. Immediately, irrigation projects should be set up in all the districts so that the people can do double cropping. After this, development projects that will make the state self-sufficient should be set up and monitored by concurrent audits at every stage before funds are released. The nexus between the politicians, bureaucrats and contractors should be broken by posting clean and strong officers in crucial, cutting edge levels. If this is carefully monitored the insurgent groups of Assam will wither away. The border with Bangladesh must be strongly fenced and fitted with an electronic screen so that infiltration is completely controlled. If this can be done on the western border, why not on the eastern wing?

In end 2005 the Supreme Court repealed the IMDT Act as unconstitutional and illegal. The Government however to preserve its vote bank has brought the provisions of the IMDT Act by amending the Foreigners Tribunal order under the rules of the Foreigners act. This is a certain recipe to revive the ULFA.

5 Ethnic Aspirations and Insurgency in the North-Eastern Region of India

H.N. Das

The idealism of nation states first made its impact felt in the late eighteenth century in Europe. Two big nation states emerged through the Italian and the German unifications. Then the break up of the Holy Roman Empire (Aka Austrian Empire) and the Ottoman Empire gave birth to several nation states particularly in Central and Eastern Europe. In the cases of Italy and Germany a number of feudal states were cemented together to form the new nation states. In the rest of Europe new nation states emerged out of the old empires. The Asian and the African nation states started coming up in the aftermath of the two world wars of the twentieth century mainly as a consequence of the fall of the British and the smaller empires which the European powers had built in the earlier centuries.

Arnold Toynbee's rather esoteric definition aptly describes "the spirit of nationality" as a "sour ferment of the new wine of democracy in the old bottles of tribalism".[1] On a more practical plane a nation is "a group of people who believe they are ancestrally related. It is the largest grouping that shares that belief."[2] Simply stated a nation state is a nation matched with territory.

Before the advent of British rule India had a chequered history. There were times when great empires brought substantial portions of the Indian subcontinent under control of one imperial power. But at other times different parts had independent kings and feudal potentates. Their territories did not always conform to the idea of nation states. Even during British times considerable areas under princely states remained outside the day-to-day administration of the Central Government. But these states were fully covered by the principle of suzerainty of the British empire till the paramountcy lapsed after transfer of power in 1947. When independence came India was divided with the creation of Pakistan. Later Bangladesh emerged out of the Indo-Pak War of 1971.

Within independent India itself fissiparous tendencies were always discernible side by side with the centripetal forces of common culture and shared traditions. All Indians harked back to the same traditions. It was through a tenuous process combined with great political acumen and the vision of a strong united India that the late Sardar Vallabhbhai Patel (first Union Home Minister) brought the 362 native states and union of states within the fold of the Indian Union through the stratagem of the instruments of accession immediately after independence. Except for Hyderabad, Junagadh, and Jammu & Kashmir, where Army had to be deployed, the entire process was peaceful.

Soon, however, problems started arising due to revival of agitations over local languages. This was inspired by the European idealism of nationhood on the local intelligentsia. The death of Potti Sri Ramalu after long fasting over statehood for Andhra Pradesh also added fuel to it. This necessitated the setting up of the States Reorganisation Commission in 1956 on whose recommendations radical changes of the boundaries of states were made in 1956 on linguistic lines except in the case of the earstwhile Bombay Presidency and Punjab both of which also ultimately had to be partitioned again, within a few years, the first on linguistic lines into Gujarat and Maharashtra and the second on linguistic and religious lines into Punjab, Himachal Pradesh and Haryana.[3]

Soon after the above-mentioned state re-organisations were carried out discordant voice were heard in many parts of India. There were sporadic disturbances also. Patriotic Indians were genuinely concerned. One American Journalist named Sellig Harrison wrote a book entitled "India — the Most Dangerous Decades" and predicted that the country would face chaos and would break up soon. But India remained together thanks to the vision and foresight of our leaders and the strong bond of the ancient civilization which has continued for five thousand years and which inspires every Indian wherever he or she may reside. The leaders also were clear about their mandate and did not hesitate to follow a strong arm policy whenever necessity arose. This provoked the American historian Paul R. Brass to remark as follows : "The one consistent principle, however, that emerges strongly in both the Nehru and the post-Nehru periods is that no secessionist movement will be allowed to prevail and that massive force will be used to suppress insurrectionary activity."[4]

The North-Eastern Region consisting of the state of Assam and some other areas formed a separate geographical entity linked to the Indian mainland only by a narrow corridor. Here the linguistic reorganization formula could not be applied in the same way because of the existence of a very large number of tribes and languages and territorial intermixture of such tribes. Therefore, differences arose among the various ethnic and linguistic groups which had small populations but strong sub-regional and racial sentiments. Popular movements all over the Region and some violence and insurgency resulted in the Union Government passing the North-Eastern Areas (Reorganisation) Act, 1971, which divided the N.E. Region into seven distinct entities all of which ultimately became states of the Indian Union. Nagaland, of course, had become a state earlier in 1964.

As the Advanced History of India remarked at that time "the reorganization of territories in North-East India was effected to enable the diverse ethnic and linguistic groups who inhabit the area to shape their own destinies without interference and to remove the feeling that they were being exploited by others."[5] This hope was belied, however, when smaller ethnic groups and sub-groups started demanding further vivisection of some of the states. Insurgent outfits also emerged demanding full independence for this or that part of the seven states and threatening to secede from the Indian Union.

It is important to realize that before independence the British Government's policy was to keep the hill people isolated. They did not allow the hill people to be integrated with the main-stream of

Indian life. This was exemplified by the Inner Line Permit system which quite successfully prevented the hill people from being swamped by others. However, this also prevented any real relationship between the hills and the plains people in economic, social and cultural fields.

After independence Prime Minister Nehru adopted a policy framework for the tribals influenced by the famous anthropologist Verrier Elwin. In fact, Nehru wrote the foreword to Elwin's famous book "*A Philosophy for NEFA*". NEFA became Arunachal Pradesh later. Nehru wrote that "the problem of the tribal areas is to make the people feel that they have perfect freedom to live their own lives and to develop according to their wishes and genius. India to them should signify not only a protecting force but a liberating one. Any conception that India is ruling them and that they are the ruled, or that customs and habits with which they are unfamiliar are going to be imposed upon them, will alienate them."[6] Elwin's philosophy has been criticized as romantic. Adverse comments have also been made about his 1939 book "the Baiga" where he had advocated for some sort of "National Park" for the tribals in "a wild and largely inaccessible part of the country." Later, Elwin regretted this and said that his suggestion was "badly put" and that "I should have realized the unfortunate connotations of the expression National Park".[7] Elwin explained that "there was no idea of keeping anything static and, in actual fact, there is continual creative development in all these fields." While translating these ideas into action the then Advisor, NEFA, late Nari Rustomji, worked under the conviction that "the hillman has, essentially, a clean, direct and healthy outlook; he is free, happily, from the morbid complexes induced by the unnatural life of city folk". Rustomji, therefore, condemned the "reckless talk of uplifting and civilizing the tribes. Officials and social workers must go to the people not as masters who dictate but as elder brothers who have suffered themselves and wish through their experience to spare others the pains they have had to endure."[8]

When the Constitution of India, 1950 was drawn up during the years following independence the then Prime Minister of Assam

Bharat Ratna late Gopinath Bardoloi personally ensured that special provisions contained in the sixth schedule relating to the hill areas were included in the Constitution. He also initiated actions for inter-mixing of the hills and the plains people through various socio-cultural activities.

In spite of all these attempts at integration, however, fissiparous tendencies made their appearance as mentioned earlier. Many factors were responsible for these developments. The desire for self-expression, the perception of discrimination and injustice, aspirations of small time politicians, better economic development of neighbouring small states and a host of other factors were responsible for the rise of sub-national and ethnic movements all over Assam and the North-East.

In the wake of India's independence in 1947 the Nagas were the first to raise the flag of revolt. They were a fiercely independent people. Even during British days many interior parts of the Naga inhabited area remained unadministered by the imperial power although the British had annexed most of what is now called Nagaland around 1832.

Way back in 1918 the Naga Club came into existence. It became the platform for Naga unity. On January 10, 1929, the Naga Club submitted a memorandum to the Simon Commission in which it pleaded, on behalf of the Nagas, to the British Government "to leave us alone to determine for ourselves as in ancient times".[9] When India became independent the Nagas demanded their own independence. Earlier they had formed the Naga National Council in 1946, which marked the beginning of political movement by the Nagas in search of their self-identity. Their struggle was based on the premise that the "Nagas had no affinity with India whether racially, historically, politically, culturally, religiously or any otherwise. Therefore, Nagaland is not part of Indian territory neither are Nagas Indians".[10] Insurgency began under the leadership of A.Z. Phizo.

It was in the Shillong Accord of November 11, 1975, that "the representatives of underground organisations" of the Nagas first "conveyed their decision, of their own volition, to accept, without condition, the Constitution of India". Later events showed that this promise was not carried out, in letter and spirit, by all the Naga outfits. Starting from late 1980, till the Government of India reached an agreement with the Isaac Muivah faction of the National Socialist Council of Nagaland (NSCN) for a cease-fire violence continued. Even after the formal cease-fire and intermittent talks sporadic incidents of violence have been recorded.

It is true that the Naga underground got divided into various groups, some of which fought against each other. But most organizations continued to demand an independent and greater Nagaland or Nagalim. They were not satisfied with Nagaland even as a full state of India. They were certainly not happy that some Naga inhabited areas of Assam, Manipur and Arunachal Pradesh had been left out of Nagaland. The basic fact is that these Naga outfits consider Nagas to be ethnically different from the other Indians and they want their right of self-determination outside India. Several rounds of talks have taken place in recent years. But a lasting solution to this vexed problem, which has plagued the North-East for more than half a century, is not yet in sight.

It was the last British Deputy Commissioner of the erstwhile Naga Hills district of Assam. C.R. Pawsey, who established the Naga Hills District Tribal Council in April, 1946, with the objective of uniting all Naga tribes under one banner. Pawsey also reported to have played a pivotal role in the formation of the Naga National Council whose policy was "to establish a sovereign independent Naga country and to develop it according to the genius of Naga democratic customs and culture". That was the beginning of insurgency in Nagaland. To quote the distinguished Anthropologist Dr. D.N. Majumdar : "During the British period, may be due to encouragement from British officers like Charles Pawsey, ethnic identity organizations grew up among many of the major tribal communities of North-East India. In fact, the ground had been already prepared by the feeling among the hill tribes that ruling class, be it the British or Indian, tended to adopt a policy of ethnic discrimination towards the hill people."[12]

In the erstwhile Lushai Hills district of Assam a similar role was played by the then Superintendent (same as Deputy Commissioner) McDonald who convened a meeting of the tribal chiefs in January 1946 and got a constitution called the McDonald Roral Khawl drafted for Lushai Hills which provided for a separate legislature and a Ministry. Later, the Mizo Union was formed as a political party. They demanded, like the Nagas, that all areas with Mizo population in the neighbouring Manipur, Tripura and Chitagong Hill tracts should be included in the Mizo district proposed by them.[13]

It was, therefore, the British administrators who planted the ideas of separation and independence in the minds of the concerned ethnic groups and organizations. This later metamorphosed into insurgencies in both Nagaland and Mizoram. The British officials named above were obviously unhappy with the decision of their home government to leave India. They made every effort to scuttle the proposal. Failing that they prepared the tribes to cause confusion and pandemonium after India's independence. But it was the factor of ethnicity which they capitalized on. In Mizoram this feeling was so strong that some secessionist groups wanted to merge with Burma (present Myanmar) because they were ethnically closer to the tribes of Upper Burma.[14]

For almost two decades after independence the tribes of Lushai Hills district simmered with discontent over many issues. They felt deeply hurt by the alleged discriminatory treatment by the Assam Government particularly during the 1959 "Mautam" (famine) in the wake of large scale flowering of wild bamboo and the 1960 introduction of Assamese as the official language. The Mizo National Famine Front, formed in 1960 to help the famine victims, converted itself into the Mizo National Front (MNF). The MNF raised the banner of insurgency on February 28, 1966 when it attacked several important government installations, looted the Aizawl Treasury and kidnapped the Sub-Divisional Officer, Lungleh. On March 1, 1966 the MNF, under the leadership of Laldenga, formally declared independence from India.

Insurgency continued for twenty long years till the Mizoram Accord was signed on June 30, 1986. The insurgent leader Laldenga was sworn in as Chief Minister on August 21, 1986. Mizoram, which had been made a Union territory on January 21, 1972, became a full-fledged state on August 29, 1988. Laldenga's Ministry lasted only for eighteen months. But since then Mizoram has been peaceful.

Tripura has been the homeland of 19 different tribes. It was a peaceful princely state under the British. For a thousand years Tripura was ruled by a dynasty of tribal origin. Its ethnic problem started with the partition of the country in 1947. Hundreds of thousands of Bengali Hindus from the erstwhile East Pakistan (present Bangladesh) came rushing into Tripura and swamped the indigenous tribals into a hopeless minority. Later even Muslim illegal migrants from Bangladesh came and swelled the non-tribal population. This created a crisis of identity for the tribals.

The Tripura Upajati Juba Samiti (TUJS) was formed on June 10,1967 to fight Bengalee chauvinism as well as the neglect of the tribals. The tribals resented the consequences of their economic deprivation and political eclipse. About the same time the leader-Hrarangkwal-revived the Sangram Union which had been formed earlier. This started the insurgency in Tripura. The main demands of TUJS included the creation of an autonomous district council under the Sixth Schedule of the Indian Constitution for the tribal people, restoration to the tribals of their land which had been illegally transferred to non-tribals, recognition of tribal Kakbarak as a state language and adoption of Roman scripts for Kakbarak. The violence that was unleashed by TUJS and some of the other insurgent outfits rocked Tripura for a long time resulting in the death of large number of Bengalee people and damages of property belonging to individuals and institutions. It also gave birth to the opposing organization — Amra Bengali — which killed a number of tribals beside fuelling the tension among the communities.

In 1977 CPI(M) came to power in Tripura. Led by an able and considerate Chief Minister Nripen Chakravorty the Communists initiated certain reforms in order to assuage tribal feelings. Kakbarak was recognized as the second official language of Tripura beside Bengalee, Kakbarak was also made the medium of instruction in the primary schools of the tribal areas, restoration was ordered to the tribals of whatever land had been earlier appropriated by the Bengalis without the permission of District Magistrates, necessary steps were taken towards fulfilment of tribal quotas in employment, enabling legislation was passed for constitution of autonomous district councils similar to those in Assam and various other welfare steps were initiated for the benefit of the tribals. An Accord was signed with Hrarangkhawl, the insurgent leader, at New Delhi in August, 1988. Sporadic violence, however, is still continuing. In the past few years Tripura has achieved tremendous progress in the economic field. The tribals have been enabled to share in this prosperity by the State Government under the Chief Ministership of Nripen Chakravorty and after him under Manik Sarkar.

Ethnicity is more in evidence in the insurgencies in Manipur. Here the Meiteis in the plains and the two main tribes of Kukis and Nagas in the hills are perpetually fighting. The Meiteis, who converted themselves into Vaishnavite Hindus in the seventeenth century and who form the majority community, feel neglected and discriminated against by the Centre. In fact, "the average Manipuri blames New Delhi for most of his woes. This sense of grievance has fanned separatist sentiment".[15]

Based on this feeling of neglect the insurgent movement took concrete shape in Manipur. N. Bisheshwar, an educated leftist extremist who had spent years in jail because of earlier terrorist activities, organized the People's Liberation Army (PLA) in the mid-seventies of the last century. The other insurgent organizations which sprung up about the same time were the People's Revolutionary Party of Kangleipak (PREPAK) and the Kangleipak Communist Party (KCP). They all believed in violence for getting a fair deal from the Centre. They wanted the outsiders (Mayangs) to leave Manipur. They practiced and propagated pan-mongoloid sentiments. As a reaction against Hinduism they prescribed revival of the old Meitei religion of Sanamahi. And all of these outfits were basically secessionists.

In the hills the Nagas and the Kukis fought. Each had its own insurgent organization. They fought against the Centre and against each other. They also had problems with the neighbouring states because the Manipur Nagas believed in greater Nagalim.

The violence is still continuing. But the scale is much less. The insurgencies in Manipur, both in the hills and the plains, are based on ethnicity as in the other states of the North-Eastern region.

In Meghalaya ethnicity was the dominant factor, besides neglect and lack of economic development, in the very emergence of the state. What is significant, however, is the fact that three principal ethnic groups — Khasis, Jaintias and Garos — decided to live together in Meghalaya. They have had their conflicts and problems but are still remaining in one state. Some sporadic violence, particularly in Shillong, against outsiders erupt from time to time. But these are not very serious compared to what is happening in Tripura or Manipur.

In Arunachal Pradesh the different tribes have different aspirations. There are pockets of dissatisfaction and many grievances. But there has not yet been any major insurgencies or violent incidents.

Assam is big and the problems are multifarious. With scores of tribes living in the plains and the hills, Assam has a long history of agitation over this or that issue. Separation of Nagaland, Mizoram, Meghalaya and Arunachal Pradesh made erstwhile Assam much smaller in area. But the problems did not diminish. The Assamese majority remained dissatisfied with the Centre. The other tribes had grievances against the Assamese and the Centre. These became more intense. The influx of millions of foreigners from Bangladesh, and some from Nepal, complicated the situation so much that the crisis of identity, which spawned insurgencies in Tripura, made its ugly appearance in Assam also. The rich mosaic of cultural variety turned into a nightmare of political maze which engulfed the state in a spate of insurgencies and consequent violence.

The United Liberation Front of Assam (ULFA) was born on April 7, 1979 in the playfield of the Ahom Kings in Sibsagar. It demanded freedom for Assam and separation from the Indian Union. The violence it unleashed in the late eighties and the early nineties has no parallel in the North-East. The damages it wrought can be compared with those in Jammu and Kashmir and Sri Lanka by their own insurgent outfits. ULFA has gone through several phases of transformation during the past quarter of a century. Its popular support has been eroded due mainly to its violence against the civil population and its aligning with ISI of Pakistan as also its tacit support to the Bangladeshis. Its cadre strength has been decimated by surrenders, arrests and deaths. It has lost its bases in Assam and it has been flushed out from its hideouts in Bhutan. ULFA's overall power is declining with its leaders and ranks getting distanced from each other. That is why ULFA has joined talks with the Government albeit indirectly through the People's Consultative Group it has formed with some of the leading citizens who support ULFA's cause. But even now sporadic violence is being perpetrated by its hardcore elements particularly against soft targets.

The Bodos have been giving vent to their grievances for a long time. But actual insurgency started only in the late eighties mainly due to the short sighted, narrow-minded and haphazard actions of the Assam Gana Parishad Government which was misguided by some self-seeking junior bureaucrats. In fact, the Government did not have any policy at all. The Bodo insurgent outfits did tremendous damage to life and property. But they hurt themselves more in the process. The Bodos have now achieved the Bodoland Territorial Autonomous Council (BTAC). It is doubtful, however, whether they will remain satisfied. They will probably try ethnic cleansing in the BTAC area where Bodos have a population of about 28 per cent only. Already the problems have started with the Koch Rajbangshis demanding their own territorial hegemony and their inclusion in the list of scheduled tribes. The Muslims have suffered at the hands of the Bodos. They are now apprehending ethnic cleansing. This will lead to more tension and conflict in the near future because the Muslims are not likely to remain passive for long. Already a number of Islamist insurgent groups have raised their heads. The Muslim Liberation Front of Assam (MULTA) is the chief among them.[16]

In order to arrive at a solution of the problem experiments have been tried in the past few decades including creation of separate states to satisfy the smaller sub-nationalities. The North-East Council and the Ministry of DONER (Department of North-Eastern Region) have been formed, both of which are pumping in more money to the Region for economic development. Beside BAC other territorial Councils for the Mishings, Tewas and Ravas have been formed to confer more powers to these tribes. Many more powers have been transferred to the already existing district councils under the Sixth Schedule of the Constitution. All these have been done in order to solve the ethnic problem. But whether these will fully satisfy the aspirations of all the ethnic groups will be seen only in the future.

NOTES

1. Arnold Toynbee, *A Study of History*, Oxford University Press, 1972, p. 34.
2. Walker Connor, "*From Tribe to Nation*", *History of European Ideas*, Vol. 13, No. 1/2, 1991.
3. Spear, Percival, *The Oxford History of Modern India*, 1970-1975, The Oxford University Press, 1992.
4. Brass, Paul R. "*The Politics of India since Independence*". *The New Cambridge History of India* Vol. IV, 1. Cambridge University Press, 1990. [During a visit to Seattle the author of this article was invited by Brass to speak to the faculty of the Washington State University in 1992. Brass delivered a series of lectures in Assam Administrative Staff College in 1994].
5. Majumdar, R.C., Raychaudhury, H.C. and Datta, Kalikinkar, *An Advanced History of India*, McMillan India Ltd., 1978.
6. Elwin, Verrier, *A Philosophy for NEFA*. Published by the NEFA Administration, Shillong, 1957.
7. Elwin, Verrier, "*The Tribal World of Verrier Elwin*". Oxford University Press, 1989.
8. Verrier Elwin quoted by Rustomji, Nari, in "*Enchanted Frontiers*". Oxford University Press, Calcutta, 1971.
9. Imchen, C.L. "*Naga Politics : Regionalism or Non-State Nation*". In Regionalism in India Edited by B. Pakem. Har-Anand Publications, New Delhi, 1993.
10. Iralu, Kaka D."*Nagaland and India. The Blood and the Tears*". Publisher not mentioned. September, 2000.

11. Majumdar, D.N.: *"Ethnicity and Regionalism in North-East India"* in B. Pakem edited *"Regionalism in India"*, Har - Anand Publications, New Delhi, 1993.
12. Pakem, B. : *"Nationality Question in the Hill Areas of North-East India"* in op.cit.
13. Marwah, Ved : *"Uncivil Wars. Pathology of Terrorism in India"*, Harper Collins Publishers India Pvt. Ltd., New Delhi.
14. Marwah, Ved. op.cit.
15. Marwah, Ved. op.cit.
16. For a detailed treatment of the emerging Islamist insurgency see : Jaideep Saikia, *Terror Sans Frontiers, Islamist Militancy in North East India*, Vision Books, New Delhi; and Jaideep Saikia (edited), Bangladesh, Treading the Taliban Trail, Vision Books, New Delhi.

PART III

ETHNO-IDENTITY IN A DEMOCRACY

6 Negotiating Ethnic Identity in a Democracy

Patricia Mukhim

The terms "ethnic groups", "ethnicity" and "ethnic conflict" have become current topics of interest because of the challenges they pose before the nation-state. The word 'ethnic' is now being increasingly used to identify groups of people who have evolved from their primitive stages of tribe and clan identity into a more cohesive group looking for a coherent political identity. Sometimes the terms are loosely adopted and do not actually carry their weight in words. Ethnicity or ethnic identity have different connotations for scholars and are different from what the ethnic communities understand themselves. As such there can be no single meaning to the term/terms. Thomas Hulland Eriksen says, "Many of us have to admit that the meaning of these terms often seem vague and ambiguous".

For social anthropologists, ethnicity and ethnic identity have been subjects of intense study since the 1960s and they continues to be focal theme for research in the 21st century. Today, there is a greater need to understand the underpinnings of ethnicity because the competition for political and economic space between ethnic groups have resulted in ethnic conflicts across the globe. Eriksen deduces that ethnicity emerges and is made relevant through ongoing social situations and encounters, and through people's ways of coping with the demands and challenges of life. He argues that social anthropology is best placed to investigate into these processes of human evolution from the primordial to the modern. Anthropology enables scholars to understand and help define ways in which ethnic relations are perceived by people which includes the way they explain and think about their own racial groups as distinct from 'others'. Anthropology also helps in understanding the world-view of different groups and how they are being maintained or contested.

Ethnicity has often been seen to be a hindrance to nationalism. Nowhere is this more visible than in the Indian subcontinent. Racial groups in this country have a strong cultural identity which they maintain is so unique that it even requires state intervention for its promotion and protection. The Sixth Schedule of the Constitution of India is a good example of state intervention in not just the conservation of a group's cultural identity but also in its promotion. Social theorists of the early twentieth century opined that ethnicity and nationalism would recede into the periphery and become insignificant in the face of rapid industrialization and modernity. But actually, globalization has thrown up severe economic challenges. Smaller groups of people living in the backwaters of a larger country and which have not experienced the levels of development that the bigger states have, feel very threatened by the open market and are unable to cope with its diverse implications. The incursion of national and international players into their hitherto 'guarded' domains to set up extractive industries and explore their flora and fauna is now threatening to dislodge their traditional concepts of land ownership and the ownership over natural resources.

The study of ethnicity is of importance to scholars because by the nineties ethnic conflicts had begun to flare up across the globe. Thirty-five of the thirty-seven major armed conflicts in the world in 1991 were internal conflicts or what we would call ethnic conflicts. The Sri Lankan one being a case in point. India's North-East today is a stage for several on-going ethnic conflicts, all of which have their roots in identity assertions. The region has over 238 ethnic communities. Each one feels stifled by the idea of living within the confines of another state whose ruling elite constitute an ethnic majority. Almost all of the ethnic movements in North-East India are violent. Scholars believe that the propensity for violence has always been there in the form of inter and intra-tribal conflicts. After independence several tribes within a particular geographical space have been integrated and made to feel they are one people. This feeling was strengthened after the states were created.

But the violence remained a superficially concealed trait. It erupted at the first opportunity when the Nagas revolted against what they perceived as a backdoor attempt by India to assimilate them, an otherwise independent people with their own administrative, political and economic systems that already have the characteristics of a mini nation in place and above all having nothing in common with the 'Indian' racial traits (Aryan or Dravidian) and/or culture. Just because a tribe or ethnic group lived within a small geographical space does it necessarily have to be subsumed by a bigger entity which itself was an emerging new nation and struggling for a national identity at that point of time. This brings us to a very interesting point. John Dunn, for example, defines the nation as a living space consisting of those who belong together by birth (genetically, lineally, through familially inherited language and culture). Watson on the other hand sees nationalism as an ideology that creates national consciousness within a political unconscious population. Paul Brass argues that ethnicity and nationalism are not given but are socially constructed terms. He says that the terms are created by the elite who draw upon, distort and sometimes fabricate materials from the culture of the groups they wish to represent in order to gain political and economic mileage for themselves and the group. Brass says if an ethnic group succeeds by its own efforts in achieving any one of these goals either within an existing state or a state of its own it has become a nationality or a nation. Therefore it would be correct to say that a nation is a particular type of ethnic community or rather as an ethnic community politicized with recognized group rights in the political system.

According to John Brass there are two fundamental processes of nation formation (a) ethnic nationalism: By transformation of ethnic group in a multi-ethnic state into a self-conscious political entity. (b) By amalgamation of diverse groups and the formation of an inter-ethnic composition or homogenous national culture through the agency of the modern state. The term nation has also undergone several metamorphoses as it is meant to be because people themselves are dynamic and are, therefore, their behaviour lends itself to different interpretations. Historian Eric Hobsbawm agrees that the old meaning of the word nation only encompassed an ethnic unit. The meaning has changed considerably with the passage of time and with emerging political dialectics and behaviour. The more recent use of the term nation suggests political unity and dependence, where the nation was seen as a body of citizens whose collective sovereignty constituted them into a state which was their form of political expression.

If we go by Dunn's definition and also correctly understand Brass and Hobsbawm's analogy then all the independent tribes/ ethnic groups of North-East India are little nations that have been submerged because they were not at the time politically cohesive to argue their case, nor were they strong enough militarily to fight back. So tribe after tribe was asked to sign the Instrument of Accession at a period in their history when they did not fully comprehend the implications. It seemed at the time that there were only two choices before these tribes. They could join either Pakistan or India. There was no option to remain as small independent nations. How correct and ethical this action of the Indian state is has never been debated by Indian civil society or by its political leaders. His process of forced assimilation was taken as a matter of right as if the people inhabiting this periphery are mere forest dwellers (*adivasis*) who could be dismissed like flies. Their opinions were not thought weighty enough to be seriously considered.

When Nehru articulated his famous tribal policy he said that the tribes should be allowed to develop according to their own genius. This has literally been taken to mean that the tribes should be left to themselves to chart out their own development paradigms. As can be seen from the various five-year plans the amount allocated for this distant periphery is just a fraction of what Maharashtra, Gujarat or Punjab have been able to wrest. By the time the backlog was addressed things had taken a different turn. The states of North-

East had begun to assume, not without reason, that they were being treated like colonies from where all the mineral and forest wealth were mercilessly extracted. Manufacturing industries were located elsewhere in the country. Hence there were little or no benefits that accrued to the region. Industrialisation is still a distant dream with only Assam having a few tea-related industries and oil refineries.

The feeling of neglect became a popular bandwagon and was soon internalized by all the tribes/ethnic communities. Taking a cue from the Naga rebels who have sustained their movement for over 50 years, other extremist groups such as the United Liberation Front of Asom (ULFA) and various other militant outfits emerged in Tripura, Manipur and Meghalaya. The Mizo insurgency which was a result of administrative failure that led to a famine was resolved in 1986 when the Mizo National Front (MNF) took part in electoral politics, but not after a bloody fight with the security forces. Mizoram is the only state which was bombed by the Indian Air Force in order to force the Mizo rebels to surrender. Even today the Central Government continues to adopt the policy of containment sometimes by launching an all-out offensive against the militants through the use of its security forces and arbitrary laws such as the oppressive Armed Forces Special Powers Act (AFSPA) to justify its repressive acts. At other times the Central Government shows an openness to ostensibly strike a dialogue with militant groups that show a 'willingness to talk'. But if the Naga peace talks are any indication of the manner in which the dialogue is proceeding then it might be correct to assume that the Indian Government is only adopting delaying tactics with the intention of tiring out the ideologues. Now the ULFA too wants to have direct peace talks with the Centre. The funny part is that the talking points are vague and do not seem to carry the mandate of the people whom the militant outfit claims to represent.

Compounding the dilemma of people in North-East India, the intellectual class and policy-makers of this country, particularly those based in Delhi have repeatedly used the refrain "join the mainstream" while trying to address dissenting groups and rebel without from the region without actually giving much thought to the phrase. For the North-East the phrase represents a stinking thinking, a worn out cliché which only shows the patronizing attitude of the powers-that-be in Delhi, whose concept of the mainstream is that large Indian mass with a common stream of thought and culture. It is almost belittling the rich mosaic of cultural diversity in the region and asking that it be painted with one single colour. It would be an understatement to say that this is akin to slaughtering the sensibilities of the people of India's North-East.

India's North-East is a mosaic in the making. The region is inhabited by people who are racially distinct from those in the rest of the country. They trace their origin to Central and South-East Asia. They constitute a very small population when compared with the rest of India. Further, the region shares about 98 per cent of its boundaries with foreign countries and only 2 per cent with the Indian subcontinent. The people of North-East India (the direction is North-East only when seen from the epicentre called Delhi) consider it an accident of history that their fates should inextricably be linked with a country whose people share no commonalities of language, custom, race and world-view with them. Naturally, the idea of being Indian has taken more time to sink in. The process is not smooth. There is a constant churning going on within the region and even today new groups of people are still trying to carve out an identity for themselves. Within the region each ethnic community is keen to establish its own identity and there lies a persistent fear in every group that they might be submerged by the bigger or stronger ones. In this environment of constant fermentation, **India is yet to develop a response mechanism which would take into account the special needs of its ethnic communities without actually fragmenting geographical boundaries.**

Ethnic groups who see themselves as minorities in the larger Indian state are facing a new threat from the continued influx of labour migrants and refugees from neighbouring Bangladesh. The state of Assam, for instance, has been battling with the problem of illegal migration of Bangladeshis who cross over the porous borders by manipulating the already fragile and corrupt-ridden system. Within no time they acquire a permanent minority status within

India and the states where they live and work in. From a status of mere survival they organize themselves politically and demand recognition by the State. This minority first becomes a potent vote bank. Subsequently, its members engage in active political mobilization to enable their members to enter the state assembly and even national parliament. With the minority tag the representatives are able to negotiate a better deal for the group.

Ethnic communities who live in regions that are vulnerable to influx from across the borders naturally live in constant fear of being submerged. Their fears are not irrational considering that they are first hand witnesses to the unfolding political scenario where people of doubtful origin are able to enter the highest decision-making bodies to legislate and influence policies merely on the strength of numbers. Since democracy is all about numbers those with bigger populations rule the roost. Ethnic minorities in the North-East are known to have a low fertility rate with an average family of 5. This is certainly no help in building a vote bank, more so if the votes are fragmented along party, clan and religious lines. Whereas in the case of the so-called minority there is very little fragmentation since religion is the crux of all mobilisation.

The picture of India's North-East is by no means simple. It is a bundle of contradictions. On the one hand are the Nagas who continue to believe that their demand for sovereignty is a just one based on sound historical arguments. On the other hand is the Indian state which sees all such demands as being secessionist in nature. The ULFA demand also mimics the Naga fight for sovereignty. Then we have smaller ethnic communities or minorities living within bigger states, such as the Karbis, Dimasas, Tiwas and Bodos who are part of the bigger state of Assam, the Kukis, Paiteis, Biateis, and the various Naga tribes such as the Thangkhuls, Maos, Pumai, Zeliang etc. living in Manipur, the Hmars, Chakmas, Reangs, Lakhers of Mizoram and the Kokborok, Darlongs etc. of Tripura. Each of these groups perceives a sense of neglect by the majority ruling elite within their own states. Interestingly even if the rulers themselves belong to a particular ethnic group they hardly accommodate the political articulations of the other smaller groups within the state. This is the dichotomy that needs to be resolved.

So while groups like the Nagas are taking on the Indian state others are engaged in pitched battles with their state of residence. Their grouse mainly is against the ruling establishment of that state. But they also look for support and intervention from Delhi because they feel the need for a third party arbiter, more so because Delhi is the dispenser of all monies and development packages. A direct confrontation with their own state does not seem to have yielded much fruit. A common strategy of all groups is to adopt the method of armed revolt. This is because the groups feel that democratic protests fall on deaf ears. Delhi responds only when the guns boom and the casualties are huge. Each time the ULFA blows up an oil pipeline or throws a bomb that kills innocent people they make it to the news and even Delhi sits up and takes notice. The groups go into an offensive intermittently. So do the security forces. But things are allowed to drift and the cauldron is kept boiling. There does not seem to be any seriousness on the part of Delhi to bring the different ethnic conflicts to a stop. Similarly, the warring groups have themselves developed a vested interest in prolonging the conflict. That gives them a valid excuse to extort and live by their own rules.

So how do ethnic groups negotiate their identity in a liberal democratic setup: This is a baffling question. Democracy has varied definitions but the most commonly accepted one is that democracy allows the full participation of people in governance. This happens through the electoral process and through a representative government. The point is that governments today are not representative of the people's views and aspirations because they are not participatory by nature. Even while we speak of grass-roots governance, planning processes are still very much conceived in the state secretariats away from the ground realities that obtain in the villages. Besides having unrealistic plans the delivery mechanisms are also faulty because they exclude people. Government functionaries do not have faith in the wisdom of the common man. In fact when suggestions were made that a 15-year vision document for the North-East should be put in place through the process of participatory methods and by asking the people in the villages what their needs and priorities are, several government officials smirked at the idea. They thought it preposterous that the villager would know what he needs. He is supposed to be an ignoramus. So these are the kind of problems that we labour with. There is a terrible disconnect between the rulers and the ruled. So in a sense, India or its north-eastern periphery is not fully democratic. Governance which actually implies a participatory mode of development is totally divorced from the people. What we have is more like an oligarchy where the ruling elite control everything.

There are two conflict areas that one foresees if the situation has to change. First, the need to make democracy in its full and inclusive form relevant to the people of North-East India. This would mean empowering the villages through more sharing of power and resources. Second, there is a dire need to decentralise governance and to make it meaningful through the full participation of people, down to the last person in the village. In both cases there will be a contest since power and the power centres will first have to be fragmented before power is judiciously distributed. In the process there could be a blood-bath. In the second case, participatory governance would mean that the capacities of people and organizations, particularly the traditional institutions would have to be enhanced so that they can make a free, prior, informed choice and give their consent about what is packaged as 'development'. Ethnic communities whose land and resources are appropriated for infrastructure development models must be adequately compensated. This necessitates that the communities and community organizations be well-versed on evaluating every development package. They must be able to vet projects and also have a good idea of the evaluation and monitoring processes. It is important that the communities learn to negotiate a good bargain and to ensure they are not short-changed. All these require large scale capacity building which has not happened over the past fifty years. People have been kept at a distance even while the ruling elite negotiate personal deals out of every development project.

India's North-East is a bio-diversity hot spot. It supports

63 per cent of the country's forests. The region has vast reserves of oil, coal, limestone and above all a strategic mineral like uranium. Naturally it has begun to attract a lot of attention from national and multi-national companies. With globalisation forcing its way into the region and global actors wanting to set up cement companies, the once cohesive ethnic communities are beginning to crack. Through a process of co-option the more progressive members of the group are inducted as board members and even allowed share-holding in these multinationals. In this way they develop a stake and are then used to defend the projects no matter how exploitative the deals are and how environmentally and economically destructive they are for the people. We have the example of Lafarge the global cement giant which is sourcing limestone from Meghalaya but manufacturing cement in Bangladesh. There is a hue and cry today as villagers have belatedly realized that Lafarge had by surreptitious means, (that is by asking the local tribals or stakeholders to purchase land and then transfer the ownership to the company) appropriated 3 lakh square metres of land in the Southern part of Meghalaya and is now its rightful owner. This land is now under mortgage to six international banks — offshore lenders as they are called — including the Asian Development Bank, in order to avail a loan of US $ 153 million.

For ethnic communities, land is a precious resource because it is linked to their cultural practices and is their very sustenance. Hence the special protection clauses in the Land Transfer Act which debars non-tribals from purchasing land in their territories. Although there are voices of dissent about such laws being arbitrary since the opposite is not applicable in the case of tribals, there is merit in what the Constitution framers have envisioned when they inserted special provisions relating to the transfer of land and resources.

Most of the ethnic conflicts or assertions for greater political space within the present dispensations have their roots in the unjust structures that have kept some ethnic groups out of the power sharing arrangements. Although the states of Meghalaya, Mizoram and Assam have their district councils for the purpose of addressing the special needs of ethnic minorities, the Councils have not been able to function effectively because of their dependence on the State Government for resources. Lack of funds or the non-timely transfer of funds by the Government to the Councils have forced them to divert money meant for one head to another. Primary schools in Meghalaya used to be administered by the District Councils. But mismanagement in the form of non-payment of teachers salaries and a poor service delivery mechanism resulted in prolonged agitation by primary school teachers who demanded that they be brought under the purview of the State Government. In this manner the Councils have lost much of their teeth.

When the 73rd and 74th Amendment Acts were passed, late Rajiv Gandhi was categorical that the states of Nagaland, Meghalaya and Mizoram should be kept out of the purview of the above Acts since they have traditional systems of governance. What was completely left out of the discourse was the urgent need to democratize these institutions since they are steeped in gender biases and are exclusive by nature in that they only include tribals. Also these institutions have not been exposed to modern influences and systems of governance but have remained closed and inward-looking, thus making them misfits in a situation where people have by and large accepted the tenets of liberal democracy no matter how dysfunctional democracy can sometimes be. Since the traditional institutions are not actually under the Panchayati Raj ministry but are actually under district councils they have not been able to access direct funding from the Centre. Yet the unwillingness of the vanguards of tradition to reform and bring in more gender sensitivity and to open themselves up to the winds of change have kept them in a *status-quoist* position neither moving forward not backwards.

What has happened as a result is that there is a huge gap between the government which is normally based in the district headquarters and the people in the villages. There are no delivery mechanisms that could bridge the gap between the people and the State Government. Governments rarely go beyond the sub-divisions. Hence villages remain obscure, unvisited territories that are left to fend for themselves. Traditional institutions have neither money nor delivery mechanisms. They cannot by any yardstick be equated with Panchayats which have well-defined powers and specific subjects on which they legislate and govern. By leaving the above three states out of the purview of the Panchayati Raj system without encouraging an alternative model of grassroot governance the Government of India has done a great disfavour to the people. Left to themselves the traditional institutions will not change. They are happy to remain where they are and their leaders enjoy the status of petty chieftains with little responsibility and no accountability. Hence the gap between the urban centres and the rural hamlets will only widen. More and more influx from the rural to the urban centres carries on unabated, creating their own sets of problems. What needs to be understood here is that the district councils have never positioned themselves as a mechanism that would take the place of local administrators. Neither have the Councils challenged the traditional institutions to adopt the enabling clauses that govern the Panchayati Raj institutions. This is mainly because to the outside world and to Delhi the district councils would like to appear to be the legitimate recipients of funds that are meant to be channeled through the PRIs. The Councils can never claim to be a PRI. They are more like a second rung legislature which carry out bits and pieces of development work.

One other problem that district councils at least in Meghalaya face is that the traditional institutions do not recognize the authority of the Councils over them as outlined by the Sixth Schedule. Proponents of traditional institutions claim that they existed much before the district councils ever came into being. Hence they resent the idea of a superimposed authority. The war of attrition carries on and neither one is co-operating with the other. But these are internal issues to be sorted out by the people. However, since traditional institutions have projected themselves as sacrosanct and as drawing their legitimacy from tradition and customary laws and practices, any critique of their undemocratic mode of functioning would immediately isolate the critic making him/her a pariah in the community. So the problem continues to fester even as people are getting more and more distances from governance.

These are practical problems about balancing ethnic identity with its ideological baggage its propensity to be glorified beyond reason, to that of a liberal democratic setup. The ethnic communities themselves want to hang on to both without perhaps realizing the damage they do to themselves. It is irrational to believe that an oligarchy can peacefully co-exist with a democracy. Both systems have different value systems and the former is almost an anachronism in most parts of the world. Perhaps the only people who gain from the dichotomous institutions are again the ruling elite from amongst the ethnic communities.

There is an urgent need to debate the existing systems prevailing among ethnic communities. Ethnicity should on no account prevent the communities from being progressive and adopting the best that democracy can offer. Of what use is one's ethnic identity if one continues to live in abject poverty? If the conservation of ethnic values and practices means that development by-passes the village then it is time to revisit what this ethnicity really means. Does it mean the continued dominance by a few ruling clans and families? Does it means a continued exclusion of half of the population, that is women, from the decision-making processes? Does it mean excluding 'others' from giving their inputs or using those others only as means for generating financial resources? These are questions that require serious enquiry by scholars who do not have a vested interest in perpetuating the *status quo*.

REFERENCES

Eric J. Honsbawm, *Nations and Nationalism Since 1870, Programme, Myth, Reality,* Cambridge University Press, 1994.

Ethnicity, Culture and Nationalism in North-East India, Agarwal M.M. (Ed.), 1996.

John Dunn, Crisis of the Nation State, *Political Studies*: Special Issue, Vol. 42 pp 3-12, 1994.

Paul R. Brass, *Ethnicity and Nationalism, Theory and Comparison*, Sage Publication, New Delhi.

The Shillong Times, Saturday, July 1, 2006.

7 Ethnic Autonomy: A Challenge to Indian Democracy (North-Eastern Experience)

Niru Hazarika

Cultural Pluralism is one of the basic features of North-East India. While enjoying the colourful social life the people of this region are also experiencing the adverse affects of it due to the appearance of ethnic-oriented discords in the fields of politics and administration. The Ethnic Autonomy question remains unanswered even today. The policies of the Government are merely changing the colour of the problems and shifting them from one place to the other.

The whole issue of ethnic autonomy centres around three concepts — Autonomy, Integration and Development. These concepts do not have similar dimensions, but they have very close relationship with the administration of a democratic state. The definitions forwarded by the scholars towards Autonomy reveal that it is not a self-contained concept. Autonomy cannot be divorced from responsibility, just as rights cannot be separated from duties. One has to earn Autonomy, it is not a gift to be received from any higher authority. The significant point is that it is not confined to a particular community, its relevance to the world across the boundary of a community cannot be denied.

The word "Integration" invites an environment in which there should be mutual respect for each other, peaceful co-existence of the people professing different religions, having different cultures and speaking different languages. It is the basic requirement of a plural society like ours to walk together on the path of progress.

The word "Development" is close to both the process and the

end as it calls for change-oriented, action-oriented and result - oriented administration. It is a dynamic process.

Background of the Ethnic Issue

During the British rule several devices were adopted for administrative convenience in the hill areas of undivided Assam, which was North-East India *minus* Tripura and Manipur. It provided enough scope for strengthening the issue of ethnic autonomy in the region. During the British rule the people of hill areas came in close contact with the plains people of the state through commercial purposes. This environment prevailed in the state even prior to the British rule. Since the hill people could not produce all the requirements for their livelihood, they used to come down to the neighbouring markets in the plains with their forest products and the products of crafts for exchange. This commercial relation, which emerged as the source of mutual understanding between the hills and the plains people in the region, resulted into even the process of assimilation. The Indian rulers also adopted the policy of non-interference in the internal affairs of the hill people.

However, considering the differences in the socio-cultural life between the hills and the plains, the British rulers thought of introducing new devices to administer the hill areas which would be suitable to their way of life. Further the problem of exploitation of the hill people by the businessmen from the plains contributed to a great extent to that thought of the Britishers.

In 1872 the Britishers realized that there was an urgent and absolute necessity of stringent control over the commercial relations between the hills and the plains by exercising special powers to lay down certain specific rules. The Government came to the conclusion that it was necessary to take special powers and lay down special rules. Accordingly, a Regulation was framed by the Lt. Governor of Bengal and approved by the Governor General-in-Council to give effect to this policy under Statutes 32 and 33 Vic. This Regulation empowered the Lt. Governor to prescribe a line to be called Inner Line in each of the tribal areas. Rules were laid down regarding trade, the possession of land beyond the line and other matters which gave the Executive Government an effective control over it. Any non-tribal seeking to go beyond the Inner Line was to obtain a pass from the Deputy Commissioner, who could lay down conditions as he thought necessary. It helped the tribal communities to save themselves from the problem of exploitation by the traders and other non-tribals. Nobody realized the adverse effect of it. Here one has to accept that when two neighbouring groups of people with manifold difference are artificially separated and prevented from easy access distrusts and suspicion are bound to emerge amongst them. This is the situation Assam is facing today.

The next administrative device was the creation of excluded and partially excluded areas. On the issue of division of excluded and partially excluded areas and the inclusion of these areas into the Reform Scheme of the British Government, the officials, non-officials and the members of the House of Commons expressed different views on the issue. Assam, with its tracts differing widely from the plains, really presented an extraordinary situation to be dealt with by the administration.

What is meant by Excluded and Partially-Excluded Areas ? The Excluded areas were the tracts where any advanced form of administration was not possible because of its nature of backwardness. These areas were to be administered by the Governor himself. The Ministers would have no constitutional rights to advise him in connection with the administration of these areas. Neither the Central nor the Provincial Legislature would have the power to make laws applicable to these tracts, but the Governor General-in-Council might direct that any Act of the Provincial Legislature should apply to the tract subject to such exceptions or modifications as the Governor thought necessary. Proposals for expenditure in the tract need not be submitted for vote in the Legislatures, Provincial or Central. No question might be asked about the tract and no subject relating to the tract might be discussed in the Assembly except with the sanction of the Governor.

In the case of Partially Excluded areas discussion in the Legislative Assembly was allowed with the previous permission of the Governor. Further application of new laws in those areas was at the discretion of the Provincial Government.

When the Government of India Bill, 1919 was referred to a Joint Select Committee, the witnesses before it also expressed different views on the issue. Sir Archdale Earle, a former Chief Commissioner of Assam expressed the view that the frontier tracts should be wholly excluded from the reform scheme. Chandranath Sarma, Nabin Chandra Bordoloi and some others expressed the view that the hill districts of frontier importance should be the primary concern of the Central Government.

However, the Government of India Act, 1919 authorized the Governor General-in-Council to declare any territory in British India to be backward area. On 3rd January, 1921, the Governor General-in-Council declared Garo Hills, British India portion of Khasi and Jaintia Hills other than the Shillong Municipality and Cantonment, the Mikir Hills, Naga Hills, Mizo Hills and the Sadiya Tracts as backward areas.

Again, the political status of the hill areas was debated before the Simon Commission. Promode Chandra Dutta was in favour of inclusion of the hill areas, while J.H. Hutton, Deputy Commissioner of Naga Hills, N.E. Parry, Superindent of Lushai Hills were in favour of exclusion.

Ultimately, the Government of India Bill, 1935 provided for excluded and partially excluded areas. The Bill was introduced in the House of Commons and it attracted the attention of almost all the members of the House. During discussion a member of the Simon Commission suggested redrafting of the list of excluded and partially excluded areas. The suggestion was supported by several members of the House including Winston Churchill. The House of Commons also felt the need of further enquiry into the question. Accordingly, the instruction was issued to the Government of India to take necessary action. The Government of Assam, while responding to the request of the Government of India, informed that the tribals in the plains did not want to be excluded — whether total or partial. Ultimately, in Assam three categories of hill areas emerged — the Frontier Tracts, Excluded Areas and Partially Excluded Areas.

Constituent Assembly and the Sixth Schedule

The Constituent Assembly which wanted to develop the nation on the basis of modern concept of justice, laws and secular education could not ignore the question of socio-cultural pluralism existing in North-East India. Even the British had to give special attention to this question. As one of the architects of the Constitution of India, Dr. B.R. Ambedkar said, "As far as the ultimate goal is concerned, I think none of us need have any doubt. Our difficulty is not with regard to the ultimate, our difficulty is with regard to the beginning. Our difficulty is how to make the heterogeneous mass that we have today to take decisions in common and march on the way which leads us to unity." Any effort to make situation analysis of public policy in Assam cannot be divorced from this explicit expression of Dr. Ambedkar.

The Cabinet Mission in its statement of 16th May, 1946 stressed that the tribal and excluded areas required a special attention of the Constituent Assembly. The Constituent Assembly also realized that the Advisory Committee should be requested to appoint a Sub-Committee on the North-East Frontier (Assam) Tribal and Excluded Areas with Gopinath Bordoloi as its Chairman. The other members were J.J.M. Nichols Roy, Rupnath Brahma and A.V. Thakkar. Later Aliba Imti was co-opted as member of the Sub-Committee.

The Sub-Committee started investigation early in 1946. The members visited all the hill areas of the state and met different tribal organizations, leading personalities of the communities including village headmen and the Deputy Commissioners and other high officials. During their visit the members found that the concept of autonomy as expressed by the people living in different hills or different groups of people living in the same hills meant differently.

Debate in the Constituent Assembly : In the Constituent Assembly which wanted to uplift the nation on modern foundations of law, individuals with secular education could not ignore the question of socio-cultural pluralism of North-East India. Even the British rulers were compelled to give special attention to this question. As one of the architects of the Constitution of India, Dr. B.R. Ambedkar said, "as far as the ultimate goal is concerned, I think none of us need have any apprehension. None of us need have any doubt. Our difficulty is not with regard to the ultimate, our difficulty is with regard to the beginning. Our difficulty is how to make the heterogeneous mass that we have today to take decisions in common and march on the way which leads us to unity." Any effort of a situation analysis of public policy in Assam cannot be divorced from explicit expression of Dr. Ambedkar.

Further they should be free from forced labour and be allowed to practice their own customs and traditions. Regarding administration they suggested that the responsibility of regular administration should be entrusted to the local people and the village authorities would carry out the village administration. Thus opinions differed from community to community on the concept of Autonomy. Naturally the Sub-Committee received different proposals for reform for the administration of the hill areas.

Observation of the Sub-Committee

The Sub-Committee observed that the fear of exploitation was one of the significant factors for demanding retention of the Inner Line Regulation in the hill Areas. Their fear of exploitation was one of the factors for not favouring the establishment of industries in their areas by the non-tribals.

They feared that due to heavy pressure from the plains people the provincial Government might not allot required fund for the development of the tribal areas. They also suggested two remedial measures — first, special financial provisions for the tribals and second the conferment of financial powers to the local council.

The Sub-Committee observed that there was an emphatic unanimity of opinion of the hill tribes that there should be control of immigration and allocation of land to outsiders. The tribal communities were worried about the problem of immigration and felt the need of protection against their encroachment and exploitation. Therefore, they repeatedly referred to the regulations like Chin Hills Regulations under which an outsider would be required to have a pass to enter the hill territory beyond the Inner Line and thus an undesirable person could be kept out of the area.

The Sub-Committee felt that the fear of being exploited by the outsiders was a justified one.

The visits to different hills of Assam helped the members of the Sub-Committee to realize that the jhuming invited problems for the hill people such as land erosion, alteration of rainfall, floods, which were the hazards of jhuming. Some tribes tried for settled cultivation. But terracing cultivation was very costly, because it required labour, suitable hill sides, irrigation, etc. Unless these facilities were provided hill tribes could not be persuaded to stop jhuming

The hill people were found to be interested in the administration of land, forests, agriculture, law and primary education. The Committee was convinced about the ability of the hill people to manage these affairs without difficulty. However, the Sub-Committee had the reservation in entrusting the financial autonomy to them, especially to accept their demand for power of taxation, raising of funds, etc. The reservation of the Sub-Committee was rooted in the feeling that there might be the demand to spend all the revenues on the district itself, in that case similar demands would come from the plains districts also. This kind of demand may affect the provincial administration very badly and it would result in multiplicity and unsound financial principles causing chaotic condition.

While highlighting the background for formulating the draft Constitution, Gopinath Bordoloi said that it was not unknown to the members of the House that the rule of the British Government and activities of the Missionaries went together. These areas were entirely excluded areas in the sense that none from the plains could go there and contact them. Further some of those areas were war zones. During the war, the then rulers and officers developed in the minds of those tribal people a sense of separation and isolation and gave them assurance that at the end of the war they would be allowed to have independent states to manage their affairs in their own way.

The people of those areas were influenced by the ideas of isolation and separation. The most serious challenge faced by the Sub-Committee was whether for the purpose of integration, the methods of force, the methods use of the Assam Rifles and the military forces, should be used, or a method should be used in which the willing cooperation of those people could be obtained for the purpose of governing these areas.

Gopinath Bordoloi mentioned that there were certain institutions among those hill tribals which, according to Bordoloi were good enough, and it would be wrong to destroy those institutions. The most noteworthy feature of the tribal society was the manner in which they used to settle their disputes. The cases which would go in the name of murder according to our Penal Code were settled by these people by the barest method of a Panchayat's decision. The boys would perform certain simple functions leaving the difficult functions of the state to the adults, while the elders would give their judgments in cases of disputes and order distribution of lands for jhuming and things of that kind. Thus the whole society was involved in the administration of the locality. This may be said as the existence of good governance which modern state is searching for. The Sub-Committee thought of not disturbing the existing system of autonomy.

Gopinath Bordoloi admitted that it was true that some of those tribal people were head hunters, but it should be understood that it happened only when there was enmity of one clan against another. Those people had nurtured a spirit of collective hatred in them for generations. Under that situation the Sub-Committee had two alternatives before it. Whether it should raise in them a spirit of enmity and hatred by application of force or whether it should bring them under the broad principles of a government by good will and love. The Sub-Committee preferred to adopt Gandhian method. With this background the Sixth Schedule was drafted and incorporated in the Constitution as a special measure to administer the hill areas providing them autonomy.

Mere incorporation in the Constitution and the creation of District Councils under the Sixth Schedule was not sufficient to achieve its purpose and the goals of the nation in Independent India. Here the state machinery fails to regulate the changes in the hill areas and to direct them towards the Ideals enshrined in the Preamble to the Constitution of India.

Status of Village Democracy

With gaining of Independence India accepted the Welfare concept of the State and the Constitution provided for a strong Centre to have efficiency in the administration and to make effective solutions of the problems arising in the states or any part of the country. The framers of the Constitution were not very confident in the strength of the rural masses and therefore, did not give much attention to the grass-roots level democracy. Till recently the political leaders of the country did not give a serious thought to it. Only under the leadership of Rajiv Gandhi, then Prime Minister of India attention was paid to this level of administration. The question of ethnic autonomy cannot be divorced from the grassroots level democracy. Negligence to this question by the leaders of independent India has contributed to a great extent in the emergence of this problem in this region.

Another factor may be highlighted here is the imbalanced development of rural India. Mention may be made of Mahatma Gandhi's vision on rural reconstruction which had two major objectives — first, economic development by eradicating economic ills of Indian villages and second, human resource development by building up the rural society on human values, truth, non-violence, love and fellow feeling. These objectives cannot be achieved without full development of all the faculties of an individual's life and removal of harmful socio-religious superstitions amongst the rural people and the obsolete customs and traditions. Gradually with the modernization of the society the customs and traditions are becoming weak and on several areas of social life these have been disappearing. But unfortunately these have been replaced by politicization of the group life in the society, emergence of hypocricy amongst the members of the elite section of the society.

While making effort for the development of the nation economic programs have been insisted upon ignoring the need of the security of human qualities. Today we are trying to build up participatory democracy after destroying the traditional democratic system at the grassroots level. Nobody can deny that economic development must be accompanied by the development of human resources based on self-service and self-governance principles, not on spoon feeding system. The ideas of Gandhi were deeply rooted in our rural and social culture which Fred Riggs interpreted in terms of Ecology and in modern academic terms of environment.

The development of villages in India demands application of the principle of decentralization in administration. India has already started immediately after independence the process of Democratic Decentralization in administration to embrace each and every citizen of the country through local level democracy. Mahatma Gandhi's concept of village "*Swaraj*" influenced to a great extent the architects of modern India who launched the Community Development Programmes in 1952. Gandhiji's constructive programme was a programme of village upliftment, social resurgence and national emancipation which indicates full-freedom not only in political field but also in the fields of economic and educational sphere of national life. His dream was to make every village self-sufficient in food, dwelling houses, in employment and education, so that it can bear the responsibility of grassroots democracy of our country. The whole concept of democracy centres round the individual and human qualities. Closely connected with the concept of democracy is truth, goodness and beauty — these three values are directly linked with intellect, will and feeling respectively — *jnana, karma* and *bhakti.* Without these values democracy cannot survive. These are the values which cannot be imposed on man from outside. The inner person must realize it and direct or regulate the behaviour of man in the society and thus one can achieve social democracy which may be termed as human society. Democracy can grow only in the human society and it is the human society which is the home of political democracy.

The primary requirement for development of a country is not merely economic process, it includes socio-cultural aspect also. Here I must say that Gopinath Bordoloi Committee realized very rightly the socio-cultural situation in the North-Eastern Region and suggested safeguard of ethnic autonomy of the hill people in the region. The North-Eastern Region is well known for pluralism in culture, language and religion. In the state of Assam alone fifteen numerically largest languages are found, such as — Assamese, Bengali, Bodo/Boro, Hindi, Nepali, Mising, Karbi, Oriya, Santali, Manipuri, Garo, Rabha, Dimasa, Mundia, Kurukh/Oraon and several others. The people belonging to different ethnic groups living in the plains of Assam were not counted by the Sub-Committee or even after independence under the umbrella of Ethnic Autonomy. There are several reasons for it — first, these groups did not give serious thought to assert for ethnic autonomy; second, the process of integration or assimilation among them was started long before India gained independence; third, they were scattered throughout the state; the state of Assam is known for its religious and caste tolerance.

In independent India social and cultural values, customs and traditions of the society influenced the whole political and administrative processes. North-East India is the typical example of it. In spite of strong system of British administration for long time the people of this region could preserve their own culture and traditions very safely. India being a developing country in the third world comprising Asia, Africa and Latin America had to begin with development administration, i.e. Rural Development Administration. It was a serious challenge to the leaders of modern India because the development invites changes and modernization of the traditional way of life. Conflict and confusion began in the minds of the people of this region, but these were nurtured tacitly by them for a decade. Since 1960 the conflicts and dissatisfactions became prominent and ethnic assertion with political flavor started amongst tribal communities of this region in both the hills and the plains. The smaller tribes lived in the remote areas being isolated from the rest of the people. Visit of the politicians and administrators to those areas were very rare, Naturally, the feeling of being neglected was intensified with the impact of science and technology. The tribal communities of the plains of Assam started comparing their status with that of the hill communities which were administered by the District Councils under Sixth Schedule.

Distortion of Traditional Democracy

In North-East India, specially in Assam a traditional village worked as essentially a democratic institution based on social customs and traditions. It had its authority over every aspect of village life in the state. It was a privilege of the village elders to occupy the positions of leadership and importance. The village was a unit by itself, self-contained, self-regulated and self-reliant in the socio-economic functions. The whole village was monitored by the village headman and the religious leaders.

The concept of participatory democracy was prevalent in traditional North-East India. In the hills there was the provision for Dormitory system for the youths in which they were trained on community life. The village defence, sharing of joy and sorrows with the fellow members, community feasts etc. were the main areas on which they were trained under the guidance of village elders. Similarly in the traditional Assam also the youth services were utilized by the elderly persons of the village during almost all the social and religious festivals, at the time of distress of a family, village defence, etc. It was common practice amongst the villagers to help the helpless people, to extend cooperation to anyone who fell ill or affected by any natural calamity. In other words they observed army like discipline in normal life. They used to work like one man and participate in each and every common issue covering the village. They moved together for cultivation, for funeral or for feast with full heart. No hide and seek technique was prevalent in their social life. In other words everything in social life was transparent. Thus among the villagers the enviable spirit of unity, discipline and social consciousness was practised.

For settling disputes or discussion on common issues generally two platforms were utilized — viz., Courtyard of the village headman and "*Namghar*", the prayer house of the followers of Saint Sankardeva. There free and frank discussions were found on the common issues of the villagers. Unfortunately, the very spirit of democratic society has been destroyed with the emergence of competitive electoral politics in modern democracy. Political violence, money and muscle power, false promises, hiring of people for political meeting at the time of election are alleged to be used as the technique to win election. The independent role of the media is also not free from suspicion. In short, the grassroots level democracy is neglected to a great extent by the leaders of the nation causing harm to Indian democracy. Further instead of emphasizing on the positive aspect of the multi-colour culture or ethnic pluralism to develop it as a resource it has been used in a negative way. Now everyday one finds complaints, cruel responses from the administration, non-accountability, lack of responsiveness of the administration etc. These have to be taken care of at the grassroots level to strengthen democracy at the higher level.

What are the Recent Trends?

Since early 1990s tribal communities in the plains of Assam are demanding ethnic based Autonomous Councils. The Government of Assam has already granted Autonomous Councils to Bodos, Misings, Rabhas, and Tiwas, while the demands of other communities have yet to be fulfilled. This is the only region in the country which is unfolding different kinds of grassroots level administrative devices. The tribal communities were confident that the ethnic based Autonomous Council was the only solution to their problems of exploitation, negligence, etc. and to safeguard their culture and languages. The government was of the opinion that by granting autonomy to them unity and integrity of the nation could be established.

Now dilemmas before the government are found in several areas — first, while granting autonomy to different ethnic groups how to demarcate the area and to ensure accountability of those autonomous institutions in the wider perspective of the nation; second, the process of decentralization may lead to disintegration, where to stop the process of decentralization and how to do that; third the question of self-determination voiced by different groups of people is very sensitive and complicated to be settled, how to be exact and scientific while analyzing it to the satisfaction of all groups of people in modern India ; fourth, the traditional concepts of "Sovereignty", "Human Rights", Welfare State", "Nation State" in the days of globalization are the inadequate answers to the challenges of modern Indian democracy. These are added by the problems caused by insurgency and counter-insurgency activities and pressures by the youth organizations. Hidden interest of the leaders, hidden relationships amongst different groups and individuals and lack of specific goals and effective control of the educational systems, emergence of money and muscle power etc. are serious ailments of the political and social life in this region.

Development, Autonomy and Democracy must go together, because all the three are interlinked and indispensable in the modern way of social life. No doubt it is a difficult task to integrate them but it is not impossible. Here one has to remember that no one mechanism can be adopted for development of a plural society like ours, no exact boundary can be demarcated while defining and granting autonomy to each and every ethnic group and no democracy whether social, political or economic can survive without the development of human qualities.

To quote Sathya Sai —

Politics without principles
Education without character
Science without humanity
Commerce without morality
are not only positively useless,
but positively dangerous.

REFERENCES

Avasthi, A. and Ramesh K. Arora (ed) : *Bureaucracy and Development : Indian Persepectives* : Associated Publishing House; New Delhi; 110005, 1978.

Barpujari, H.K. : *North-East India; Problems, Policies and Prospects*: Spectrum Publications, New Delhi, 2000.

Bordoloi, B.N.; *Alienations of Tribal Land and Indebtedness*; Tribal Research Institute, Ghy, Assam, 1986.

Dahl, Robert, A. : *Democracy and Its Critics* : Orient Longman Ltd., New Delhi, 1991.

Dutta, P.S. : *Autonomy Movement in Assam* : New Delhi, 1993.

Gupta, N.L. : *Human Values in Education* : Concept Publishing Company, New Delhi, 2000.

Hazarika, Niru : *Ethnic Autonomy Question in N.E. India* : Spectrum Publications, Delhi, 2005.

Rao, V.V. : *A Century of Tribal Politics* : S. Chand and Company, New Delhi, 1976.

Rao, B. Shiva (ed). : *The Framing of India's Constitution*; four vols.

Memorandums and documents available in the offices of different youth organizations of Assam.

PART IV

Ethic Conflicts : Understanding and Resolution

8 Ethnicity, State and Identity : From Confrontation to Co-Existence

Nani G. Mahanta

The search for identity is a powerful psychological driving force which has propelled human civilization. Identity is evocative: we are after all dealing with a myth or an imagined community which has all the power necessary for political mobilization. Identity has also been defined as an abiding sense of selfhood, the core of which makes life predictable to an individual (Northrop, 1989: 55). To have no ability to anticipate events is essentially to experience terror. Identity can be conceived of as more than a psychological sense of self; it encompasses a sense that one is safe in the world — physically, psychologically, socially, even spiritually. Events that threaten to invalidate the core sense of identity will elicit defensive responses aimed at avoiding psychic and/or physical annihilation.

What seems to be the unanimous view is that ethnicity and identity conflicts will be the dominant form of violence and war in the coming years. Ethnicity itself can be enhanced and reformulated under conditions of modernization. Myths of origin, enemy images, demonizing the other, are old and traditional myths of long historical duration. Most ethnic groups do have a myth of origin, a history of the group, chosen enemies, and stories of traumas. It is at this point that the intersection between modernity and the revival of myth and ritual is of interest.

Inevitability of Ethnic Identity and Response of Nation-State

The protagonists of Nation-State — Political leaders and political theorists of all persuasions have argued against explicit recognition of cultural identities — ethnic, religious, linguistic, racial. The result, more often than not, has been that cultural identities have been suppressed, sometimes brutally, as state policy — through religious persecutions and ethnic cleansings, but also through everyday exclusion and economic, social and political discrimination.

Globally the ethnic identity politics is on the rise. In vastly different contexts and in different ways — from indigenous people in Latin America to religious minorities in South Asia to ethnic minorities in the Balkans and Africa to immigrants in Western Europe — people are mobilizing anew around old grievances along ethnic identity. People want the freedom to practice their religion openly, to speak their language, to celebrate their ethnic or religious heritage without fear of ridicule or punishment or diminished opportunity. It is a simple idea, but profoundly unsettling. States face an urgent challenge in responding to these demands. If handled well, greater recognition of identities will bring greater cultural diversity in society, enriching people's lives. But there is also a great risk.

These struggles over cultural identity, if left and ignored become one of the greatest sources of instability within states and between them — and in so doing trigger conflict that takes development backwards. Identity politics that polarize people and groups are creating fault lines between "us" and "them". Growing distrust and hatred threaten peace, development and human freedoms. Ethnic violence destroyed hundreds of homes and mosques in Kosovo and Serbia. Struggles over identity can also lead to regressive and xenophobic policies that retard human development. They can encourage a retreat to conservatism and a rejection of change, closing off the infusion of ideas and of people who bring cosmopolitan values and the knowledge and skills that advance development. Managing diversity and respecting cultural identities are not just challenges for a few "multi-ethnic states". Almost no country is entirely homogeneous. The world's nearly 200 countries contain some 5,000 ethnic groups. And confrontations over culture and identity are likely to grow — the ease of communications and travel have shrunk the world and changed the landscape of cultural diversity, and the spread of democracy, human rights and new global networks have given people greater means to mobilize around a cause, insist on a response and get it.

Socio-economic injustices

India's nation-building project that sought to create a pan-Indian identity has gone awry. It would be wrong to bring unity of the state by asking the ethnic communities to think in terms of citizenship and forget their cultural root. This is indeed a difficult proposition. In multi-ethnic state like Assam and other North-eastern states of India, we have no way out but to develop a multicultural policy that recognizes the distinctiveness of each and every community at the same by giving sufficient choices to develop a sense of unity. Further splinterisation of these states can be prevented only by allowing each and every community to develop culturally, socially, politically and above all economically. Going beyond the contractors, politician and the elites, development process must reach the common people doesn't matter whether he is a Bodo, immigrant Muslim or caste Hindu resident of the state. Cultural diversity is here to stay — and to grow. States and the society need to find ways of forging national unity amid this diversity. The world, ever more interdependent economically, cannot function unless people respect diversity and build unity through common bonds of humanity.

Ethnic based identity is bound to be there in North-East (NE) India and they are likely to proliferate. Rather than looking at these issues as 'problems' approach should be to look at the structural issues and address them accordingly. Thus we must realize that such ethnic 'unrest' is bound to be there especially when politics is based on 'first past the post system' and politics is essentially 'who gets what when and how'. The identification of the political parties with the interest of the majorities by appealing to the categories such as 'ethnic', 'linguistic'or a combination of some or all of them is problematic. Such a situation not only puts pressure on the less powerful communities to organize its separate identity, but also 'deepens the hatred between the well defined communities or nationalities, particularly when the nation-building is organized and measured in terms of the 'will of the majority' which exercises state power.

Ethnic upsurge is not always bad — it gives hitherto unrepresented groups a chance to be heard and listened to. A look at the present coalitional politics in Assam shows how it generates a feeling of competitiveness among the power holders for performance. The constituent of present ruling coalition — the Bodo leaders want to deliver — otherwise people will also reject them — the way they had done with the once powerful ABSU.

Identity is not Static: It is Multi-Layered

Here in NE India, we urge for respecting diversity and building more inclusive societies by adopting policies that explicitly recognize cultural differences. Individuals can and do have multiple identities that are complementary — ethnicity, language, religion and race as well as citizenship. Nor is identity a zero sum game. There is no inevitable need to choose between state unity and recognition of cultural differences.

A sense of identity and belonging to a group with shared values and other bonds of culture is important for individuals. But each individual can identify with many different groups. Individuals have identity of citizenship (for example, being Indian), gender (being a woman), race (being of Tibeto-Burman origin), language (being fluent in Bodo, Assamese and Hindi), politics (having left-wing views or regionalism) and religion (being Hindu or Muslim). Identity also has an element of choice: within these memberships individuals can choose what priority to give to one membership over another in different contexts. Sociologists tell us that people have boundaries of identity that separate "us" from "them", but these boundaries shift and blur to incorporate broader groups of people.

"Nation building" has been a dominant objective of the 20th century, and most states have aimed to build culturally homogeneous states with singular identities. Sometimes they succeeded but at the cost of repression and persecution. If the history of the 20th century showed anything, it is that the attempt either to exterminate cultural groups or to wish them away elicits a stubborn resilience. By contrast, recognizing cultural identities has resolved never-ending tensions. For both practical and moral reasons, then, it is far better to accommodate cultural groups than to try to eliminate them or to pretend that they do not exist as some writers would make us believe. Countries do not have to choose between national unity and cultural diversity. Surveys show that the two can and often do coexist.

In case of Assam there are substantial numbers of people who prefer to call themselves both as an Indian as well as Assamese and while some of them preferred to have one identity. This has come into picture from a survey by the Centre for the Study of Developing Societies (CSDS), New Delhi.[1] The question that was asked was — how do you identify yourself? It is very clear from the above data the people of Assam would more prefer to call themselves as Assamese or both as Assamese and Indian. What it clearly establishes is people believe in a more federal identity than one political identity.

	Frequency	*Per cent*	*Valid per cent*
Assamese	596	38.5	38.5
Assamese and Indian	336	21.7	21.7
Indian	444	28.7	28.7
Other identities	135	8.7	8.7
DK	38	2.5	2.5
Total	**1549**	**100.0**	**100.0**

The same survey was again conducted by CSDS in the year 2006-March. The main findings of this survey are as follows —

1. 39 per cent of the total surveyed considers them as only Indian.
2. 14.7 per cent considers them to be only Assamese.
3. 41 per cent consider both as Indian and Assamese.

Contesting Xenophobic and Regressive Ethnicity

Struggles over identity can also lead to regressive and xenophobic policies that retard human development. They can encourage a retreat to conservatism and a rejection of change, closing off the infusion of ideas and of people who bring cosmopolitan values and the knowledge and skills that advance development. For it is often the suppression of culturally identified groups that leads to tensions. The UNDP report 2004 makes a case for respecting diversity and building more inclusive societies by adopting policies that explicitly recognize cultural adopting policies that explicitly recognize cultural differences — multicultural policies individuals have to shed rigid identities if they are to become part of diverse societies and uphold cosmopolitan values of tolerance and respect for universal human rights.

Thus, what needs to be contested is the craze for mono-ethnic homeland that is exclusionary and does not bear the existence of others. In North-East India the craze for ethnic exclusiveness and reorganizing space in exclusive ethnic terms has created a tussle between the State and community on the one hand and the community-community on the other hand. The clash over Nagalim or 'Greater Nagaland' and reaction by the ethnic groups in Manipur, Assam and Arunachal Pradesh; the reaction of the Non-Bodos like the Koch-Rajbangshi, the Rabhas, etc. in the Bodo Territorial Council, the recent Karbi-Dimasa clash in Karbi Anglong are a few examples of such quest for exclusive home land. The State by creating innumerable tribal district councils accentuates such tendency for exclusivity by relying on a 'tribal to tribal' approach. While the existing identities as of now will have to be recognized, fragmentation will have to be halted. Or else we may soon end up facing innumerable demands for tiny home republics. Though the contemporary world appears to be completely divided on ethnic lines yet the parochialism of the ethnic orientation should not be overlooked. The universal humanitarian values take a back seat when the reality is perceived from ethnic point of view. The exclusive rights claimed by the ethnic identities on the basis of indigenous status are also problematic because no community can conclusively prove that they are the original inhabitant of an area. They can merely claim. The evidence about authenticity is rather insufficient and definitely not verifiable.

What is missing in such mono ethnic territorial space is effective communication among the communities. The recent ethnic clashes between the Karbis and Dimasas in Karbi Anglong that had claimed more than 100 lives make us the need to think about inter-ethnic accommodation. Surgical vivisection of territorial space into some mono-ethnic homelands seems to be the guiding principles of ethnic politics in North-East India today. Viewed thus, our solution to conflicts is marked by the same craze for reorganizing the space — albeit according to the same binary principle. The prospects of peace according to this discourse are decided in a game that is admittedly of zero-sum character. In the midst of such uncertainties the state is believed or legitimized to play a dominant role as it goes to the old dictum of liberalist principle of the State as the neutral umpire among contending forces. Thus a conflict between the State and community becomes a conflict between communities. In this tussle between justice and justice — injustice seems to be the end result.

Ethnic Identity from Liability to Co-existence

To consider the ethnicity based identity as an asset in North-East India, the following steps need to be considered —

> Constitution of a *State Social Council* may be in the line of upper house. Question is to how we can accommodate the burgeoning demand of the ethnic groups. For that we need to explore socio-political structure that can satisfy the Bodos, the Rabhas, the Karbis, the Dimasas, the Tiwas, the Chutias, the Koch-Rajbangshi, the Tai-Phakes, the Matak and Moran, the Ahoms, and the minority groups like the Bengali Hindus, the Muslims, the Nepalis and the Adivasis. Even the smaller groups like Singphos, Tai-Phakes, Lichus and others would soon take up arms — because their main grievance is that they are not being heard. Unless we work out a comprehensive structure that can at least satisfy the basic socio-cultural and economic needs there will be continuous turmoil in the state. Thus how the Asomiya middle class and elite accommodate their demands

and the growing aspirations of the smaller groups and nationalities will be the single most factor that might generate violent conflict in Assam.

In order to give them a greater share in the state of affairs we propose for the constitution of *State Social Council* in each state of North-East India with a proportional representation from each and every community of the state.

Nature and Functions of the Proposed *State Social Council* in Assam: A Conceptual Elaboration

- The proposed ethnic council is a socio-cultural body that would look into the distinct issues of the ethnic groups of Assam and would also address the common socio-cultural concerns of all nationalities.
- This will not be a replication of the political and economic works of the existing seven tribal councils or the panchayti raj institutions in the state. The proposed Council shall essentially look at the identity issues and other socio-cultural issues so that it can address their concerns.
- Apart from the members from the ethnic community, a few distinguished sociologists, anthropologists, historian, social scientists or any other persons having expert knowledge on ethnic, demographic history of Assam and the North-East should be nominated by the Governor of Assam as neutral representative of the government and people of Assam.
- The ethnic council is a Dialogue forum where the respective communities can raise their issues of concern and can meet with other communities and this will help to understand each other's view points while protecting ones own interest.
- It is mandatory for the government to accommodate the advice/recommendations of the members in the council while formulating policies that might affect the groups in that area.
- The council is modelled in the consociational model where

the principle of proportionality, mutual veto, grand coalition and consensus methodologies will be followed while arriving at decisions.

- The main purpose of joint or collective session is to understand each other and appreciate each other's view points democratically in a healthy atmosphere which is lacking in Assam today. A fascist, inward looking devoid of understanding each other's concerns is growing on in Assam and the North-East. In such an atmosphere a healthy democratic dialogue is the only answer to these vexed issues where the state can't alone enforce a decision.

What is the Importance of such Interaction/Dialogue among the Ethnic Communities of Assam?

Today the communities who are at loggerheads with each other due to various reasons need to initiate a dialogue among the affected communities. The issues like claiming the territories of other states or communities, the fear of being treated as the second class citizens in the homeland politics, etc. should be included in such dialogue. An overnight solution may not come — but it will help in understanding the minds of each other. If carried on for a longer period a desirable solution might come up. In Conflict Resolution literature, this process is known as informal problem — solving approach or workshops, where a third party assists conflicting parties to find solutions to their problems. The philosophy of these dialogues is not to force the parties to accept a settlement, but to provide an informal atmosphere, where the parties can exchange their perspectives about their needs and conceive a solution that satisfies the needs of those involved in the conflict.[2] The third party (nominated experts) creates an atmosphere, establishes norms all conducive to free and open discussion in which parties address each other in order to understand their differing perspectives. They are encouraged to deal with analytically rather than polemically — to explore ways in which their interaction helps to exacerbate rather than to blame each other while justifying their own. They are to understand each other's concern, needs, fears, priorities and constraints. The primary objective of such workshops/dialogues/joint sessions is to build channels of communication that enables the parties to learn more about each other. This process, in other words, transforms the negative stereotypes and images constructed during the development of the conflict. This dialogue is the basis of the resolution of social conflicts, as communications between parties can heighten conflicting parties understanding each other's needs, leading the parties to create new social structures and institutions that resolve conflict.[3] An agreement, which would essentially come from the civil-society side, would make an ever-lasting impact in the conflict prone areas of the North-Eastern India.

What is missing in North-East India today is that the doors of dialogue have been virtually closed down. The democratic space has been gradually getting diminished both at the instance of the State and the militant groups. This has more to do with the fact that the entire identity politics has been hijacked by the militias. The insurgent groups irrespective of their ideologies and principles work under extreme authoritarian and military principles. The civil society initiative which was so vibrant in Nagaland has now been reeling under the pressure of NSCN-IM. The reality is NSCN-IM has stopped all civil society dialogues that Naga Hoho took under the leadership of Niketu Iralu and Charles Chasie and seven more members. Even the constitution of the co-called People's Consultative Groups (PCG) by ULFA should not be constructed as representatives of the Civil Society. The most important qualification of all the members has been their unflinching support to the organization. Where are the representatives from women, minority groups and other ethnic groups of the state not to talk about their critics? This I believe is a valid question since ULFA claims to represent the 'people of Assam' and 'not the Assamese'. At the same time let us not be very euphoric about the civil society initiatives as we have outlined above. If these initiatives are not conducted in sustained manner and not regulated by neutral mediators it could end up in a quarreling platform. Nevertheless, our objective is to find a democratic space that can address the identity issues of various ethnic groups in the region.

A Robust Look South and South-East Policy

That amongst others can integrate the communities culturally? In the mainstream writings, psychological alienation and economic under-development have been underlined as primary causes behind insurgency in India's North-East. Consequently, more funds and recognition of national heroes of the region like Lachit Borphukan, Sukapha, Chilarai, and Sankardeva at the national level are prescribed to break this psychological and economic barrier. While some of the suggestions certainly have its relevance, such causal analysis can hardly reflect the reality of the situation. In order to resolve some of the conflicts, one needs to understand the psyche of communities of the region who have resisted integration with the national mainstream. The Nagas, for example, emphasize that they are simply not Indian. They talk more about integration of their communities and separation from India, which consequently would give them a chance to be a part of the community. They visualize an identity which is different from the Indian identity. The futuristic talk of economic development and of North-East India joining the 'national mainstream' contrasts sharply with the vision of the militias that mostly hark back to history and emphasizes the region's historical autonomy from mainland India. For instance, Assamese independentist intellectuals, according to one writer, 're-read, re-interpret and even re-create history' in order to make the case that "Assam had always been a free nation."[4] The names of the region's numerous ethnic militias evoke the memory of independent old kingdoms. Some of these new histories emphasize the region's historical ties with South-East Asia. For instance, in recent years there has been a powerful movement of cultural revivalism among the Ahoms of Assam — the westernmost of the Tai-speaking people spread in mainland South-East Asia. Apart from economic opportunities, trans-national region building can bring important dividends in terms of North-East India's political troubles. The politics of recognition is a recurrent theme in the politics of ethnic militancy in North-East India. Prof. Sanjib Baruah argues even limited cooperation between India and Myanmar can improve conditions in North-East India. For instance, it can make a difference in the current Naga peace process that could end one of the world's oldest armed conflicts. Since Nagas live on both sides of the Indo-Myanmar border, a proposal that might be able to capture Naga political imagination and break the deadlock in the peace process is one that would bring the Nagas of Myanmar into the picture. That, of course, would involve taking the Myanmarese government into confidence. Ethnically, the large majority of the indigenous population of North-East India belongs to different subgroups of the Mongoloid stock whose other cognate branches are found in South-Western China and South-East Asia. The Assam-Burma border was the meeting place of races, cultures, and languages of South and South-East Asia. Taking these points of similarities between the culture of North-East India and South-East Asia into consideration, scholars like Robbins Burling and Peter Kunstadler justify the inclusion of Eastern India in a social and anthropological study of South-East Asia. The border region is inhabited by over a dozen distinct ethnic groups spreading over the whole belt of the Patkai range. Some of them are the Singphos (called Kachin in Myanmar), Usus or Yobins, Tangsas, Noctes, Wanchos, Tutsas, Layos, Khamtis, Tai Phakes, Duanias, Shyams, Khamyasgias, Turungs, Bodos, Mons, Deoris and others with a population over a lakh.[5]

Economic Empowerment or Good Governance

Economic empowerment or good governance is a must for the North-East India. If we analyze the causes for the growth of insurgency in the region, it becomes clear that the factors such as under-development, unemployment, lack of agricultural infrastructure, lack of access to government departments, Flood, corruption, communication, lack of heath care, etc. are some of the basic problems that after being neglected for decades have acted as the greatest incentive for the youth to join the militancy. All this eventually means that the economies do not stir and fail to meet the growing aspirations of the people, particularly the younger generation. This, in turn, provides a fertile ground for grooming various militant groups or a spurt of popular uprisings. In some sense, lack of growth and disturbed environment feed on each other. This is exactly what is happening in most of the North-Eastern states.

Let us look at the situation in Assam. Assam's economic situation is such that it can't generate high growth and more employment to the twenty lakh educated/uneducated unemployed youths in Assam. For our research on ULFA, we had the opportunity of interviewing 120 surrendered ULFA cadres at various points of time.[6] If we analyze the interview with the surrendered militants and the field visits make it amply clear that insecurity of the youths with full energy and frustration contributed to the growth of insurgency in Assam. Let us paraphrase some of the experiences of ex-rebels as to why they had to join insurgency out of frustration —

- The unemployed youths mostly in the rural areas have nothing to do — they pass on most of their time by playing carom, cards or just loitering in the areas.
- In many occasions, some youths open up a small grocery shop to be closed down due to lack of sale.
- Some of them apply for government loan to be given up later on after spending considerable time by running from one government department to another for a minor loan of Rs. 20,000.
- Many of the small scale sector business like poultry, piggery, dairy farming, pischiculture, power loom, wheat mill, rice mill, tractor, cycle repairing, TV mechanic, etc. had been closed due to lack of entrepreneurial skill, power failure , non-payment of loan, flood, etc.
- Many of them were frustrated by the corrupt officials. The peon would not pass on the application without being bribed, the dealing assistant wouldn't forward the application without some reward — the officials would ask them to come again and again for the same work , the typist wouldn't type without a good amount being given — otherwise the letter gets lost from the file.
- There is no value of merit for many of the educated unemployed applied for government jobs. The conditions for being employed into the government job is a hefty amount

to be paid to the politicians through middle man or having excellent relations with the politicians.

- A few of them systematically went for rabi and kharif agricultural production. They undertook these ventures because there is heavy demand of these agricultural products in the urban areas. But due to over production thousands of kilograms of agricultural produce were destroyed. By the time these products came to the market they were rotten — so they gave up next year.

All these conditions were made worse by a brutal, insensitive police and security personnel. The continuous harassment of the rural people by the security forces made them flee their original place for a long time. These are all basic human security issues which compound the insurgency issue in Assam. Continuous heaping of all those issues for many days, months and decades have given these frustrated youths to look for an alternative — and that was provided by ULFA. ULFA was ever-ready to accept them as their cadres and fight the Indian State for a better future. Having argued we don't want to minimize the role of 'ideology', 'colonial legacy', 'exploitation of the centre', 'feeling of not being a part of India' etc. as important factors in the sustenance of ULFA or present socio-economic situation in the state. But anyone who is in the field or has the touch of reality especially in places like Kakopathar (Tinsukia), Nalbari, Dhemaji, Kokrajhar, etc. realize that the vast educated unemployed in Assam today which is more than 23 lakhs are directionless and act as the fertile breeding ground for social unrest in the state. Interesting fact is it's not that these are strong support base of one particular group like ULFA — they are accessible to all groups who provide them some material benefits or some productive engagement. They can be used for processions in Kakopathar which had resulted in the killing of nine people on 9th February, 2006 few days back one would see them in Congress, AGP or BJP rally in Guwahati and Dibrugarh and so on.

NOTES

1. Sandhya Goswami, Obtained through the coordinator in charge of North-east, 2005.
2. Carlos L. Yordan, *Instituting Problem-Solving Processes as a Means of Constructive Social Change, Online Journal of Peace and Conflict Resolution,* issue-Nov. 1998, No-1.4
3. *Ibid.*
4. Udoyan Misra, *The Periphery Strikes Back: Challenges to the nation-State in Assam and Nagaland,* (Shimla: Indian Institute of Advanced Study, 2000), p. 62.
5. S.N. Barua, *Tribes of Indo-Burma Border*, (Margherita, 1991).
6. Nani G. Mahanta, *Assam-portents of violence and hope for peace* — Peace Studies Paper series, 03 by Peace Studies of Omeo Kumar Das Institute of Social Change and Development, July, 2005.

9 Naga Peace Talks : New Parameters, Fresh Challenges : The Issue of Sovereignty vs. Autonomy

Udayon Misra

The attempt to arrive at a peaceful negotiated settlement of the oldest and most protracted insurgency in post-independence India is clearly proving to be a major challenge both to the Indian nation-state and the National Socialist Council of Nagaland (IM). The Naga struggle, like many other identity struggles in the north-eastern region of the country, has thrown up certain central issues relating to the federal structure of the nation and its capacity to include within its ambit the wishes and aspirations of those small nationalities which were only partly covered by the British administration and whose involvement in the freedom struggle was minimal. In the traumatic years immediately following indepen-dence when the Partition led to one of the greatest exodus in human history involving untold human misery, New Delhi didn't seem at all politically equipped to tackle the Naga demand for independence raised by the Naga National Council under the leadership of Angami Zapo Phizo. For, the general mood of those in power then seemed to be in favour of a centralised unitary structure which they thought would be better equipped to hold the country together. In such a context, it was but inevitable that the refusal of a small nationality to unquestioningly become a part of the Indian Union was looked upon with suspicion and distrust by New Delhi. This, despite the fact that independent India's first Prime Minister, Jawaharlal Nehru, possessed a deeper and more comprehensive understanding of the Naga issue than any of his colleagues in government. This is adequately reflected in the letters that were exchanged between Nehru and the NNC secretary, T. Sakhrie, in the period immediately preceding independence. It is indeed an irony of history that Nehru's understanding of and sympathy for the Nagas notwithstanding, military operations in the then Naga Hills district of Assam commenced in the early fifties, thereby initiating a period of strong-arm tactics and human rights violations which further alienated the Naga population from the rest of the country and created conditions for long-term and protracted insurgency to thrive. In the past fifty years and more, the Indian nation-state has learnt quite a few lessons from the continuing insurgency in Nagaland and State manoeuvres have ranged from the use of military force to the creation of a separate state for the Nagas and the introduction of representative forms of government. And, today, it is evident that the Indian nation-state has travelled quite far from those early days of the turbulent fixities in the Naga Hills to a stage where it is engaging itself in discussions relating to the type of relationship that the Nagas would like to have with the Indian Union. This is clearly a measure of its confidence born out of its experiment with representative democracy, reinforced by a Constitution which has time and again proved its resilience and power of accommodation. The very fact that New Delhi has been holding parleys for several years now with an organization which is committed to carving out a Naga homeland outside the Indian Union through armed struggle is proof enough of the changing priorities and expanding parameters of the Indian state. It is certainly no mean achievement for the Indian state to have reached this point of dialogue with a small nationality at war with the Government of India. This becomes even more strikingly clear when one compares the position of the smaller nationalities in many a neighbouring country which secured independence from foreign rule around the same time as India but whose initial experiments with representative democracy finally gave way to authoritarian regimes and military dictatorships.

Nine years after the announcement of the cease-fire, the Government of India and the NSCN (IM) seems to be finally moving towards working out a framework which may bring about an end to the protracted struggle in Nagaland. This framework envisages an autonomous *Nagalim* within the Indian Union, although the NSCN(IM) has been insisting that it has not deviated from its stand on an independent Nagalim outside the Indian Union. But, the NSCN(IM)'s assertions about a sovereign *Nagalim* notwithstanding, it is becoming increasingly clear that the issue of a sovereign Naga homeland outside the Indian Union is finally being marginalized in favour of an arrangement which would guarantee greater autonomy for the Naga people. The peace talks between the NSCN(IM) and the Government of India have reached a stage where the issue of working out maximum autonomy seems to have become the first priority, overriding two other issues which have been central to the peace talks: (a) the question of self-determination or sovereignty for the Naga people; and (b) the integration of all Naga-inhabited areas of Assam, Manipur and Arunachal Pradesh in Nagalim. This has become clear from the NSCN(IM) statement following the June 22-24 round of talks in the Hague where the idea of a Jammu and Kashmir style of autonomy seems to have been favoured. Although the NSCN leader T. Muivah has, in subsequent interviews, denied having made any compromises on the right of the Nagas to an independent homeland, yet the Bangkok round of talks held in July 2006 has made it amply clear that the NSCN(IM), while continuing to talk about sovereignty, is willing to be party to an agreement which would ensure a large measure of autonomy for the Naga people within the Indian Union. According to reports, the proposed framework envisages a relationship between the Nagas and the Indian state on the basis of an "asymmetric federalism" which would be different from the existing relationship between the Indian Union and the federating states. While the NSCN has been insisting that the Nagas have a separate Constitution, the Indian side is of the view that Naga aspirations for autonomy could be accommodated within the Constitution of India. Both the sides would begin by analysing the different Articles of the Constitutionof India so as to find out what would be applicable specifically to the Nagas. The subjects or competencies to be managed separately by the Government of Nagaland and the Centre and to be managed jointly by both would have to be demarcated before a final agreement is reached. From all this it appears that a major restructuring of Centre-State relations would have to be done in order to make the proposed framework feasible. The question, therefore, would inevitably arise: If the Nagas have a "unique" history which calls for a radical overhauling of Central and State powers, then what about the other nationalities which have been struggling for their rightful place within the Indian Union? This is an aspect which New Delhi can never overlook, especially in view of the developments in Kashmir or for that matter in Manipur or Assam.

In this context, it needs to be remembered that the NSCN (I-M), while quietly working towards an arrangement ensuring greater autonomous status for the Nagas, has all the while kept the issue of sovereignty very much alive. This is obviously being done to bring pressure on the Government of India to secure greater concessions for the Naga people. Moreover, as part of these pressure tactics, the NSCN(IM) seems to have given a new thrust to its efforts to further internationalise the Naga issue. This was evident in the June 2006 talks in Holland when the NSCN made it plain to the Indian representatives that it would not hesitate to seek third party intervention in the Naga issue. For instance, when the Indian delegation raised objections about the NSCN(IM) sending an emissary to China and of one of its members addressing the London-based organization called the "Parliamentarians for National Self-Determination" (PNSD), Mr. Muivah categorically stated that it was well within their rights to send their representatives to "any part of the world". He accused the Indian government of trying to "contain" the Nagas and supported the need for third party intervention in solving the Naga issue. This assumes significance in the light of the NSCN(IM) recently addressing the PNSD and strongly calling for British intervention in the Naga issue because the former colonial power had a "moral responsibility" to ensure justice for the Nagas. Third party intervention in the Naga parleys has taken on a new significance with the involvement of the Hong Kong based international expert on constitutional law, the

Kenyan Indian Yash Ghai and of the head of a Dutch NGO, Mr. Van Walt. All this has added a new dimension to the issue of sovereignty which is being sought to be redefined in the context of New Delhi's negotiations with the NSCN(IM) — something which is bound to have its effect on the insurgent groups in the North-East, particularly at a time when the Centre is trying to open up a dialogue with the United Liberation Front of Asom (ULFA) which has been insisting that the issue of sovereignty would be central to any negotiations. In the light of all this, any agreement based on the concept of "shared sovereignty" which would have sub-national Constitutions is bound to strengthen the position of those insurgent groups fighting to break away from India. Interestingly, in recent weeks, especially as news of the Centre's dialogue with the NSCN(IM) started filtering in, the sovereignty issue has resurfaced with renewed vigour in Assam and Manipur. For instance, the United Liberation Front of Manipur (UNLF) has geared up its campaign for a plebiscite to achieve that state's separation from India. Given these equations, it remains to be seen as to how far New Delhi will be able to proceed on the path of shared sovereignty or sub-national constitutions.

Thus, it is important to note that while working towards greater autonomous status for the Nagas within a relatively loose Indian federal structure, the NSCN(IM) has kept alive the issue of sovereignty so as to keep up its pressure on New Delhi. Interestingly, after each round of talks, the NSCN leadership makes it a point to repeat that the organisation's commitment to a sovereign Naga homeland remains unchanged, notwithstanding the clear movement towards greater autonomy. The other point on which the NSCN(IM) has brought pressure on the Centre is that of the territorial integration of all the Naga-inhabited areas in Manipur, Assam and Arunachal. This demand has the support of all sections of the Naga people and is being vigorously pursued by the NSCN (IM) with the hope that the emotive appeal of Naga integration would deflect any possible criticism of the NSCN leadership for backtracking on the issue of sovereignty. Whether such territorial integration would be possible, given the huge popular reactions against it in Manipur as also the resistance of Assam and Arunachal, is, however, a separate matter.

In order to understand the inherent dichotomy between sovereignty and autonomy as has become evident in the peace negotiations, it would be necessary to go back to the years immediately preceding India's independence when the Naga National Council raised its demand for self-determination. In these early communications between the NNC secretary and the Indian Prime Minister, the NNC had not spelled out its parameters of an independent Naga homeland, with the emphasis being on protecting and preserving the "Naga way of life". This was exactly why there was a great deal of confusion among the Naga representatives over the issue of self-determination as spelled out in the Hydari Agreement which was almost signed one year prior to independence. It was only after the ascendance of Phizo within the NNC and the marginalisation of the moderate voices, that the Hydari Agreement was finally rejected over the interpretation of a particular clause which referred to the relationship which the Nagas would be having with the Indian Union. Consequently, the idea of a sovereign Naga homeland outside the Indian Union was promoted by the Phizo-led NNC which declared Naga independence on August 14, 1947. Once the NNC decided to launch its struggle for an independent sovereign Naga homeland, Phizo's organizational skill succeeded in marginalizing those voices within Naga society which were not in favour of breaking away from India. And, with the Naga "plebiscite" and the election boycott, the Naga National Council emerged as the unquestioned political force of the then Naga Hills district of Assam. The Government of India's response to the NNC demand and the subsequent course of the Naga struggle under Phizo gave a new meaning to the concept of Naga self-determination which got increasingly enmeshed with the idea of a sovereign The NNC's position was soon to be defined in the following terms: (a) that historically, the Nagas had never come under foreign domination and that even during the British period only a small part of Naga territory came under British administrative control; (b) that since it was never a part of the India which emerged during British rule, the question of seceding from the Indian Union did not arise; (c) that the Naga struggle was not a secessionist movement but one for independence. While all these positions are open to interpretation, yet the construct about the Nagas being a sovereign nationality was gradually strengthened during the course of the Naga struggle led by the NNC. This construct quite often did not take into consideration the fact that there existed strong contradictions within the different Naga tribes and that the idea of self-determination did not carry the same connotations for all the tribes which gradually became a part of the emerging Naga nationality. The fact remained that while the NNC-led movement attracted large number of Nagas cutting across most of the clans and tribes, yet it cannot be said that not all Nagas shared the NNC vision of a sovereign Nagaland. It was because of these differences over the question of sovereignty that the Government of India succeeded in working out the 16-Point Agreement with the Naga People's Convention which paved the way for the formation of the State of Nagaland as per the thirteenth amendment of the Constitution of India. A close look at the Sixteen-Point Agreement would show that it provided for a large degree of autonomy for the Naga people and laid down specific provisions for safeguarding their identity and culture in a highly plural and diverse country. For instance, Clause 7 of the Agreement specifically stated that no Act or law passed by the Union Parliament affecting the religious and social practices of the Nagas, their customary laws and procedure and judicial system was to have any force unless specifically approved by a majority vote in the Nagaland Legislative Assembly. Clause 8 stated that every tribe would retain power of rule-making and administration of its own affairs through local bodies like the Village Council, the Range Council and the Tribal Council. These bodies were also to retain their power to deal with disputes involving breaches of customary law and their usages. When the Nagaland state was formed, the thirteenth amendment of the Constitution incorporated most of the points made in the Sixteen-Point Agreement, with Clause 37A stating that no Act of Parliament would affect the (a) religious and social practices of the Nagas;

(b) Naga customary laws and procedure; and (c) administration of civil and criminal justice involving decisions according to Naga customary laws; (d) ownership and transfer of land and its resources etc. Thus, certain very clear provisions for autonomy were spelt out when the state of Nagaland was formed. Therefore, the quest for self-determination of the Nagas must be seen in the light of all these developments and the provisions for autonomy for Nagaland laid down in the Constitution itself.

It is significant that during the first civil society intervention in the conflict situation in Nagaland in the form of the 1964 Peace Mission headed by Jayprakash Narayan, the issue of self-determination took a central stage. The Peace Mission proposals clearly stated that it "appreciates and understands the desire of the Nagas for self-determination and their urge to preserve their identity". But it also emphasised the need for peaceful settlement of the Naga issue and stated that the "Naga Federal Government could on its own volition, decide to be a participant in the Union of India and mutually settle terms and conditions for the purpose". The Peace Mission also stated that "the Government of India could consider to what extent the pattern and structure of the relationship between Nagaland and the Government of India should be *adapted and recast*, so as to satisfy the political aspirations of all sections of Naga opinion"(emphasis mine). This gains a lot of relevance especially in the context of the NSCN(IM)'s demand for a radical restructuring of the present federal structure. Judging by the recommendations of the Peace Mission, it appears that its emphasis was on a autonomous status for the Naga people within the Indian Union. The Peace Mission was also aware of the fact that there was no unanimity amongst the Nagas on the question of a sovereign Naga territory and noted "that a section of the Naga people accepted the status of a statehood conferred upon Nagaland as being in their best interest". Further the Peace Mission while respecting the rights of "all subject peoples to self-determination", drew the attention of the Naga Federal Government "to certain historical processes that had taken place to give birth to the Union of India and to the emergence of the great concepts and ideals underlying the Union

Constitution". The observations of the Peace Mission make interesting reading in the light of the fresh parameters and new challenges that are emerging in the present Naga peace process.

Therefore, the present pulls and counter-pulls over the questions of sovereignty and autonomy that seem to have marked the present peace process, need to be seen against all these experiments aimed at providing a large and effective measure of autonomy to the Naga people. Whatever the legalities of the Naga National Council's original position on self-determination/sovereignty, the situation today has undergone major changes not only in relation to the Nagas' relationship with the Indian nation-state but also in the post-September 11 international arena where greater emphasis is being laid on internal self-determination with maximum political autonomy as against external self-determination or secession. Although the NSCN(IM) seems to have usurped the multiple Naga voice by claiming to be the sole representative of the Nagas, yet the fact remains that there is a substantial section of Naga civil society which is prepared to work out an autonomous relationship within the Indian Union. This view, for instance, finds expression in S.C. Jamir's article, "The Bedrock of Naga Society" which has come in for sharp criticism from the NSCN(IM). Jamir, interestingly, echoes many of the views expressed by the Rev. Michael Scott, one of the members of the Peace Mission who happened to earn the ire of the Government of India, for his open sympathy for the Naga cause. Scott, in a note prepared in 1965 entitled "Bearings on the Future of Nagaland", asks the Nagas to consider what they really meant by independence, and says that "independence conceded to Nagaland might stimulate secessionist tendencies, which would threaten the integrity of India as a whole". Referring to the Naga demand for independence, Scott observes:

> "... As compared with African or colonial territories, Nagaland under the present setup has the ownership of land and settlement under its control. Nagas cannot forcibly or constitutionally be deprived of their land as the indigenous people of South Africa have been deprived of..." That there is lack of unanimity on

the question of a sovereign Nagalim is evident in the position adopted by another faction of the NSCN led by Khaplang. The NSCN(K) has gone to the extent of dubbing the Tangkhuls as "terrorists" and has issued quit notices on them. The NSCN(K) move has brought to the fore the contradictions inherent in Naga society and the lack of unanimity over certain major issues. The NSCN(IM) needs to realise that it cannot expect to usurp the Naga voice by claiming to be the sole representative of the Naga people. There are plenty of faultlines in Naga society and these find reflection in the politics of the Naga underground. Therefore, while discussing the issue of sovereignty and its impact on the Peace Talks, one would have to keep in mind the process of the emergence of different Naga tribes into a nationality. This process was no doubt hastened by the Naga struggle. But it would be premature to conclude that there is unanimity over the issue of sovereignty amongst the different segments of the Naga population.

The present scenario in Nagaland is such that no single organization, however strong, may be said to represent the entire Naga people. Not only the NSC(K) which has had major clashes with the NSCN(IM), other sections owing allegiance to organizations like the NNC also have their differences over the question of Nagaland's relationship with the rest of the country. Thus, it would be wrong to treat the entire Naga society as one, homogeneous whole. The strength of Naga society lies in the variety of its tribes and their distinct traditional structures which have combined in a certain historical process to give shape to a clear Naga identity. Therefore, it would be wrong to try to merge all these distinct identities under the umbrella of one organization — the NSCN(IM) for example. The very democratic structure of Naga society, made of all the different tribes, would not permit this. This is clearly reflected in the civil society response to the peace process. The problem today is not just of keeping the talks going and finally, working out a settlement with the Government of India. There is perhaps an even greater problem of bringing the rival groups to the negotiating table. Just as a united Naga nation has emerged and consolidated during the entire course of the Naga struggle, similarly it was inevitable that this long and protracted struggle would give rise to varying viewpoints about the type of freedom which would be best for the Nagas. For instance, the Naga National Council, which at one time virtually moulded the destiny of the Naga people stood discredited in the eyes of the NSCN(IM) who sharply attacked the lineage of Phizo and did not shrink from calling him a traitor to the Naga cause. Therefore, it would be simplistic to give any particular organization a hegemonic role in Naga society today. This is clearly reflected in the civil society response to the peace process. Cutting across the divides of clan and tribe, of political agendas and priorities, civil society groups in Nagaland represented by organizations like the Naga Hoho and the Naga Mothers Association, to name just two, have emerged as major pressure groups in the peace process. Quite often, it has been the pressure mounted by these civil society groups that has kept the peace talks going. For instance, there have been occasions when the NSCN(IM) threatened to withdraw from the talks. But the civil society groups made it clear that the under no circumstances was the road to peace to be abandoned. Civil society groups have come to represent a Naga nation which is a synthesis of the modern and the traditional, of the consensual and the representative, and made up of divergent viewpoints and attitudes where the sanctity of both societal and individual space is maintained. It is, therefore, inevitable, that the influence of Naga civil society is bound to be a major factor in the peace process. And, judging by the statements made by Naga civil society groups from time to time, it is evident that sovereignty is not a major issue with them; peace with dignity is.

Therefore, given the historical background of the different experiments with autonomy within the Indian federal structure that have marked the history of the Naga people since India gained independence from the British and the present lack of unanimity amongst the Naga people over the question of a sovereign Nagalim outside the Indian Union, it is not at all surprising that the issue of sovereignty is being marginalized in favour of more acceptable and effective forms of autonomous relationship with the rest of the country. Whatever the limitations of India's experiment with representative democracy, the fact remains that the struggle of the small nationalities has led to the expanding of the parameters of the Indian nation-state and a redefining of the concept of Indian nationalism itself. Therefore, if the NSCN(IM) fails to work on the possibilities that have been made available to it, then there is every chance that it would, in the near future, lose its present position in Naga politics. The overall mood in Nagaland today is in favour of a negotiated settlement based on greater autonomy and territorial integrity. No insurgent group, however strong, can really afford to ignore this while drawing up the parameters of a solution to the Naga issue.

10 Ethnic Problems and Inter-state Border Problems in North-East and Solutions

N. Changkakoti

Introduction

Out of about 7 crore tribal people in the whole of India, belonging to around 360 tribes, North-East India comprising the seven sisters, namely, Assam, Meghalaya, Nagaland, Manipur, Tripura, Mizoram and Arunachal Pradesh is the home of around 1.3 crore ethnic people. Incidentally, India's tribal population is the highest in the world. Our Constitution has not defined the term "Tribe". But Article 342 of the Constitution empowers the President, in consultation with the Governors of concerned States, to draw up a list of the tribes inhabiting our country. Thus Scheduled Tribes are those tribes as the President may by public notification specify. However, Encyclopaedia Britannica explains the word 'tribe' as a group of people speaking a common language, observing uniform rules of social organization and working together for common purposes such as agriculture, trade and warfare. Other typical characteristics are a common name, a contiguous territory, a relatively uniform culture or way of life and a tradition of common descent. Encyclopaedia Americana defines the term "Tribe" as a group of families who have a feeling of community through occupying a common territory and following similar custom. It also says that tribe and tribal are covenient terms for indicating that a people still follow custom rather than state law.

Ethnic Problems and Legal Provisions

Our First Prime Minister Pandit Jawaharlal Nehru displayed great understanding when he made the observation regarding the tribal people that "they possess a variety of culture and are, in many ways, certainly not backward. There is no point in trying to make them a second rate copy of ourselves......The tribal people should be helped to grow according to their genius and tradition".

Accordingly, many special provisions have been incorporated in our Constitution to enable our ethnic minorities to grow according to their genius and tradition and to protect their interests. Thus,

(i) Measures for the advancement of the Scheduled Castes and Tribes are exempted [Art.15(4)] from the general ban against discrimination on the grounds of race, caste and the like contained in Art 15.

(ii) While the rights of free movement and residence throughout the territory of India and acquisition and disposition of property are guaranteed to every citizen, in the case of members of the Scheduled Castes and Tribes, special restrictions may be imposed by the state as may be required for the protection of their interests. [Art.19 (5)]

(iii) The claims of the members of the Scheduled Castes and the Scheduled Tribes shall be taken into consideration, consistent with the maintenance of administration, in the making of appointments to services and posts in connection with the affairs of the Union or of State. [Art. 335]

(iv) Article 338 of the original constitution has been substituted by the Constitution (65th Amendment) Act, 1990 to set up a National Commission for Scheduled Castes and Tribes (in place of a special officer) to investigate all matters relating to the safeguards provided for the Scheduled Castes and Tribes under the Constitution and to enquire into any related complaints and to report to the President. The President shall cause all such reports to be laid before each House of Parliament along with a Memorandum explaining the action taken or proposed to be taken on the recommendations relating to the Union. Similar action will be taken by the Governor of a State if it is concerned with any matter relating to a State.

(v) The President may at any time, and shall, at the expiration of ten years from the commencement of the Constitution by order appoint a commission to report on the administration of the Scheduled Areas and the Welfare of the Scheduled Tribes in the States. The order may define the composition, powers and procedure of the Commission and may contain such incidental or ancillary provisions as the President may consider necessary or desirable. [Art. 339 (1)].

(vi) The executive power of the Union shall extend to the giving of directions to any such state as to the drawing up and execution of schemes specified in the direction to be essential for the welfare of the Scheduled Tribes in the State. [Art. 339 (2)]

(vii) Financial aid for the implementation of these welfare schemes is provided for in Art. 275 (1) which requires the Union to give grants-in-aid to the states for meeting the costs of schemes of welfare of the Scheduled Tribes and for raising the level of administration of the Scheduled Areas in a State to that of the administration of the general areas of that state.

(viii) Special provisions are laid down in the Fifth and Sixth Schedules of the Constitution read with Art. 244 and 244 A, for the administration of areas inhabited by Scheduled Tribes.

Over and above these, there is a general Directive in Art. 46 that the state shall promote with special care the educational and economic interests of the weaker sections of the people and, in particular, of the Scheduled Castes and the Scheduled Tribes, and shall protect them from social injustice and all forms of exploitation.

Besides, there are temporary provisions for special representation of and reservation of seats for Scheduled Castes and Scheduled Tribes in the House of the People and State Legislative Assemblies. Further, there are also many state laws, rules and regulations for fulfilment of the same objective.

Reasons of Tribal Distrust of Non-Tribal People

(a) The tribal people of North-Eastern India, particularly inhabiting the hills feel that their language, way of life, customs, ethos etc. are quite different from those of the people of the rest of India and they have no emotional links with them. They were also not under any Indian political set up before Britishers forcibly merged their land in British India. Therefore, when the Britishers left India, a large section of them felt that their communities should be free to decide whether it would be advantageous for them to remain within India or to become independent countries outside India.

(b) Because of the routine and generally apathetic approach of the Government towards the problems and grievances of the tribal and all other common people and also the condescending behaviour of Government officials towards the common men, the Government failed to win the hearts of these simple people and make them feel that the quality of governance in free India will be better than the administration during the British rule. One example should suffice. During the period when present day Mizoram was a part of Assam in the name of Lushai Hills District, a big famine called 'Mautam' in Lushai language, had struck the District in 1959-60. As, in those days, there used to be no Superintendent of Police in the District and Deputy Commissioner used to be in charge of Police Department also, I was sent by Government to assist the Deputy Commissioner in maintaining law and order in those difficult days. I had found that the flow of relief materials like rice etc. from the Government was very slow and intermittent causing considerable suffering and resentment among the local people. Not to speak of any Minister of the Government of Assam, no senior officer of the Government visited the District during the crisis period to help the Deputy Commissioner in mitigating the suffering of the people. Goverment thus lost a golden opportunity to demonstrate its compassion and empathy for the Mizo people. On the other hand, lots of relief materials like milk powder etc. arrived from abroad which was highly appreciated by the people.

(c) Government of Assam adopted certain short-sighted policies taking into account the interest of the majority Assamese speaking people, ignoring the susceptibilities of the tribal people. Let me give one example. In 1960, Government of Assam passed a bill making Assamese the state language of Assam, brushing aside the objections of the tribal people and other non-Assamese speaking people. Though even today, English is continuing to be used as the official language of Assam, the passing of this bill became another strong reason for a number of ethnic communities of the state to intensify their agitations for achieving for their territories separate political status outside Assam.

(d) The tribal people discovered that the Governments led and manned mostly by non-tribal people are not sincere in preserving their primary status in any particular area and in protecting tribal land, whatever may be the lofty provisions in this respect enshrined in the Constitution and therefore they felt that they must acquire enough political power to protect their interests. Let me give two examples.

 (i) As a sequel to the partition of British India for creation of two independent countries — India and Pakistan in August 1947, lakhs of Hindu refugees from the territories included in East-Pakistan and now Bangladesh, migrated to Indian Union and most of them were settled in Tripura, causing alienation of most of the tribal land, reducing the indigenous Tripuri tribals to the status of minority and making them pathetically dependent on the mercy of the new settlers for the preservation of their identity and culture.

 (ii) In 1947, the then Assam Government under the leadership of Late Gopinath Bordoloi, who was a rare

Champion of tribal cause, had amended the Assam Land and Revenue Regulations of 1886 to incorporate a new chapter (Tenth Chapter) therein, with the laudable objective of protecting the land of all backward classes which included tribal land also. On the basis of the regulations in this Chapter, Assam Government had created altogether 31 belts and blocks within the first five years from 1947 to 1951. At present there are 17 belts and 30 blocks on paper in Assam. As these belts and blocks were formed in the areas predominantly inhabited by tribal people, these are popularly known as "Tribal belts and blocks". However, it is a matter of grave concern that as per the estimate of the Government of Assam itself, more than six lakh bighas of Government land falling within the boundaries of these belts and blocks have been grabbed by non-tribal encroachers and successive Governments, swayed by vote bank politics, have hardly done anything to prevent it.

(e) As corruption increased with the passage of time in the functioning of the Government machinery and more and more developmental funds pumped into the economy did not reach the actual beneficiaries, the economically backward tribal people yearned for more and more political power in their hands as a panacea.

Some Encouraging Trends

Nevertheless, after many a twists and turns in the agitations — some peaceful and some violent — resorted to by different tribal communities in the North-Eastern region for different forms of self-rule, it is encouraging that most of these ethnic groups have given up the demand for secession from India and have reconciled to some form of self-rule like statehood, district council setup or autonomous councils with varying degrees of political power. Even the most powerful faction of the Naga hostiles, namely,

NSCN (IM) group is, nolonger, demanding independence and is now negotiating with Government of India for an honourable agreement with the demand for greater Nagaland. ULFA, which had been carrying on Guerrilla warfare against the Government since last 25 years, for liberation of Assam, is, most likely, to come to the negotiating table soon and under pressure of public opinion, is also, most likely to give up the demand for sovereign Assam, remaining content with a special status for Assam with some more political and financial powers. In Manipur, however, there is no sign so far of People's Liberation Army and other extremist groups giving up their armed struggle for creation of an independent Manipur and the situation needs to be handled with a human face.

Some Suggestions to Solve the Tribal Problem

Governments must keep in mind that if they do not back their words with deeds and honour the agreements so far arrived at with the extremist groups, in letter and spirit, they or some other groups may again take up the path of violence. For permanent peace in Nagaland, negotiations with the hostiles are yet to be concluded satisfactorily, without creating new problems. Again, even though many political entities have been created such as tribal states, district councils, territorial councils, autonomous councils to fulfil the aspirations of bigger tribal communities for self-rule, it is certainly not possible to satisfy such demands of all ethnic groups, however small. At the same time, steps have to be taken to ensure that these small tribal groups do not become victims of ethnic cleansing indulged in by any other stronger tribal group or any non-tribal community. In view of the above, it is also suggested that :

(a) The National Council for Scheduled Castes and Scheduled Tribes as provided for in the Constitution should be constituted with a retired Supreme Court Judge as Chairman and it should have a strong monitoring wing to closely monitor the implementation of various schemes for upliftment of different ethnic groups in the North-East strictly as per sanction and without any corruption. The

Commission may also be advised to examine and recommend if any new legal or other provisions need to be made to ensure that the interests of other small ethnic communities also get due attention and they can also grow according to their genius and tradition without any hindrance and in every tribal village whichever politico-administrative structure, it may be, shares a sense of participation in self-governance.

(b) Special arrangement should be made for selection of only those officers of different Departments for service in the tribal areas who are not desk bound, have affection and sympathy for the tribals and feel no difficulty in living in an environment without modern facilities. Such selected public servants should be given a special Tribal Area Allowance and should not be posted in such areas for more than five years.

(c) As the tribal people are very much dependent on land for their livlihood and the land at their disposal are becoming insufficient to sustain their increasing population, educational and vocational training facilities for the tribal youth should be increased considerably without delay to enlarge their employment opportunities.

(d) In Manipur, even if the situation does not permit withdrawal of the Armed Forces Special Powers Act, in spite of the recommendation to this effect by the special committee set up for the purpose 2/3 years ago, there is scope for amending the same to reduce scope for misuse of the powers given by the Act. This should be done immediately and urgent steps should be taken to considerably enlarge the scope of employment of Manipuri youth to prevent them from being recruited by the extremist organizations.

Inter-state Border Problem in the North-Eastern Region

(a) Assam-Nagaland

At the commencement of our constitution, in parts A and B of the table below paragraph 20 of the Sixth Schedule under head "Tribal

Areas" two areas inhabited almost entirely by Naga Tribes within the state of Assam were mentioned. These are :

(i) The Naga Hills District in Part A
(ii) The Naga Tribal Area in Part B

In the year 1957, Government of India passed The Naga Hills - Tuensang Area Act, which came into effect on 1st December, 1957. Section 2 of this Act says that "as from the commencement of this Act, there shall be formed a new administrative unit in the state of Assam by the name of Naga Hills-Tuensang Area comprising the tribal areas which at such commencement were known as the Naga Hills District and Tuensang Frontier Division of the North-East Frontier Agency". The Act also stated in Section 3 that the Naga Hills-Tuensang Area shall comprise the areas which at the commencement of the Constitution were known as the Naga Hills District and the Naga Tribal Area. Subsequently, Government of India passed the State of Nagaland Act, 1962 which came into effect on 1st December, 1963. Section 3 (1) of this Act says that "As from the appointed Day, there shall be formed a new state to be known as the State of Nagaland comprising the territories which immediately before that Day were comprised in the Naga Hills-Tuensang area and there upon the said territories shall cease to form part of the state of Assam". It follows as a logical corollary that the boundaries of the new State is exactly the same as was the boundaries of combined Naga Hills District and the Naga Tribal Area which was subsequently known as Tuensang Frontier Division of North-East Frontier Agency. There has been no change in the boundaries of Naga Hills District since the erstwhile British Government had issued Notification No 3102 R dt. 25th November, 1925 in supersession of all previous Notifications, defining the boundaries of the Naga Hills District and, therefore, this District of Assam became a part of newly created Nagaland State on 1st December, 1963 with this boundary only. The details of this Notification were based on survey operations conducted between 1916 and 1923 and the boundaries have been very clearly defined and located with reference to Hill ranges, rivers, streams and boundary pillars.

In 1960, there was a meeting between Government of India and Naga Leaders to discuss sixteen point memorandum submitted by them about creation of the new State of Nagaland. The Naga Leaders had laid claims to certain reserve forest within Assam, on the plea that these forests had in the past formed part of the Naga Hills District, Government of India, however, had made it clear that it was not possible to go beyond the 1925 Notification and had pointed out the provisions in Articles 3 and 4 of the Constitution prescribing the procedure for the transfer of areas from one state to another. Soon after the creation of Nagaland State in 1963, Government of Nagaland started claiming some territories of Assam, particularly Reserved Forests in the then Sibsagar (now Jorhat, Sibsagar and Golaghat) District and also the North Cachar Hills District of Assam. Simultaneously, encroachments on the reserved forests of Assam increased in accordance with the claim. This created considerable tension in Assam Nagaland border areas, endangering the lives and properties of innocent people. In the year 1971, Government of India, in consultation with the Government of Assam and Nagaland, appointed Shri K.V.K. Sundaram, the then Chairman of the Law Commission as Adviser in the Ministry of Home Affairs and was given the following task : "The Adviser will ascertain the facts regarding the Assam-Nagaland boundary and the need for any adjustment, having regard to all the facts of the situation, including the provisions of Section 3 of the State of Nagaland Act, 1962. He will consult the Chief Ministers of the two State Governments. and such other persons as he considers necessary. He will try to bring about an agreed solution likely to promote the welfare and interests of the people of the two states and to create faith and goodwill between them. He will also put forward suggestion, if necessary, to maintain peace and tranquillity in the border areas pending his final advice."

Shri Sundaram, after detailed survey of the border areas of Assam claimed by Nagaland, thorough scrutiny of the justifications put forward by Nagaland Government in support of their claim of Assam's land and meeting all concerned persons of both sides, submitted his report in 1978. In his report, except Nagaland's claim on Desai valley reserve, Shri Sundaram rejected all other claims of Nagaland for inclusion of North Cachar Hills, Mikir Hills, Sarupathar Thana elaka of Golaghat District, and all other Reserved Forests of Assam in erstwhile Sibsagar District as unjustifiable. On the other hand, he observed in his report that "although the plains area around Dimapur was rightly taken out of the Naga Hills district in 1898, it was put back in that District in 1913 for no good reason. If the boundary question was allowed to be reopened on purely historical grounds, Assam would be justified in asking for the retransfer of this traditionally Mikir-Cachar tract."

While Assam Government accepted the report, the Government of Nagaland rejected it. As Government of India has not put its feet down for honouring the report by Nagaland Government, encroachments continued unabated. At present, total area of Assam's land encroached from Nagaland side is 54150 Hectares of Forest land and 1030 Hectares of Revenue land. Further, Nagaland Government have established three of their sub-divisions, namely, Tizit in1984-85 in Abhoypur RF, Newland in 1987 in Rengma RF and Kohoboto in 1991 in Diphu RF within the territory of Assam.

It is unfortunate that Government of India has not taken a firm stand on the issue and meanwhile many innocent people have lost their lives and a number of clashes between Nagaland Police and Assam Police have also taken place and the relations between the two states have become very much strained. If necessary, Government of India may constitute another boundary commission with prior commitment of both Governments to accept the findings of the commission to resolve the issue. This is such an issue that Hon'ble Supreme Court's intervention can be sought through a Public interest litigation petition.

(b) Assam-Meghalaya

The State of Meghalaya came into existence on 21st January, 1972 on the basis of the North-Eastern Areas (Reorganisation) Act, 1971. It comprises the erstwhile United Khasi and Jaintia Hills District and Garo Hills District of Assam. The state has common boundary with the following Districts of present day Assam :

(i) Goalpara District
(ii) Kamrup District
(iii) Nagaon District
(iv) Karbi Anglong District
(v) North Cachar Hills District and
(vi) Cachar District.

Soon after Meghalaya State was formed differences between the two State Governments regarding some stretches of the Inter-state boundary came to the fore. As the differences could not be resolved at lower levels, a meeting was held on 26th May, 1983 in Shillong between the Chief Ministers of Assam and Meghalaya, in which the following decision was taken :

"It was decided that a Joint Official Committee be formed with the Chief Secretary, Assam, and the Chief Secretary, Meghalaya as joint convenors to identify the areas of differences on the Assam-Meghalaya boundary. The Chief Secretaries will be assisted by such officers as they consider necessary. At a subsequent stage, if necessary, a representative of the Survey of India may also be associated with the Committee. The Committee will submit its report within a period of two months, i.e. by the end of July, 1983.

It was agreed between the two Chief Ministers that instructions will be reiterated to all the concerned authorities to maintain peace on the border and not to take any action to precipitate matters."

The Committee met four times and finalised its report on the 16th November, 1983.

The Joint Official Committee identified the areas of differences and classified them sector-wise as follows : —

"Sector 1 - Boundary between Garo Hills district of Meghalaya and Goalpara district of Assam.

Sector 2 - Boundary between Jaintia Hills district of

Meghalaya and Karbi Anglong district of Assam.

Sector 3 - Boundary between East Khasi Hills district of Meghalaya and Karbi Anglong district of Assam.

Sector 4 - Areas where the question of retransfer is involved, viz.; retransfer of Block I and Block II of the Karbi Anglong district of Assam to Meghalaya.

Sector 5 - Boundary between Cachar district of Assam and Jaintia Hills district of Meghalaya.

Sector 6 - Boundary between the districts of East and West Khasi Hills of Meghalaya and districts of Kamrup and Nowgong of Assam."

Except for the differences in Sector 4 and Sector 6, differences in the other sectors could be resolved through demarcation on the ground of the common boundary by joint survey parties with the assistance of Survey of India, where necessary in accordance with the relevant Notifications regarding which there was no dispute. As regards Sector 4, the difference between the two Governments about whether the two blocks should remain in Assam or transferred to Meglalaya has not ended. The matter can certainly be settled on the basis of whether Khasi-Jaintia population or the Karbi population were in the majority on the date of creation of Meghalaya. For resolving the differences as regards Sector 6, the Government of Assam and Meghalaya, by two idential resolutions dated 19th October, 1985 referred the matter to a committee headed by Mr. Justice Y.V. Chandrachud, former Chief Justice of India. The committee after examining in detail the representations of both the Governments and after hearing the counsels of both the Governments submitted its report on 27th July, 1987 wherein the committee rejected all the claims of the Government of Meghalaya to certain Khasi inhabited areas inside Assam. There is no further efforts on the part of Meghalaya Government to include these areas in Meghalaya. Though the situation in the entire border is normal at present, the two Governments should sort out the remaining differences urgently with a spirit of give and take and meanwhile refrain from doing anything illegal to alter the *status quo* so that no untoward incident recurs as had happened earlier.

(c) Assam-Arunachal

Section 7 of the North-Eastern Areas (Reorganisation) Act, 1971, by virtue of which Arunachal Pradesh was first created as an union territory with effect from January 20, 1972 and which was subsequently upgraded as a full-fledged state on February 20, 1987, mentions the territories of this state as follows : —

> "On and from the appointed day, there shall be formed a new Union Territory, to be known as the Union Territory of Arunachal Pradesh comprising the territories which immediately before that day were comprised in the tribal areas specified in Part B of the table appended to Paragraph 20 of the Sixth Schedule to the Constitution (but excluding the areas covered by Notification No. TAD/R/35/50/109 dt. 23rd February, 1951 issued by the Governor of Assam under the proviso to sub-paragraph (3) of the said paragraph 20 and known as the North-Eastern Frontier Agency and thereupon the said territories shall cease to form part of the existing state of Assam." Part B of the table appended to Paragraph 20 of the Sixth Scheduled to our Constitution mentions the following territories :
>
> 1. North East Frontier Tract including Balipara Frontier Tract, Tirap Frontier Tract, Abor Hills District and Mishmi Hills District.
> 2. The Naga Tribal Areas.

Notification No. TAD/R/35/50/109 dt. 23rd Fbruary, 1951 issued by the Governor of Assam under the provison to sub-paragraph (3) of Paragraph 20 to the Constitution of India, covers a clearly specified area in the plains portion of the Balipara

Frontier Tract, Abor Hills, Mishmi Hills and the Trip Frontier Tract and these plains areas thus do not form part of Arunachal Pradesh. In North-East Frontier Area (Administration) Regulation, 1954, the Naga Tribal Area mentioned in Part B of the Table appended to Paragraph 20 referred to above, was renamed as Tuensang Frontier Division and this area was transferred to the new administrative unit known as Naga Hills-Tuensang area in 1957, which became the separate state of Nagaland on 1-12-1963. Arunachal Pradesh has a common boundary with Dhemaji, Lakhimpur, Sonitpur, Darrang, Tinsukia and Sibsagar Districts of Assam.

While the Notifications specifying different sections of the boundary of Arunachal Pradesh are quite clear, there could be differences here and there as regards exact ground location. To avoid any misunderstanding over this matter, as early as in 1969, at an official meeting between the Chief Secretary, Assam and the Adviser to the Governor of Assam for erstwhile North-East Frontier Agency, it was decided that the boundary should be surveyed by the Survey of India and the ground demarcation by Survey of India was to be on the basis of sets of maps showing the Assam-Arunachal boundary signed by both the Governments. Upto 1973-74 field season, a total length of about 396 kilometres of the boundary was demarcated, out of which Assam did not accept pillar positions in about 25 kilometres and Arunachal Pradesh did not accept demarcation in about 111 kilometres. Of the total length of about 308 kilometres of the undemarcated boundary, only 93 kilometres could be demarceted by Survey of India till 1984 and work could not proceed further due to violent resistance from local Arunachalis to prevent the eventuality of their coming under the Assam administration. In fact, though there were violations of Assam territory by the Arunachalis since long, a series of encroachments by Arunachalis and Arunachal administration inside Assam territory, intimidation and harassment of people living on the Assam side of the border by the Arunachalis took place in quick succession since the beginning of 1978, disturbing the peace and tranquillity in the border area. Such encroachments were very noticeable in Kimin, Dirpai, Likabali, Dullungmukh and Jonai areas. Arunachal

Administration established a circle office, PWD and Forest offices in Kimin well inside Assam, constructed a Health Centre and Staff quarters at Telem in Jonai area and built a Anchal Samiti House at Likabali without any permission from Government of Assam.

Without going into further details, it needs to be stated that the situation demands urgent intervention by Government of India to undo any illegalities committed by any of the Governments involved and to enable the Survey of India to complete the work of ground demarcation of the boundary in the next field season itself by providing required security and logistical support from the resources of Government of India. On the other hand, any village of Arunachali tribals which will fall within Assam boundary after ground demarcation, should be given due facilities by Assam Government to develop according to their culture and tradition in conformity with the constitutional and other provisions for development of scheduled tribes.

(d) Assam-Mizoram

Mizoram had become a full-fledged state of the Indian Union on 20-2-1987 as a sequel to the signing of the historic memorandum of settlement between Government of India and Mizo National Front in 1986. Earlier Lushai Hills District of Assam was renamed as Mizo Hills in 1954 and after the promulgation of North-Eastern Areas (Reorganisation) Act, 1971, it had become a Union Territory by the name of Mizoram with effect from 21-1-1972. Thus the Assam Mizoram inter-state boundary is the same as the old inter-district boundary between old Cachar District and Lushai Hill District of Assam. This boundary was notified under Notification No. 2106 AP dated March 9, 1933. This boundary has not been changed after our country became independent and Mizoram State Act accepted this boundary Notification. Actually, therefore, there can be no boundary dispute between the two states. But the problem arose because of encroachments in the Reserve Forest areas of Cachar district by people from Mizoram and the efforts made by Mizoram Government on its own to change the border in their favour on untenable historical, ethnic and such other factors. The problem will be over once, Government of Assam extends its effective administration in the border areas and Mizoram Government, refrain from dishonouring the legal provisions as regards its boundary with Assam. At present, there is, of course, no fresh encroachment and tension in the border areas.

11 A Blueprint for Ethnic Reconciliation in Tripura Decommission the Gumti Hydel Project for a Start

Subir Bhaumik

At 10,039 sq.kms., Tripura is North-East India's smallest state. But this was not always so. Maharaj Bijoy Manikya is said to have taken bath in seven large rivers of East Bengal, which means he controlled a large swathe of land between hill Tipperah and Bangladesh's present capital Dhaka. The Manikyas controlled much of East Bengal's Comilla region during medieval times — a region my ancestors hailed from. Their governance was marked by fairness and balance in handling of ethnic aspirations. With royal patronage, tolerance and multi-culturalism flourished in an area divided by ethnicity and religion and torn by conflicts born out of it. Not surprisingly, therefore, readers of "Tripura Observer" (an Agartala-based English Daily) in 2000 voted Maharaja Bir Bikram as "Tripura's Man of the Millennium" in preference to those who have led the state since the end of the royal order.

Even after the advent of the British , when the Tripura kingdom was restricted to its present hill confines, Bengalis and indigenous tribes-people lived in peace. No riot, not even sporadic ethnic clashes were ever reported between Bengali settlers and from princely Tripura. If the Manikyas welcomed Bengali professionals or peasants to modernize their administration or increase their land revenue through spread of settled wet-rice agriculture, they also created the tribal reserve, that, in many ways, is the precursor of the Tripura Tribal Areas Autonomous District Council.

The Partition unleashed a wave of migration from East Pakistan to Tripura and other states on its borders. Though the indigenous tribes-people in the state never enjoyed a decisive majority like in neighbouring Chittagong hill tracts or the Mizo hills, they accounted for anything between 50 to 60 per cent of the total population. In the three decades after Partition, the indigenous tribes-people were reduced to below thirty per cent of the state's population, a situation which left them completely marginalized in both self-perception and reality.

The influx intensified the land alienation of the tribes-people and added to their collective sense of loss and marginalisation. Almost all writers on Tripura insurgency have identified land alienation amongst the tribes-people as the major cause that has fuelled the violent insurgency that has eaten into the vitals of an once vibrtant state.

As long as the tribals had enough land and the Bengali population was limited to certain urban or semi-urban pockets or rural areas around the capital, land alienation of tribals did not emerge as a major problem. That began to change with the Independence and the merger of princely Tripura in the Indian Union. Between 1947 and 1971, 6,09,998 Bengalis displaced from East Pakistan came to Tripura for rehabilitation and resettlement. Since the total population of the state in 1951 was 6,45,707, it is not difficult to gauge the enormous population pressure created on tiny Tripura by the Partition. During this period, the State Government primarily resettled the refugees on land under different schemes, some enabling the refugees to settle down with financial assistance and some just helping them buy land.

The operation of these schemes accelerated the process of large scale loss of tribal lands. The pauperization of the tribals can also be discerned from the growing number of tribal agricultural labourers in three decades since the Partition. In 1951, cultivators constituted 62.94 per cent of the total tribal workforce in the state while only 8.93 per cent were in the category of agricultural labourers. But in 1981, only 43.57 per cent of the tribal workforce were cultivators and the number of agricultural labourers had risen to 23.91 per cent. But it would be wrong to assume that tribals alone became landless paupers and their lands were taken over by

Bengali settlers who grew at their expense — a stereotype that tribal extremist groups seek to create.

It is true that tribals account for 41 per cent of the agricultural landless labourers in Tripura — but the rest are non-tribals, almost wholly Bengalis. It is true that the per centage of landless agricultural labourers in Tripura's rural workforce has sharply risen from 4 per cent to 20 per cent in 1971 to 29 per cent in 1981 — but it is also true that the rest are Bengalis and that's almost in keeping the population ratio of the two communities in the state. Of the nearly half a million agrarian population in 1951, 2.5 per cent were rent receivers, 97.5 owner cultivators, 11.6 per cent tenant cultivators and 6.4 per cent were labourers. In 1981, agricultural labourers had become 29 per cent of the total rural workforce. In 1961, 16.9 per cent of the tribals and 29.9 per cent of the Bengali settlers controlled much of Tripura's land. The World Agriculture Census (1970-71) shows that in Tripura 11 per cent of the total population controlled 46 per cent of the total land while 70 per cent of the population controlled 28 per cent of the operational holdings.

But while the Bengalis who came were used to sharp class differences in the erstwhile homeland — East Bengal — the tribes-people were not. At an individual level, they lost lands mostly to Bengalis, rich or poor. Studies made by the Law Research Institute in Guwahati in certain areas of Tripura shows the huge land loss suffered by the tribes-people at the hand of the Bengali settlers. The study analysed the land transfer pattern in seven scheduled and seven non-scheduled villages in South and West Tripura. In the seven non-scheduled villages, out of the total 240 plots transferred, 145 plots were transferred by tribals to non-tribals (read Bengalis), 76 by tribals to tribals and 19 by non-tribals to non-tribals. So sixty per cent of the land transfers were from tribals to non-tribals. In the 7 scheduled villages, the position was worse. Out of 282 plots transferred, 191 were transferred from tribals to non-tribals (68 per cent of the total land transfers). Of the villages under study, the heaviest tribal to non-tribal transfer took place at Hawaibari on the Assam-Agartala road.

One has to go to Teliamura, once a small village but now a

vital road junction connecting West, North and South Tripura. Gunomoni Sardar, the grandfather of the INPT leader Debabrata Koloi and former TNV military wing chief Chuni Koloi, owned almost seventy per cent of the lands in Teliamura. He was a great friend of my grandfather, Kashinath Bhowmik, who established the police in Khowai town, from where Teliamura was covered those days. In 30 years, Gunomoni Sardar's descendants have hardly got a few hectares left for themselves by the side of the TRTC bus stand on the Assam-Agartala Road. Under the Congress administration, some Bengali refugee leaders even set up "land cooperatives" like the Swasti Samity in North Tripura. These cooperatives violated the Tribal Reserves regulations and began to take over large swathes of tribal land, a process that was legitimized by conniving bureaucrats. The Communist Party mobilized the tribesmen and even took the matter to the court to secure a favourable verdict that was not honoured by the bureaucracy. Angry at such rampant loss of their traditional lands, large number of tribal youths took to the jungles and the first significant underground group in post-Merger Tripura, the Sengkrak or the "Clenched Fist" was born.

The Sengkrak movement, Tripura's first manifestation of overt ethnic militancy, started in1967 as a direct fallout of the large scale of alienation of tribal lands, accentuated through state patronage. The ruling Congress government backed the forcible occupation of tribal lands in the Deo valley by Bengali settlers grouped into an organization called the Swasti Samity and the Reang tribesmen organized themselves into a militant group to hit back at the new Bengali settlers. This writer conducted a correlation analysis between land alienation and tribal insurgency in August 1984 by choosing to interview the family members of 84 extremists of the Tribal National Volunteers. These family members had been gathered at a government hostel as part of Chief Minister Nripen Chakrabarti's "Motivation Drive" to facilitate the return of the guerrillas to normal life. It was found that sixty-four per cent of the families had suffered loss of land to Bengalis while thirty-two per cent of them were from families of jhumias or shifting cultivators who were under increasing pressure to find fresh lands for cultivation due to the growing occupation of hill stretches by Bengali refugees. Only four per cent were from families with enough land that had not been lost to the settlers.

In settled agricultural areas like Khowai and Sadar, all within one hundred kilometres of the state's capital Agartala, between twenty to forty per cent of the tribal lands have been alienated by the end of the seventies, when tribal insurgency gathered momentum. In some parts of South Tripura district, as much as sixty per cent of the tribal lands were alienated, sold in distress conditions as a sequel to an unequal economic competition with the Bengali settlers.

The land loss at the level of the individual was further compounded by large scale loss of tribal lands to huge government projects like the Dumbur Hydro-electric project, where an estimated 5000 to 8000 tribal families lost their lands and only a small per centage of them possessing title deeds to prove ownership managed to secure rehabilitation. The pauperization of Dumbur's once prosperous tribal peasantry and the huge benefits that Bengali urban dwellers gained by electricity and Bengali fishermen gained by being able to fish in the large reservoir was not lost on a generation of angry tribal youths who took up arms and left for the jungles to fight an administration they felt was only working in the interests of the Bengali refugees. Insurgent leader Bijoy Kumar Hrangkhawl, now back to mainstream politics after his Tribal National Volunteers (TNV) returned to normal life following an accord in 1988, used to refer to Nripen Chakrabarty as the "refugee chief minister" of Tripura.

The heartburn over steady land loss on an one-to-one basis was further exacerbated by the submergence of a huge swathe of arable lands owned by the tribals in the Raima valley as a result of the commissioning of the Gumti hydel project in South Tripura. This project not only disturbed the fragile ecology of the Raima valley in the South district of Tripura, but also left a permanent sense of loss in the tribal psyche. All tribal organizations including the Communist backed Gana Mukti Parishad fiercely protested the commissioning of the Gumti hydro-electric project in 1976. But the Congress government crushed the protests. It was determined to augment Tripura's deficit power supply – but it ended up augmenting the catchment area of tribal unrest by dispossessing thousands of them of their only economic resource and collective symbol, their land. A thirty-metre high gravity dam was constructed across the river Gumti about 3.5 kms. upstream of Tirthamukh in South Tripura district for generating 8.60 megawatt of power from an installed capacity of 10 megawatt. The dam submerged a valley area of 46.34 sq.km. This was one of the most fertile valley region in an otherwise hilly state, where arable flatlands suitable for wet rice agriculture is a mere 28 per cent of its total land area. Official records suggest 2,558 tribal families were ousted from the Gumti project area – but these were families who could produce land deeds and were officially owners of the land they possessed. Unofficial estimates varied between 8,000 to 10,000 families or about sixty to seventy thousand tribes-people displaced by the project. In the tribal societies of north-east, ownership of land is rarely personal and the system of recording land deeds against individual names is a recent phenomenon. So, most of those ousted by the Dumbur failed to get any rehabilitation grant and were forced to settle in the hills around the project, returning to slash and burn agriculture called jhum. The Left government has recently announced that all Dumbur Oustees, wherever they are, will be covered under Kutir Jyoti Programme. A list of 500 Dumbur Oustee families supplied to the Power Department. The Department has given connection to 114 families who do not have power connection under Kutir Jyoti Programme. But what these families need more than free electricity is arable land and resources to earn their livelihood from it.

The dam destroyed the once surplus tribal peasent economy of the state. Tripura's leading economist Malabika Dasgupta has shown in her study on the Gumti hydel project that "attempts either to protect the environment to the exclusion of considerations for the well-being of the people or to improve their level of well-being without consideration for the environmental impact of such policies can neither protect the environment nor improve the standard of living of the people."

The Gumti, Tripura's principal river, is formed by the confluence of two small rivers, Raima and Sarma, the former flowing out of the Longtharai range, the latter originating from the Atharamura range. Before the dam, the river Gumti flowed southwards through a gorge in the Atharamura range beyond the confluence point of Raima and Sarma. It spilled over a series of rapids which were locally known as the Dumbur falls at the point of Tirthamukh (literally Pilgrim's Point), a place considered holy by the tribals and also the Bengali settlers who would bath in the river during the *Pous Sankranti* every winter. Beyond Tirthamukh, the Gumti flows westwards up to Malbassa village and then changes direction again, cutting through the Deotamura range. After crossing the Deotamura, it flows for another 60 kilometres before it enters Bangladesh. After flowing about 80 kilometres through eastern Bangladesh, it joins the Meghna river which flows into the Bay of Bengal.The upper catchment of the Gumti comprises of eleven Gaon Sabhas — nearly sixty villages in all — in the Gandacherra block of Tripura's newly formed Dhalai district.

The upper reaches of the catchment area is steep and hilly, located on the east of the river, but as it flows towards Tirthamukh, it is flanked by small flat-topped hills locally called *tillas* with many *lungas* or lowlands between them. And as it comes down to Tirthamukh, the Gumti valley waters huge flatlands all the way along its course into Bangladesh. Before the commissioning of the hydel project, the upper catchment supported a small population of tribals. The small Bengali population practised wet-rice cultivation around Boloungbassa and Raima and some were into trading while the tribals, originally almost all slash-and-burn agriculturists called jhumias, had began to settle down to wet-rice cultivation, having learnt it from the Bengali farmers. The Kings of Tripura had settled some Bengali farmers even in such remote areas to encourage tribals to pick up wet-rice cultivation and abandon jhum which is ecologically damaging. Before the Dam, the hills around the present project area were sparsely population and the area was almost wholly under dense forest cover supporting wildlife. The Tripura Gazetteer of 1975 talked of sighting "large herds of Indian elephants in the Raima-Sarma region along with some tigers and bears in the dense forests." Dasgupta says the area "was an abode of deers, bears, wild boars, tigers, elephants and a wide variety of jungle cats." The vegetation was rich, so was the flora and fauna. But after the hydel project was commissioned, not only did almost half of the tribal families displaced by the Dam move into the hills in the river's upper catchment area, but the roads built to first transport construction material and then to support the Hydel project opened up the rich forests of the area to the illegal loggers. The surplus-producing tribal peasentry were not only angry for having lost their rich flatlands and *lungas* – they were forced to revert back to slash-and-burn jhum cultivation that has, in Dasgupta's opinion, "caused irrepairable damage to the ecology of the upper catchment of the Gumti."

Illegal logging by businessmen backed by politicians has further damaged the ecology. During two extensive trips into the Gumti valley in 1985 and 1998, this writer found extensive felling of trees and no presence of forest guards to check it.The tribal insurgents of the National Liberation Front of Tripura or the NLFT have not banned tree felling, as some North-East Indian rebel groups like the National Democratic Front of Bodoland or the NDFB has done. They have encouraged it. In large parts of the Gumti valley upstream of Tirthamukh, tribal villagers told this writer that the NLFT had allowed loggers to operate freely so long as they paid them off. Relatives of some insurgent leaders were in the business, entering partnership deals with the Bengali-owned saw mills of Amarpur, Udaipur and Sonamura. So the tribal insurgents who had capitalized on the community's anger at the large scale displacement at Gumti were now collaborating with the most exploitative segments of settler society to raise funds. It is my contention that (a) the present ethnic conflict that pits the Bengali settlers against the indigenous tribes-people in Tripura has much to do with the large scale land alienation of tribals because land is seen not only as the prime economic resource in a rather backward pre-capitalist agrarian society like Tripura but also as the symbol of the ethnic preponderance; (b) the psychological alienation of the tribes-people was further aggravated by the Dumbur hydel project which, in one stroke, contributed the most to the ongoing process of land alienation; (c) the Dumbur hydel project has caused huge damage not only to the ecology of the Raima-Sarma valley but also to ethnic relations in the state; and (d) that the project is now a white elephant and can be decommissioned to make way for large scale land reclamation that can be used to resettle landless tribes-people in a major gesture of undoing injustice.

Why the Dam must go?

The Gumti hydel project must be decommissioned for four reasons:

(a) The Gumti hydel project is now not producing more than seven megawatts of power even in the peak season when the reservoir is full during monsoon. The State Government says that by investing Rs. 1.18 crores, it has been able to restore the output to the original installed capacity of 10 MW. It also says that while the running cost of the project is around Rs. 3 crores per annum, it rakes in nearly Rs. 21 crores through sale of electricity. Officials in Tripura Power department describe the project as "very profitable." But experts say the siltation levels will continue to increase and unless the reservoir can be dredged, there would be no rise in output. The power output from this project will progressively diminish.

(b) With huge natural gas reserves now discovered in Tripura and major gas thermal power projects in the pipeline (including one with the capacity to generate 500 MW against the state's current peak demand of 125 MW), it is a wastage of funds to invest in the Gumti hydel project. If the state can produce three times more electricity than it now uses , there is a strong case for decommissioning the dam that will free a huge area for other pressing causes. An ideal power strategy for Tripura would be to produce around 500-600 MW of electricity, feed half of that into the North-Eastern Grid, use 150 to 200 MW within the state keeping in mind the rising demand, and sell the balance of 100 MW to Bangladesh as the NEEPCO's former chairman P.K Chatterji had suggested.

In the long run as Bangladesh augments its own power capacity, the surplus Tripura power could be used locally in the event of major industrialization or fed into the regional grid for neighbouring perpetually power deficit states like Mizoram which lacks the gas reserves of Tripura. Since more than 45 sq.kms. can be reclaimed from under water if the Gumti hydel project is decommissioned, a huge fertile tracts of flatland would be opened up for farming and resettlement of the landless tribal peasentry of the state. The fertility of this land is likely to increase after so many years under water. Atleast 30,000 tribal families, perhaps the whole of its landless population, can be gainfully resettled in this fertile tract. Before the dam, this area's fertility was a talking point in the state. After so many years under water, this is likely to be very fertile. Tripura is a food deficit state and turning this area into a modern agrarian zone will solve the state's food problem for ever. Needless to say, the entire tribal landless population of the state, estimated at between 25,000 to 27,000 families, can be gainfully resettled in the Gumti area, once the entire land in and around the reservoir area is reclaimed. Each family can be given atleast one hectare of prime agricultural land – thrice the average land holding size in Tripuira. The problem of tribal land alienation can be tackled in one go. Solution of conflicts need both symbols and substance — this gesture could provide both. Never before has a development project been dismantled to preserve the interests of the indigenous peoples. Since this project is proving to be a bit of white elephant, it is not very difficult to justify its decommissioning in view of its potential to solve the problem of tribal landlessness in one stroke.

If the entire or almost the entire tribal landless population can be gainfully resettled in the Gumti project area, it will free the hilly forest regions from human pressure. Since most of these landless tribals practise jhum or slash-and-burn which is dangerous for ecology of the hills and the forests, it is essential to settle this entire population in wet plains like the Gumti area. The hills cannot take the high pressure of human settlements — the plains can. So from an ecological viewpoint, the resettlement of the landless tribals of Tripura in Gumti project area will be welcome. The state's forest cover, now receding, will improve, degraded forests may be turned into gainful plantations by large scale private investments. The area likely to be reclaimed in Gumti project area should be used only for resettling tribal landless — a compact area in keeping with Maharaja Bir Bikram's tribal reserve concept.

This decommissioning proposals should be implemented before ethnic polarization between Bengali settlers and indigenous tribes-people snowballs beyond control. The state is still ruled by the CPI(M)-led Left Front, a left-of-centre coalition which has support both amongst Bengalis and tribes-people. Tribal parties and militant groups will support the dam's decommissioning and Bengali extremist groups are not yet around to resist it. A political dialogue can be initiated to create the proper climate for decommissioning and the creation of an alternative economy.

Even the security agencies have a benefit from this settlement — a happily settled tribal population, easily monitored, is less of a headache for police than if it is spread out over a huge hill region with a poor economy that creates empty stomachs and angry minds. Otherwise the graph of insurgent violence in Tripura, very considerable for a small state, cannot be controlled. According to police statistics, more than 3,000 people including 158 school teachers were kidnapped and 1697 people (including security personnel) were killed between April 1, 1993 and February 15, 2003. The figure has risen further after February 2003.

I would argue that the Bengalis can buy peace through the process of ethnic reconcialition that decommissioning of Dumbur hydel project and redistribution of the lands reclaimed from the project can start off. That is because the root cause of the tribal insurgency can be addressed. The tribal peasentry can be substantially empowered through this relocation of priorities. If the Dam goes, some Bengali fishermen in the area may feel upset at the loss of the Dumbur lake (as the Gumti reservoir is popularly known). But in the larger interest of ethnic reconciliation, the dam must go. Tribal insurgency in Tripura, now largely criminalized, must be fought relentlessly. The tribals must be reminded that these insurgents never addressed grassroot development issues like land. They have focused only on power-sharing concerns or resorted to mafia-style extortions rather than look at strategies for the empowerment of the tribal peasentry. Only such empowerment can lead to percolation of the fruits of development and make it an equitable process.

REFERENCES

A Study of the Land System of Tripura, Law Research Institute,1990.

B.K. Hrangkhawl's letters to Chief Minister Nripen Chakrabarty, 1983-87, available with the writer.

Dasgupta, *Ibid.*

Findings of the study was used for a PTI special report, 18th August, 1984.

For a detailed account of the Sengkrak movement, see Subir Bhaumik, *Insurgent Crossfire: North-East India,* Lancers, Delhi, 1996.

Harihar Bhattacharya, *Communism in Tripura,* Ajanta Publishers, Delhi, 1999.

In Tripura, the tribals were never a decisive majority but they were always in majority prior to the Partition, constituting just over fifty per cent of the population. But by 1981, they were barely accounting for thirty per cent of the population. See Tripura Census Reports, 1951 to 1981.

J.B. Ganguly, *Problem of Tribal Landlessness in Tripura,* in B.B. Dutta and M.N. Karna (eds.), Land Relations in North-East India, Peoples Publishing House, Delhi, 1987. Website of the Tripura Peoples Democratic Front (TPDF) in www.geocities.com.

Progress Report on 25-Point Tribal Development Package (1999 to 2002) Malabika Dasgupta, *The Gumti Hydel Project of Tripura,* Economic & Political Weekly, 7 October,1989.

The writer has collated the statistics available with the Tripura Land Revenue Department and the Agriculture Census Reports. The Land Revenue department had entertained applications from tribals for restoration of their alienated land-holdings. The percentage figures given are a result of this collated exercise.

PART V

Perspective on Ethnic Issues

12 Rephrasing the Identity Question in Manipur

Pradip Phanjoubam

Another round of the Naga peace talks was held recently at the Hague. Thanks to an active media following the event, we already know more or less the stance of either side of the negotiating parties. In many ways there was always a foreknowledge of the conclusion of every rounds of these talks. Only the desperately optimist can believe there would be a breakthrough. Hence no great political insight would be needed to predict the deadlock is not just about to end. It can even be imagined there having evolved some vested interest in having the deadlock continue. If not for anything else, some officials and interlocutors from either side can continue to make paid trips to various destinations in the world in the name of these parleys. But these are merely side shows and the extra expenses incurred we suppose will be small change for the Government of India. What is on centre stage is the peace talks and its progress or the lack of it. It is sad but true that whatever progress that have been claimed so far have been more illusory than real. At best they were placebos. It is even sadder to acknowledge the inability to imagine a possible way out, given the visible inflexibility of attitudes all around.

For one thing, believing it is possible to win sovereignty through negotiation would be simply too preposterous. But even the half way house of an integrated Naga homeland remains a distant dream for very many factors. The most immediate of these problems is that this homeland includes territories of three other Indian states, Arunachal Pradesh, Assam and Manipur and one foreign country,

Myanmar. Myanmar is a different story and beyond the scope of the present parleys to settle, but of the Indian states that are the hurdle, there can be no denying Manipur is the most problematic, and this precisely because the issues here are extremely entangled. As we have said in an earlier editorial this week, on the different notion of territory held by the different communities in the state, there is somewhat a clash of civilization situation, with these communities, from their respective standpoints, based often on mythology, ancestral values or emotions, claim a stake on the same bit of territory. As events in the past one decade or so have proven, it is not an easy matter to pass a verdict on. If it was, a lot of the vexing problems would have been a thing of the past.

I am firmly of the opinion now that it is time for all, not just those making the parleys, but also those who feel that their interests would end up compromised by it, to begin thinking out of the box. To begin with the Manipur integrity and Naga integration face-off for instance, cannot people begin thinking beyond the perimeters of these "imaginings". Indeed, the answer we all seek may very well be outside of these closed worlds.

Maybe it is a non-territorial "imagining" that is needed to be engendered. If not for the intended symbolism of the UNC's recent call for private schools in four hill districts to affiliate to the Nagaland state board, perhaps the move could have been the beginning of the kind of new "imagining" I suggested. In such an ideal situation, schools in Manipur can affiliate to the Central Board or to Nagaland Board or Assam Board, or wherever, just as schools in Nagaland can affiliate to the Manipur Board etc., depending on which is convenient and which is to the best benefit to the future of the students. This is an age in which boundaries, even if they exist physically, are dissolving. As for the symbolisms of such resolutions, let us be honest, in real terms they are bland. There was another similar resolution earlier of a certain no-tax campaign, whereby all in these hill districts were called upon not to pay the Manipur government any tax and instead pay them to the Nagaland government. Again, apart from the symbolism of antagonism, we all know how flat the whole thing was, knowing fully well what the tax revenue generated from these hills is. It is a little over

Rs.14 lakhs a year from about 94,000 Naga households. Neither must the Manipur Government been worried about the sum, nor the Nagaland Government thrilled.

Clash of Civilisations Fatalism

There can be few more pleased with the publication of Amartya Sen's new book "*Identity and Violence: Illusion of Destiny*" than those burning the mid-night oil on ways to resolve the question of identity and violence in the north-east at this moment. Many of us are happy that a man of such renown has thrown such a lot of light on a matter of gravity that we, by force of circumstance, have been trying to grapple with and interpret to the best of our abilities in all these years. My newspaper have been among those which have been arguing that much of the conflict situations we face are on account of very many traditional world-views juxtaposed in a single modern time frame. On the question of the notion of territory and its ownership, for instance, we had discussed at length how a settled agriculturist, a nomadic shifting cultivator, a feudal polity or a modern democracy would see differently. From their different standpoints, the same stretch of land may be seen as belonging to each of them. This overlap, results in friction and in extreme cases, conflicts. Can there be anyway to decide which of these different standpoints are just and which not? In the Manipur integrity and Naga integration conflict for instance, between the man sitting on top of the mountain peak claiming the entire mountain ranges to be his, and the man sitting in the valley below, claiming the same mountain ranges also belong to him, where must the verdict go? Indeed, where can the verdict go? In making these claims, both have invoked their individual traditions of "time immemorial".

Given this adherence to impervious traditional views, intellectually and logically inaccessible to each other, can there ever be a common ground on which the issue is put up for discourse and settled? On a smaller canvas, this is what the theory of "Clash of Civilisations" is about. We had also argued that what is needed is for all parties to emerge out of these insular worlds and evolve a common platform of scientific, humanitarian rationality on which these issues can be thrashed out together to the mutual benefit of all concerned. Failure to do this would amount to accepting "Clash of Civilisations" as a human destiny – our destiny.

Sen's book further debunks the assumption that the "Clash of Civilisations" predicament is intrinsically a human destiny. In most of the bloody clashes that the world has seen, be it the Hutu-Tutsi clashes in Africa, the Serb-Muslims-Croats clashes in the former Yugoslavia, the Nazi pogrom against the European Jews, or the present day bitter antagonism between what are supposedly "Western" and "Islamic" worlds, there isn't anything so grand as destiny but extraneous and arbitrary factors such as politics, economics, demagogic incitements etc. These may have made for extremely compelling factors, but the mere fact that they were compelling does not necessarily mean that they were proofs of conflicts being destiny ordained and unavoidable. Sen attributes such fatalistic approaches to the causes of conflicts, to a somewhat vain hunt for intellectual profundity in explaining social situations.

We can ask the same rhetorical question that Sen poses as explanation and illustration of his arguments to try and have a grip of our own situation. Was the Kuki-Naga clashes of the early 1990s destiny, or was it Machiavellian politics? Was it something that would have happened whatever the circumstance, or was it a by-product of electoral equations, underground power game, economics of land ownership and trade routes etc.? If it was destiny, why did it happen in the 1990s and not a century ago? Is the present day friction between the Nagas and Meiteis destiny? Is the hill-valley duality destiny? Or are they again by-products of human shortcomings? We prefer to wallow in Sen's optimism and basic generosity of heart that makes him see that embedded in all conflict situations is not destiny, but rationally and amicably resolvable human issues.

Identity Not Intrinsic

The intriguing nature of identity continues to fascinate scholars and politicians alike even to this day. Endless reams of newsprint spent on the subject as well as endless series of scholarships on it haven't been able to bring about a conclusive answer to what must be one of the most vexing problems of the modern world. If it were not so, there would be no need and reason why new thoughts and books on the subject still has a huge market. Identity still matters, and sometimes for what are seemingly unintelligible reasons. What then are the deciding factors of identity? Is it language, race, ethnicity, religion, geography, culture? While all of them are constituents, none or any permutation and combination of them, seem to be sufficient explanation for the phenomenon of identity. Yesterday quite a few of the deliberations at the memorial function of the 18 young men and women who lost their lives in June 18, 2001 uprising to save Manipur's territorial integrity were revealing in this regard. Some leaders of the many smaller tribes in the state especially were emphatic about identity being a matter of choice, asserting they would in the present juncture neither want to be identified with the Nagas or the Kukis or any other generic groupings independently. We also know how many others in the past have, by the same principle, chosen to belong to anyone of these generic groupings, and these choices have today come to stay. The point however remains that at one point in time, identity was a rather volitional choice than destiny.

Benedict Anderson, in his influential 1983 book "*Imagined Communities*" has more examples of this paradoxical idea of "choosing or else assigning identity". The question of the Mulattos, the Caucasian European settlers in Latin America, mostly Spanish and Portuguese, who immediately lost not just their citizenships of their mother countries once they settled in the South American colonies, but also their primary Spanish or Portuguese identities is one such. Although speaking the languages of their mother countries, belonging to the same race and espousing the same cultures, they were presumed to have acquired a separate identity, and the distinctions came to be rigorously and sometimes brutally maintained. Similarly, it would be worthwhile noting that the war of independence that Americans fought was against their own forefathers. There was yet another reference in a different context to the phenomenon in yesterday's deliberations by a Meitei Pangal. In 1947, when India was partitioned, some Bihari Muslims opted to migrate to the then East Pakistan, believing idealistically they were choosing to be part of a Muslim nation. They soon found out that they had walked into what was primarily a Bengali nation. When the Bangladesh war of independence commenced in 1971, they ended up siding with Pakistan. Today these Bihari Muslims, numbering about 10,000, are an issue for international human rights organisations like the Amnesty International to tackle, having been deprived of even Bangladesh citizenship, although *bona fide* residents of the country since the time of its birth. We in the north-east also know how a conflict between religious and linguistic identities at the time of the Indian partitition lead to the unfair situation of the Hindu districts of Sylhet and Manmesing ending up as a part of East Pakistan.

The point again is, there is nothing intrinsic about identity. It is a matter of choice. Let us then stop all these cock and bull stories of "time immemorial" affiliations and blood brotherhood as the basis of identity. If a genetic mapping of the peoples in the region were to be done, we are sure a lot of the identity myths would be blown apart. Let the separateness of identities remain, but if everybody was open enough, these separateness should be no cause for any fundamental conflicts of interests, as many are making it seem to be. "Identity as a choice", also offers hope. It means, we can evolve rational choices rather than the blind, impulsive ones adhered to by most. Once the issue is put up on the rational, discursive space, meaningful discourses and negotiations can begin. The postulate of layered identities by Amartya Sen in "*Identity and Violence: Illusion of Destiny*" says as much. One can be a Meitei, a Manipuri, a north-easterner, an Indian, an Asian etc., in widening concentric sets, without anyone of these components coming into conflict with each other.

Rational Identity

Manipur is not new to the notion of ethnic clash. By that virtue, it would not be difficult for anybody who follows conflict issues here to appreciate the arguments in Samuel P. Huntington's influential "Clash of Civilisations and the Remaking of the World Order". In fact, reading the text of this theory alongside the unfolding events in our state, as well as the world at large uncritically would make it seem as if the "Clash of Civilisations" is a truism rather than an intellectual assumption. A lot many however challenged this notion from the time the book hit the stands and put up very interesting and often disturbing questions like can war be a human destiny? Can conflicts be an essential feature of civilizations? Shouldn't civilization and civilized behaviour be about avoiding conflicts? etc. But all these appeared more like desperate appeals, posing little threats to the popular imagination generated of the supposed reality of the "Clash of Civilisations". But this equation has been shaken up seriously since March 2006 release of economics Nobel Laureate, Amartya Sen's latest book "*Identity and Violence: Illusion of Destiny*", (Penguin).

Sen does not go into the familiar argument of "civilizations do not clash" but attacks what he calls the flaws in the assumption of identity, be it civilisational, national, ethnic groups or individuals. None of these identities in reality bears a singular attribute but on the contrary have multiple and plural affiliations. As for instance, a person can be a journalist, an admirer of the world of academia, a Meitei with no ill-will towards the Nagas or Kukis, a Hindu admirer of Christian humanity, a nascent yoga enthusiast, a football fan, a jazz lover, a father, a husband, a Manipuri etc., all at the same time and without any of the attributes militating against any other. This logic works right up to the civilisational identity. What the "Clash of Civilizations" theorists and practitioners have done is to segregate these identity attributes into separate boxes, often making them mutually unacceptable, and identifying just one amongst them as fundamental, unique, destined and hence overwhelming. Most often, the attribute thus singled out is religion and at other times race. Hence, under the treatment of the "clash" fundamentalists, the Meitei identity or the Naga identity would become "unique" islands intellectually inaccessible to each other, leaving only the option of a clash as the negotiating ground, since all other identity attributes that could have served as the meeting platform have been eliminated as insignificant. The complexity and richness of identities become reduced to mono-linear and supposedly self-contained worlds of West, East, Christian, Islam etc.

Sen blasts this notion in very many ways, and in a particular instance, with a touch of his characteristic humour. He reinforces the strength of his contention that identity is also very much a matter of rational choice rather than pure destiny, by imagining a plausible identity dilemma of a man who is a linguist and a vegetarian. At an official dinner, his identity as a vegetarian would definitely be what is practical and important. Before taking seat at the table, he would probably voluntarily declare his vegetarian identity if he is not asked if he belonged to that identity group. At a linguistic seminar, his other identity would likewise become more prominent. Similarly, somebody can be a Meitei first in Imphal, but probably he would be a Manipuri first in Chennai, and if he were to be in Rome, it would make little sense for him to persist in being Meitei first. The chief question that emerges is, if identity is also a matter of rational choice, what is the identity most rational for us all in the conflict situation we are in. The liberal accommodative one or the rigid inflexible one that is doomed to lead to a "Clash of Civilizations".

Tragi-comedy

Manipur's quest for an answer to its many conflict situation often reduces to the farcical. The chief minister, Okram Ibobi, was put through some embarrassment in Senapati district headquarters recently. Some people in the crowd displayed a banner that welcomed him to what they chose to call Senapati – South Nagalim. In a sequel photograph juxtaposed alongside a picture of the banner in the vernacular "Naharolgi Thoudang", the amused, and to that extent dismissive, smiles on the faces of the chief minister and his cabinet colleagues, counter-balanced the affront pretty well, we had thought. For the silent laughters almost mocked and turned the table around, reducing the entire manoeuvre somewhat to a tragi-comedy, leaving the audience unsure of whether to be in rage or laughter, or more precisely, overcome with pity. In fact, it was a mixture of all of these uncertain emotions. Had Ibobi reacted in rage and resorted to the violence vested in the state that he is the chief executive, the script would have been entirely different, and definitely would have played into the hands of those trying to provoke extreme reactions. Obviously there are plenty who disagree with us, but we would still insist such a response would not have been the right answer.

In fact, the problem with Manipur today is, we have not been able to find the right answers to many of the most vexing problems staring us in the face. Apart from the confrontationist stances, has there been a Meitei answer to the Greater Nagaland question, conversely has there been a Naga answer to the Manipur integrity question? Has anybody tried honestly to find an answer to the Kuki question or those of any other community? Should we not also try rephrasing these questions, or better still go beyond their immediacy and take a more objective overview of the entire gamut of unfolding events? Must it all end when somebody's sanity snaps at somebody else's provocation and an orgy of violence engulfs us all?

Discourse on Legitimacy

A two part, edit page article in *The Telegraph,* by Pratap Bhanu Mehta after a routine India-China cooperation summit in Beijing recently, contains some very absorbing argument on the sources of legitimacy for different forms of governments. The comparison between India and China, in this regard, is loaded with lessons. These lessons can very well be for Manipur too and hence this invitation for further reflection, although we are aware most would have already read the original article. One of the chief contentions is that the governments of China and India by necessity draw their legitimacy differently and from different sources. Being a democracy, India puts a premium on representation. There is beauty in this but it nevertheless dilutes the question of accountability. It ensures participation of all different sections of the people in the governance process but this itself becomes the primary end justice, leaving the question of performance, the other vital functions of any government, as secondary. Consider this. The official counter against the charge that the north-east occupies only a peripheral space in the Indian national consciousness and hence neglected, is that everyone of the north-eastern states is represented in all the institutions of the Indian state, administrative as well as legislative, hence the question of neglect, or injustice, at least at the institutional level, does not arise. The fact that the north-east still remains backward does not seem to be considered a factor in assessing the legitimacy of the government system. It is as if representation is all.

In another arena, this logic has in recent times acquired a new hue in the wake of Mandal-II. The point again is, ensuring representation may be a necessary condition for the larger understanding of justice, but the questions remain – is it sufficient condition? On the smaller canvas of Manipur too, and we are sure all other states as well, the source of government legitimacy is drawn from similar wells and are invariably beset with the same flaws. Take the case of the hill-valley divide. Here too, as all of us know, the fierce contest for representation is at the crux of politics and is indeed treated as the only legitimate route to systemic as well as social justice. Every community wants as much handle in the government as possible and the equilibrium struck between the numerous pulls and pressures from these demands is what constitutes a stable government. However, after this equilibrium is reached, the other important considerations of accountability and performance are somewhat pushed into the background.

Again, here too, as in the case of the larger canvas of the Indian Union, the counter argument against discrimination charges by any community or region, most specifically by the hill districts, is the proportion of representation. That the hills have been very much a part of the political and administration processes in proportionate measures, and that even two Nagas have been chief ministers. These are facts, but must not government legitimacy also take into account performance? Why then have the hill districts lagged behind in development? These questions should be made answerable by state leaders, regardless of whether she or he is from the hills or the valley.

By contrast, the challenges of legitimacy before the government in China are different. Its leaders are nominated ones hence the only way they can win this legitimacy is through performance and accountability. Because of this, the nature of their motivation and drive are radically different. This onerous expectation has even led China in recent times to treat Capitalism and Communism not as ideologies, but as instruments of development, to be administered in measured doses as per the developmental needs of the society. In our situation, this quest for legitimacy would be somewhat similar to that of a President's Rule scenario when a nominated Governor runs the civil administration. He too must have to seek his legitimacy through performance and accountability alone. No state can know this better than Manipur. The Chinese system too has its flaws, but we have no doubt many will agree that there are lessons in it that can benefit our own outlook to what should constitute good governance.

Nurturing Creativity

Following the welcome discussions on intellectual freedom and responsibility in setting the agenda of public debates on social issues, initiated by the First Arambam Somorendra Memorial Lecture this year, the need now is also to explore if there is anything beyond. This question is essential for apart from intellectual freedom, there must also be something as intellectual honesty. The task is not simple, considering the contentious idea thrown up in a classic and much quoted essay on the subject by Bertrand Russell "The Harm That Good Men Do." In deference of good men in this world, of which there are innumerable, it would have been far easier for mortals like us to swallow the idea if Russell had toned down his intellectual irreverence and had inserted the word "can" in the titled of his essay and made it "The Harm That Good Men Can Do." For good men do not always equate with intellectual clumsiness or are by nature bumbling gawks, out of tune with the times. If history is full of short-lived, disastrous careers in the harsh game of politics for good men, there have also been exemplary leaders who actually altered the definition of politics and indeed the fate of humans on earth. We do not have to go far to find a living example, for there is the living legend of Nelson Mandela, in South Africa. Many would contend he is not of South Africa alone, but of the whole world, for today the goodness of his iron-willed politics has come to infect practically everybody. There have been so many others in whom a basic humanity combined with the power of politics. Closest to mind is a colossal leader who paid with his life to abolish slavery in America – President Abraham Lincoln. Gandhi would fall in the same category but he was more of a saint than a politician. Some would even classify him as a fit candidate for Russell's essay, for if his politics held sway without being tempered by the pragmatic scientific outlooks of his younger followers, India's goal would probably have been to reduce itself to an idealistic, and for that reason, impossible "village republic".

The challenge before our intellectuals today, (the officially designated ones who have chosen academia as their career especially, but also the non-academic scholars in all other walks of life), is not just about opening up the space for debates with the intent of raising the bar of the general intellectual understanding of the place's political and social predicaments, but also to define the parameter of this space itself. The assumption is, outcomes of these social debates will ultimately influence and shape vital public issues, including our politics, for the better. These debates must have to be informed, open and honest. While openness and honesty are personal characteristics, the earlier attribute of being informed can be best achieved by career intellectuals, for the demands of their profession require them to keep abreast with the most current thoughts in the social sciences as well as the exact sciences. It is for this reason that the academia must bear the major responsibility in this project. The discourses must also be intensely probing or else our social prognoses will remain incomplete. The logic and wisdom of the advice of old, "never hide anything from your doctor or lawyer" must apply here too.

It has been said that in the world of art, the age of criticism and the age of creativity alternate. If this segmentation is too radical, at least it needs to be acknowledged that there is an active and direct dialectic between two enterprises, each informing the other and in the process growing together. The absence or deteriorating standard of one will impede the progress of the other. This dialectic however cannot be confined to the world of art alone. This is why we argue that committed intellectuals must treat it as a duty to sustain continually, an incisively critical atmosphere to form the background against which political ideas and initiatives can shape and grow. Just as the critic and the artist must nudge each other in the quest for creative excellence, the intellectual and the activist (into the broad category of which we would include the politician) must act as each other's foil too.

Mapless Solution

A lot has been said about how only meaningful civil society dialogues can be the medicine for the present day friction between various groups in the North-East region. Unfortunately, meaningful dialogues have been virtually a nonstarter everywhere. There are no signs any new initiative will take shape either, considering there has not been any sincere effort to build a platform on which ideas can be shared and expanded, dialectically. The Manipur example is illustrative. The current face-off between Naga civil society campaigners for Naga unification and those who believe in the spirit of a cosmopolitan Manipur with all its territory intact, in particular the Meiteis, is a live demonstration of how this dialogue cannot happen. Neither side is willing to budge an inch from their original stances that in the first place resulted in the friction, ensuring that the potential for conflict remains high. In the present deadlock, both sides see a win by either side as a loss of the other. Nothing can be more dangerous than this. The challenge then is to find a situation where each's vision and aspiration is not a threat to the other: A "Game Theory" situation in which any two or more contesting parties can end up winners simultaneously and in complementary ways.

For this to become possible, an intellectual platform must first be constructed on which all the conflicting interests can stand together and discover each other's mental and emotional wavelengths. In constructing such a site where ideas can exchange, interact, enrich each other and multiply, the foremost task before all parties, in our opinion, is to secularise the agèndas before us, most specifically that of identity. That is to say, the most important pillar of such a problem solving discourse must have to be the ability to convert our ethnic issues into civic ones (a suggestion adopted from one made by Sanjib Baruah in "Durable Disorder" although in a slightly different context). The first advantage of such an approach would be that it would make many of the problems at hand quantifiable in real terms and hence addressed and tackled in real terms too. Perhaps the most important mechanism of tackling these then would become contained in the administration and reforms within it. After all, despite all the rhetoric and polemics on ethnic affinities and brotherhood, at their very crux, most of the problems in the region ultimately boil down to the failure of the administrative mechanism leading to the birth of desires for new orders. At its very basic, the Naga integration question, or the objection to it from Manipur, Assam and Arunachal Pradesh, are also about restructuring the administrative ambits. The spiritual aspects of human bondages between individuals and communities are also important constituents, but what we are suggesting is, an imaginative administration can ensure that none of these develops into mutually hostile interests. While the former must as far as possible remain in private spheres, the latter must be the governing principle of public life. This, we have come to be convinced more than ever now, is the formula for peaceful coexistence of a diversely multi-cultural, multilingual, multi-religion and multi-ethnic state like Manipur, and on a larger canvas, India.

If there is an important succour to draw from the past, it is not in the shape of all the jingoism we see flying around so flagrantly and wildly. On the other hand, it is the realization that like the "Nation State", hard map drawing is a legacy from Europe. In the pre-colonial world outside of Europe, the boundaries between civilizations, kingdoms, village communities, etc., were more frontiers than precise lines of demarcation marked by boundary pillars and zealously guarded by professional soldiers. In this world of yore, cultures overlapped and melted into each other naturally and effortlessly. Perhaps the solution to our problems is not in redrawing of physical maps but in modelling an administration that drew on the virtues of the seamless adjustments cultures and communities made in a mapless political reality.

Rightness of Things

Ratan Thiyam's new play, "*Kurukshetragi Peerang*", (The Tears of Kurukshetra), revolves around just one word of Panchali (Draupadi) – "dharma". The play is based on the Mahabharat, but it is not straight out of the narrative of the Hindu epic. On the other hand, it is an extrapolation of what might have been the nature of the agony suffered by those who survived the war, especially the women. The chief characters are hence, Gandhari the mother of the 100 Kaurava brothers who lost the war and their lives, Kunti the mother of the victorious five Pandavas brothers but lost a son, Karna, born out of wedlock and therefore abandoned at birth, and Panchali, the polyandrous wife of the five Pandavas, who made her husbands vow revenge for the public humiliation she received in the court of the Kauravas, triggering off the devastating war between the cousins. The grief of the three ladies are awesome and convincingly portrayed, but in the fight to overcome this grief, it is the younger woman, Panchali, who stood tall. While the two elderly women wanted to leave the palace and seek refuge from their misery in exile in the forest, Draupadi remained firm in her resolve to stay back, take the full blast of the consequences of the devastating war, and do her best to heal the wounds not just to her immediate family but to the people of the kingdom her five husbands now ruled. This, she comes to the conclusion, was what she and her family owed to the people who went through the war for no fault of theirs, and hence her "dharma", following which will be the only salvation for her as the queen.

We write of the play not with the intent of reviewing it but simply because of the reminder of the term "dharma" and its relevance in politics, not the least today's politics. We are not trying to understand the term within the casteist Hindu parameters where each caste category is expected to be satisfied with doing well what their respective castes supposedly destined them to do. On the other hand, we are interpreting, as much as we believe the director of the play was also interpreting, the term in the more universal sense of doing what is "right" and "fit" in any given circumstance. The understanding "dharma" is not strictly religious but there is a definite ring of religiosity in it, and in the same sense, in the understanding of "right" action in any given circumstance, there is the same ring of religiosity without being religious. This understanding would be more akin to the concept of natural justice and because of the commitment to justice and truth, its proximity to religiosity. Very often what we do may not be "wrong" but at the same time the same action may not be the "right" thing to do. It may not be "wrong" for legislators to switch party loyalty, but beyond legality and conventions, we also know intuitively that this is not "right". Hence, while it may be well within the permits of religion and morality for the virtuous Pandavas to destroy their wrongdoer cousins, there was something simply not "right" about the devastating war that razed a kingdom so totally. The magnitude and scale of the physical as well as spiritual devastations simply dwarfed any justification of the war even on moral grounds. This was the reality Thiyam made his characters confront on stage. This is also the reality of any war anytime although it is difficult for anybody in a war situation to see this because wars and hatred make those involved so myopic to the larger ethical question of the "rightness" of things.

To be ethical then, in our opinion, is to be able to see this "rightness" of action and deed not just through the prism of any defined religion or legal frames, but through a filter fashioned from the realization of the common human predicament. It will also not be easy to hit this "right" decision for it is a moving target. The only way to arrive at this truth will have to be through relentless, sometimes agonizing self-questioning, as indeed the women in Thiyam's play are made to go through.

To be Manipuri

Just what does it mean to be Manipuri? Innocuous as it may sound, this question signifies a multilayered problem both at the semantic as well as at the ontological levels. At its most basic, the problem is one of deciding whether the term refers to the domicile statuses of people living in the state called Manipur or else is securely bonded to the identity of the dominant community, the Meiteis? That is to say, should Manipuri signify a community or should it be a kind of citizenship status? Should it be an intuitive under-standing or a legally definable term? Before going into the other nuances of the problems, uncomfortable as these few questions and their derivatives are, our civil society, in the midst of the identity churnings it is immersed in, must honestly address and seek and answers to them. Unless and until this issue is settled conclusively, we for one are of the opinion that all the talk of emotional integrity will remain hollow. If our voice matters in setting the agendas and tone of the discourses in our civil society, we would definitely at this stage call attention to this proposition. Let us openly thrash out what this term can and should mean and exorcise the demon within our society. If possible, let us give it a fresh mould so that it becomes a faithful mirror of all its constituents. In a way, our problem is one faced by all multi-ethnic, multi-cultural societies. On a larger canvas, India is beset with it too and the effort of liberals in the country has been to make the Indian identity more inclusive in letter and spirit.

Our own perception of the problem as on the Manipur canvas is that the nomenclature Manipuri is too closely associated with the Meiteis, even at the cost of excluding other communities. This may not have happened out of any intent, but through impersonal historical and other circumstantial forces, nevertheless the fact remains that it is today lacking in inclusiveness. Imagine a scenario in which a person from Manipur, belonging to any of its many communities other than the Meitei, identifying himself as a Manipuri anywhere outside the state. We also know it for certain that many actually do, sometimes out of a sense of political correctness but very often also because of a genuine affinity with the place and its spirit before it plunged into its present identity imbroglio. Because of the image of "Manipuri" projected outside in all these years, the first set of queries this person is likely to face would be about Ras Lila, Pung Cholom, Thang Ta, INA memorial,

Manipuri cuisines etc. all of which have come to bear, or else have been given, Meitei signatures. If the inquiries carry on, our hypothetical non-Meitei person would probably be obliged to make a qualifi-cation that he or she is from Manipur but not a Meitei, distancing herself a little from the identity "Manipuri" perforce. Herein then is the failure of the "Manipuri" identity as it stands today. For this reason, we do not get all too piqued by those from Manipur who do not identify themselves as "Manipuris" when outside the state, for in the gesture we can read a deeper, even essential, identity crisis.

The remedy as we see it can come only from an open, uninhibited discourse in our civil society. Ultimately, an under-standing must come about whereby the Meitei identity is just a set within the bigger set of the "Manipuri" identity, to use an analogy from mathematics. Our self-questioning must be honest. As for instance, why cannot the Manipuri Sahitya Sabha have a non-Meitei language section where literatures in these languages are sought to be developed? Why cannot the "Manipuri" cuisine, as and when projected outside during cultural festivals etc., include a meat category? Until such a time as a more composite and more politically and ethnologically correct "Manipuri" identity emerges, perhaps more prominence should be given to the link between show-cased cultural achievements such as the Ras Lila, Thang Ta etc. and the Meitei identity subset, than to their link with the larger "Manipuri" identity set so that the latter is not usurped by the Meitei identity altogether.

PART VI

Issues of Identity and Governance

13 Ethnicity and Self-Governance in the North-East

B.D. Sharma

Background

The quintessence of the pre-independence tribal scene can be said to comprise three basic elements :

(i) a system of self-governance guided by the traditions and customs of the people with almost no exotic intervention;
(ii) considered intervention at the highest level in matters concerning the system and the legal frame; and
(iii) realisation of the need for protection against the articulate neighbours and even the functionaries of the State exemplified by the 'excluded area' approach and even total ban on entry into the same through stringent inner-line regulations.

We may begin with the very first issue of self-governance, which, in the case of tribal areas, has to be accepted as the central element.

Self-Governance at the Village Level

That community at the village level in the tribal areas is a functioning unit is universally acknowledged. That it has been managing its affairs in accordance with its customs and traditions effectively and that too in the spirit of a true democracy, is also beyond doubt. The ideal setting was succinctly described even after more than a decade of independence by the Scheduled Areas and Scheduled Tribes Commission as in the following :

> "The decision of their Councils is law to the tribals. The sanction behind it is both necessity and faith; necessity because there in far-flung areas social equilibrium and stability have to be maintained by some responsible agency and the Council is that agency; faith because with the tribals their social customs and religious rites are the essence of their existence."

The principle of exclusion or non-regulation was the formal expression of this realisation by the *Raj.*

The policy to be pursued after independence was expressed most eloquently by Pandit Nehru in his famous *Panchasheel.* It was accepted as the corner stone of State's policy on tribal affairs in that early phase. Even on the larger canvass of the national life, a republic-like system at the village level, simulating the village republic of the hoary past, was accepted by the Founding Fathers and duly enshrined in the Constitution as Article 40. *Therefore, there could not be even an iota of doubt about the ideal and the objective for the tribal areas in respect of self-governance.* It had to be an integral part of any frame, which might be designed for the tribal areas in general. That is not all. It had to be accepted as the firm foundation for building a new system with necessary scope for variations of design and detail depending on the local situation. Yet, no explicit provision was made either in the Fifth Schedule or even the Sixth schedule to ensure that necessary space was created within the formal System for this living entity at the village level, the Village Council or the *Gram Sabha* and that the new edifice was built there on in real terms.

Sixth Schedule X-rayed

The provisions of the Sixth Schedule, however, on careful examination, reveal the nature of prevailing confusion and ambivalence as also the yawning gap between the intension of the Founding

Fathers and the hardware of democracy. The warning of Pandit Nehru about the limitations of written words and terms and his plea for being guided by the spirit proved to be a mere palliative. For example, under paragraph 3 of the Sixth Schedule, it is the District Council or the Regional Council, as the case may be, which has been endowed with the necessary law-making powers concerning '(e) the establishment of village or town committees or councils and their powers' as also '(f) any other matter relating to village or town administration including village or town police and public health and sanitation.'

This provision in the Sixth Schedule, on the face of it, would appear to be unexceptionable. What we have here is an autonomous district or region. The governance of these autonomous units is in the hands of the Autonomous District Councils or the Autonomous Regional Councils therein, as the case may be. The Autonomous District/Regional Council is constituted under paragraph 2. It can comprise not more than thirty members. All members thereof 'shall be elected on the basis of adult suffrage', except those nominated by the Governor, whose number cannot be more than four. Thus, the norms of representative democracy are largely honoured.

It is, however, important to note that what we have here is a transformation from the traditional system to the formal system. In this case the transformation on the face of it is not arbitrary or just superimposed. It is envisaged to be effected through a process of consultation with the traditional system by the Governor. The 'rules for the *first constitution* of District Councils and Regional Councils' shall be made under sub-paragraph (6) of paragraph 2 by the Governor 'in consultation with the *existing tribal councils* or other representative tribal organisations within the autonomous districts or regions concerned'. The traditional councils can be said to have been given due honour. These rules cover, *inter alia,* the composition of the District Councils, matters concerning elections and conduct of business. The District or the Regional Council, after its first constitution, may make rules on the said subject under sub-paragraph (7) with the approval of Governor.

Here is the real twist, which perhaps went unnoticed in the

flurry of freedom and euphoria of democracy. The democracy after independence in general got equated with 'representative democracy' in a meticulously defined frame reduced to writing in the form of laws and rules made there under. It was a great event for the nation as a whole, which had carried the imperial yoke for more than a century. But the significance of the traditions and customs in the system of self-governance at the village level particularly in the tribal areas was not fully appreciated even though they have to be accepted as an integral part of the frame of law in a truly democratic polity as discussed earlier.

Implications of Formalisation

This vital omission and confusion would need a detailed analysis. The Constitution in the Sixth Schedule envisaged replacement of the traditional institutions of self-governance, which had retained full autonomy in these tracts by virtue of non-regulation or exclusion thereof, by a set of formal institutions. There are many facets of such a transformation. *Firstly,* let us consider the scope of the two sets of institutions, the traditional and the formal. The scope of the new formal Councils is set out in paragraph 7. It comprises almost all affairs concerning the day-to-day life of the people such as management of resources, *albeit*, excluding reserved forests, civil administration and social matters like marriage and divorce. Nevertheless the fact remains that the scope of the powers of the new Councils is *prescribed and definitive*; it is not open-ended. All that is not enumerated in this paragraph is deemed to vest with the State. It is not the other way round, as should be expected as natural in a true democracy. In the case of a true democracy certain specific aspects can be taken over by the State, whose number has to be kept at the bare minimum leaving the rest to be handled by the people as per their traditions and customs. This is the frame, which was actually in vogue in the excluded areas before independence.

Secondly, comes the question about the way even the matters enumerated in paragraph 7 of the Sixth Schedule are to be handled in the new situation. The last arbiter in matters concerning the traditions and customs of a people naturally is the community. As noted earlier, it is the dynamics of *parampara,* which has been the moving spirit of the grand procession of all cultures and civilisations until the onset of the modern State. But now in the new frame, a formal institution has been endowed with the responsibility as also the authority to settle the parameters of governance in all those matters, which had been governed by the *parampara* of the people earlier. *What is crucial in this change is the implicit premise that the parameters of governance of the community in the specified matters can be settled by a body other than the traditional institutions of the people.*

The scope of this change itself in practice can be highly variable. At the one end, the new formal authority can even decide that all matters concerning the specified matters will continue to be dealt with by the traditional institutions in accordance with their traditions and customs. This will be a 'no-change' scenario even after the formal system takes over from the traditional. At the other end of the spectrum, a situation can be visualised in which every aspect of the people's life gets formally defined by law, leaving no scope for the vicissitudes of the so-called people's autarchy under the name of *parampara.*

Even those who swear by traditions and customs of the people sometimes talk about codifying the same. They hardly realise the serious implications of such a proposition. The first point in the above proposition is about the scope of the proposition, that is, 'what and whose traditions and customs are to be codified?' The traditions and customs are so variable over space and time that by the time one reaches the other end of the spatial spectrum of a tribal tract the situation may be totally different even though the continuum from one end to the other may be faultless, unbroken. Any codification of customs of a people, therefore, has to be an exercise in generalities. Significant variation of the codified version from the reality, particularly in respect of the smaller sections of a community, is inevitable in this process. Moreover, codification of customs, by itself, would bring about a total change in the nature of ultimate authority in matters concerning the traditions and the customs of a people. After codification the concerned community or group is no longer the last arbiter about what its custom is. A book may be flung in the face of the most revered persons, genuinely accepted by the people as their wise leaders, on questions of social norms and traditions, by a zealot, not always moved by honourable considerations. The bewildered community may have no answer except that they may decide to burn the book, chastise the zealot and revolt against the System, which may be forced on them with best intentions without realising its implications, a recurrent phenomenon in the living tribal societies.

The irony is that in this formal setting, on the one hand, the community loses the natural endowment concerning self-governance even in that limited prescriptive frame. There is no gain on the other side either. Even the new institutions are not really autonomous as their name would feign to suggest. Not only the laws on the specified items, but even the rules governing the constitution of these formal institutions and the rules of game for their own working, are beyond their competence which they themselves cannot finally decide. In the instant case of the Sixth Schedule these rules have to be approved by the Governor. In fact, thus, what we have is the *'end of autonomy';* there is not real autonomy by any stretch of imagination in the new frame, as the name would suggest.

Territorial Jurisdiction

The next question is about the geographical expanse of the jurisdiction of the formal institutions established under the provisions of the Sixth Schedule. Those institutions become the formal centres of powers and responsibilities. The tribal communities are generally associated with a territory over which each community, or part thereof, have been exercising effective command. Therefore, *the self-governing system not only relates to a community or a part thereof but also to a territory or a part thereof. Particularisation, not generalisation, is the guiding principle of the Constitutional schema of administration concerning the tribal areas and the tribal people.* The Constitution envisages district as the unit for the new System. There is no formal definition of district. It can be as large as a State; it could as well be a small tract comprising a few hundred villages. That a district may not comprise the same tribe all through and it may be necessary to carve out a smaller tract therein for other social groups has been incorporated as a part of the Sixth Schedule Scheme itself. A district can have one or more regions within its geographical jurisdiction, which may be as autonomous as the district itself with reference to the entire canvass of autonomy discussed in detail above.

Again, this formal frame of the Constitution in principle may be considered as adequate to accommodate all geographical areas related to each tribe or a part thereof as a separate unit, that is, as a district or one or more regions therein, as the case may be. Nevertheless the fact remains that the process of delimitation in this case is formal and proceeds from above. Therefore, it is bound to be influenced, if not governed, by considerations of formal administration. The possibility of each tribe, or part thereof, being accommodated in this formal process as per the people's perception and their sensitivity is rather small and unpredictable.

To the extent there is dissonance on this count, the organic and dynamic character of the community will stand undermined. It would give way to formal processes, which have their own dynamics. The most ominous aspect of the new dynamics is the disregard for the community and ascendancy of countless vested interests, which enter these areas under the cover of the formal frame, which the people are unable to understand.

To cap it all, like all other formal structures in a democratic polity, the new Councils comprise people's representatives chosen by them on the basis of adult suffrage. Besides the issues of delimitation of constituencies, which of necessity have to follow a number norm, and not societal zones, this System has the inevitable implication, that is, installation of the principle of vote, or the number game, at the centre of the stage. The serious implications of this proposition, which not only look so simple but even natural in a democratic polity, were never made explicit, nay not even considered in any detail in respect of the traditional community organisation of the tribal people.

The formal system basically accepts 'the atomised and inorganic view of society'. The tribal system, on the other hand, is built on the foundation of community life. The essence of community life is complementarity of roles of all its members, ideally set in a frame dedicated to lasting harmony. The community can never be at war with itself: one part of it fighting the other (*albeit* democratically), and the majority ruling over the minority. Nevertheless this issue was not faced squarely after independence even as a general proposition, not to speak about the tribal situation. There was no doubt an uneasy feeling about something going wrong amongst sensitive leaders like Jawaharlal. Yet, their search for the missing key remained confined to the lighted area of formal institutions in total disregard of the vast expanse of traditional system, simply because it was dark over there.

The Scheduled Areas and Scheduled Tribes Commission, comprising persons deeply concerned with tribal affairs, did pose a decade later some important questions in clear terms such as 'Is the principle of election to Tribal Council contrary to tribal tradition?' 'Will the elective principle enunciated for statutory Panchayats create any rivalry or jealousy in the tribal villages, so as to disrupt the existing cooperative feeling amongst them?' The Commission after due consideration did take a categorical stand about the existing traditional Councils. They should continue in all homogeneous tribal areas where they are strong and alive. It was also clearly stated that 'it will not be necessary to introduce new statutory Panchayats in such places'. *But the Commission failed to take note of the negation of this principle in the scheme of the Sixth Schedule itself with built in transformation from the traditional to the formal in the form of Autonomous Councils for the district or the region, as the case may be.*

The most anomalous, nay, unseemly and indecorous aspect of this transformation in the Sixth Schedule was that it was to be done 'in consultation with the existing tribal councils'. The judgment had been passed by the August Assembly. The existing tribal councils enjoying allegiance of the people had to go. They had to give way to the Autonomous Councils established under the authority of the Constitution. The new Councils were also vested with necessary powers there under. This fiat was reminiscent of the suppression of the traditional village system in the country as a whole in the beginning of the British Rule, but with a difference. The insolent rulers then did not even take a formal note of the *'being'* of the community except in tribal tracts where they faced revolts and rebellions. The suppression of the community in that situation was unilateral. It became effective on the dot with the enforcement of concerned laws. In the new setting after independence, however, perhaps in deference to the spirit of democracy, the *being* of the tribal councils was recognised. They were also given the honour of being consulted by the high priest of the new system, the Governor himself. They could perhaps express their wish about the way their *Last Rites* were to be performed. But the judgment about their virtual dissolution itself was final. That was to be an act of self-sacrifice on the altar of democracy in fulfilment of the dreams of countless millions. Could there really be any case for a choice?

Village Councils Remain Supreme

The Autonomous Councils have been established in the North-East in accordance with the provisions of the Sixth Schedule. It was presumably done in consultation with the existing tribal councils. It is a moot question whether the people who were consulted really knew what they were being consulted about. In their perception that exercise may have been one more ritual like a series of other rituals relating to some events up there which were really beyond their comprehension and, therefore, of no real concern to them. All they could have imagined was the fact that there was a Parliament; there was an Assembly; so here was one more body to be known as Autonomous District Council, all of the same mould. In their perception, so far as their day-to-day life was concerned, there could be no change unless they themselves decided about the same. They had resisted all sorts of attempted intrusions even by the most powerful Empire successfully for more than a century. Therefore, there was no reason for them to visualise any change to their disadvantage now particularly when the overbearing white man had disappeared from the scene. Their own representatives, irrespective of their positions up there, be it the Parliament, the Assembly or the District Council, could have no special position back home in *their* system which was governed by *their* customs and *their* traditions. There was no place for any exotic intervention irrespective of the genus to which it belonged.

The inevitable result was that the Autonomous Councils in the Tribal Areas governed by the Sixth Schedule largely remained irrelevant so far as the people are concerned. They were visualised by the people as a part of that state whose jurisdiction was not extended to these areas earlier by virtue of 'non-regulation' or 'exclusion'. Any activity which went against the well-established customs and traditions of the people, be it management of resources, or raising of taxes, by the State or the Autonomous District Council, was deemed as an uncalled for intrusion. It was successfully resisted without much effort through the sheer inertia of their living tradition. The exotic bodies including the State and the District Council could, however, operate in those aspects which, in the perception of the traditional society, were till then no-man's land like education or health services. The provisions of the Sixth Schedule, therefore, have remained largely ineffectual as no one could dare to intrude into the jurisdiction of the traditional Councils, not to speak of challenging their authority.

This situation has particularly prevailed in matters concerning the village system which was functioning like a republic. The irony is that under paragraph 3, the Autonomous District/Regional Council has been vested with all powers concerning Village Councils including their establishment, functions and powers. These Councils at the district or regional level in general, however, could not acquire legitimacy in the people's perception. Therefore, *their formal powers remained irrelevant in relation to that system at the village level, which is rooted in the traditions and customs of the people with unwavering allegiance on their part.* In fact, these 'irrelevant', 'autonomous' institutions proved to be a boon in disguise for the traditional Village Councils. Even though the formal jurisdiction concerning Village Councils is vested with the Autonomous District Councils, they had little time or energy to attend to that side. They remained engrossed, like the Panchayat Raj Institutions elsewhere, in their dealings with the State Governments, that too mostly concerning the so-called developmental activities. These activities do not comprise the real hard core of self-governance particularly in the tribal areas with a self-sufficient economy amidst rich natural resources.

Thus, in the Sixth Schedule areas, the traditional system of self-governance at the village level has remained, more or less, intact after independence. The scheme of transformation from the traditional to the formal system described as autonomous, proved to be cosmetic. It could not affect the traditional system. Rather, the weak formal structure of Autonomous District Councils provided immunity to the traditional system against the possible intervention from the more powerful forces, which could emanate from the laws enacted by the State Legislatures or the Parliament.

14 Communities in Search of Identities in Sikkim

A.C. Sinha

Sikkim joined the Indian Union in 1975. Till then, the Government of Sikkim recognised two ethnic blocks: Lepcha-Bhutia on the one side, and the largely (immigrant) Nepalese on the other. From among the Nepalese, Damai, Kami and Saraki were recognised as the Scheduled Castes and allotted a seat in the State Council and the Buddhists among the Limbus (Tshongs) were allotted another seat in the State Council in 1967. The Government of India accorded status of Scheduled Tribe to the Lepchas and Bhutias and the status of the Scheduled Caste to Damai, Kami, Manjhi and Saraki in 1978. This was done to provide constitutional framework to accord with what had been in practice since 1952. The Indians of Nepali Origin (INO=Nepamul or simply the Nepamul; Sinha, A.C. and T.B. Subba:2003) were busy in consolidating 'Nepalese solidarity' in Sikkim. They were agitated on the issue of doing away with the seat reservation for the 'Nepalese' in the State Assembly and demanded that all the 'General' seats in the State Assembly be declared as the 'reserved' for them, a demand, which was found legally unacceptable by the Supreme Court in India. In 1980s B.N. Mandal Backward Commission Report was submitted and after a good amount of debate, it was accepted for implementation in 1990s. Sikkim could not remain untouched from these developments. Demands were made to declare various communities enumerated as the 'Other Backward Classes' (OBC) and, many of the communities from among the Nepamul social commonwealth not being satisfied with the provisions of being among the OBC, further demanded to be identified as the scheduled tribes. The paper tries to report on those developments in the State of Sikkim.

For that purpose, the author feels that it is imperative to understand the legal and *dharamshashtric* stipulations of the Nepalese social structure, which continues to be relevant for the Nepamul. *Secondly*, it is also necessary to understand the on-going *janajati movement* in Nepal, because demand for tribal status by the various Nepali communities in Sikkim is largely influenced and inspired by such developments in Nepal. *Thirdly*, we have tried to briefly review the anthropological tradition of defining a community as 'tribe' and see how the concept of scheduled tribe emerged as a political nomenclature, and not a scientific anthropological one. *Fourthly*, we have subjected the Sikkimese situation in the context of the demand for Scheduled Tribal status by the various communities. And lastly, we have briefly mentioned our limited field experience with a view to verifying the claims of the various communities the status of Scheduled Tribes. At the end, we comment on the ethnic scenario in Sikkim and report how new formations are emerging because of the availability of the legal and constitutional framework.

Traditional Social World of the Nepamul Sikkimese

Communities like the Limbu, Lepcha, and Magar lived within the present boundaries of Sikkim prior to the consecration of Phuntsog Namgyal as the first Chogyal (king of righteousness) in Sikkim in 1641. However, Sikkim's boundary with Nepal was fixed in 1817, although Sikkim had a claim over Limbuan, the land east of river Arun in east Nepal. Similarly, Nepal staked its authority over Morung, the low-lying foothills below Darjeeling hills. However, there are no historical evidences or references to indicate that the other communities from among the Nepamul were in Sikkim before 1641. Hence they must have come to Sikkim during its subjugation by Nepal for some years in the end of the 18th century and more prominently after the Treaty of Segowlee signed in 1815. Bulk of the ethnic cousins of the Nepamul Sikkimese continues to reside in Nepal and are governed by prevalent social and civil codes of that country. Though there were Buddhist rulers at times in certain regions and some of the Nepamul communities claimed to have their kings in the past, Nepal had been known as a Hindu kingdom for centuries. Way back in the 14th century, King Jayasthiti Malla got the caste system codified and imposed it in Kathmandu valley over a basically egalitarian ethnic base. This was done with an eye to boost economic development by introducing professional specialization through occupational castes (Bista 1970: 56-57). Prior to consolidation of the Gorkha kingdom, Nepal was divided into sets of polities from west to east: *Baisis* (conglomeration of 22 principalities), *Chaubisis* (conglomeration of 24 principalities), Nepal (Malla rulers of Newar extraction at Patan, Kantipur and Kathmandu in the Kathmandu valley), Rais (Khambuan), and Limbus (Limbuan). Within Chaubisis, there was a small principality of Gorkha, which was destined to change the history and political structure of Nepal.

It may be noted that Nepal had a multiplicity of ethnic communities from the ancient times. In the words of Dor Bahadur Bista, "owing to lack of communication between different groups each remained in its traditional areas, isolated from other groups until quite recently...People with so many different origins and cultural backgrounds cannot possibly be arranged into a strict social framework. However, the values of the Hindu caste system tend to pervade the entire Nepal situation" (Bista 1980: xii-xiv). The western hills in Nepal were the home of Magars and Gurungs. Northern hills were abode of the Buddhist communities such as Sherpa, Tamang and Bhutia. The industrious Newars inhabited the Kathmandu Valley. Eastern Nepal was the domain of Kirata communities such as Limbu, Khambu (Rai), Yakkha, Sunuwar and Lepcha. In such a socially complex situation, there used to be small rulers in almost every mountain top or river valley. Writing in 1896, the District Recruitment Officer to the Gurkha regiments in British India, Eden Vansittart informs that among 'the aborigines of Nepal, Magars, Gurungs, Newars, Sunuwars, Rais, Yakkhas, Limbus, Tamangs and Lepchas may be counted. He also notes that Rais, Yakkhas and Limbus belong to the Kirata group' (Vansittart

1896:56). Furthermore, he records that while some Damais and Sarkis are recognized as "Gurkhalis", only 'fighting classes' consisting of the Thakuris, Khas, Magars and Gurungs are counted among the 'Gurkhalis'. Another recruitment officer, Major C.J. Morris, wrote in the same vain some four decades after Eden Vansittart in 1933 that 'Gurkhas are grouped into a large number of tribes': Thakuri, Chetri Gurung, Magar, Rai, Limbu, Sunawar, Tamang (Morris, C.J.: 1993:28). Though bulk of the recruits for the British regiments are obtained from Magar and Gurung tribes, Rais, Limbus and Sunwars are enlisted for the Gurkha regiments of the British Indian Army. With exception of certain tribes, all the Gurkhas speak Nepali, their lingua franca. Inter-tribal marriages cannot, strictly speaking, take place except between the Rais and the Limbus.

During the medieval period of its history, Nepal was divided into a series of castes and tribes and many of them spoke their own tongues. Further more, there were Buddhist Newars, who were themselves divided into castes. This was also the period, when Muslim rule in India was on decline and the British East India Company, perceived by the Nepalese rulers, to be a Christian entity, was emerging on the political scene of the subcontinent. Nepal was seen within Himavatkhand as the northern extension of Bhratkhand, the classical India of epic period. The king of Gorkha, Prithvi Narayan Shah, whose ancestors claimed to have migrated from Chittorgarh in Rajasthan to Nepal and who claimed to be 'the king of the Magars' (*Magarat ko raja mai hum*), laid the foundation of a strong Hindu kingdom. He consolidated Nepalese State into a Hindu kingdom in third quarter of 18th century by uniting 60 political units, termed it as 'real land of the Hindus', not polluted by the Muslims and Christians (*asal Hindustan),* 'a garden of four estates and 36 castes' (*4 Varnas and 36 jatis*). In his famous *Dibya Updesh* he exhorted his people thus: "...if the members of the council of nobility (*bharadar*) eschew luxury (the sound of) my sword will ring out on all four sides of (my kingdom's) boundary markers. If they take to (a life of) luxury, the country is not earned out of my small pains; it is a garden of all castes, if they have sense to realize it. All (those) of this garden, high and low, belong to the four *vernas* and thirty-six *jatis* (castes), since it is the pure land of the Hindus, should not abandon the customary religion of (their respective) lineages. (They) should redeem the master's (king's) salt…"(Sharma, P.R.: 1997:479).

A Garden of four *Varnas* and 36 *Jatis*: A Collectivity or A Hierarchy

Prithvi Narayan was a visionary in the sense that he could rally a broad cross-section of Gorkhali society inclusive of the Brahmins, the Khas, the Gurungs, the Magars, and others to his cause. His army comprised men of all the castes and social groups, an integration of some sort. The Gorkha kingdom was administered on *dharamshashtric* rules. The king, the Brahmins and the cows were above the laws. The regions vanquished by him, apart from being allotted to army commanders as *jagirs* (fiefs), were permitted to continue their customary laws and their traditional rulers were invariably not disturbed. It is a common knowledge that Gorkha kings acknowledged the continuation of 'tribal' rulers by conferring titles of '*Subba*' (revenue collectors — *Subedars* — governors in Urdu) on the Limbus, Rai (the honoured ones) on *Khambus* and *Mukhia* (the headmen) or *Dewan* (minister) to the Yakhas. Marshal communities were encouraged to emulate Khatryia style of life by adopting titles such as Singh, Rana, Jung, Bahadur, etc. and inter-marrying in Khatryia families. Many of the clan names turned out to be the titles in course of time. In this context, tribes' relaxed attitude to sex and institution of polygamy among the rulers played decisive roles. After the death of Prithvi Narayan Shah in 1775 at the age of 47 years, his successors over-ran the territories between river Sutlej in the west to river Teesta in the east and Kuti pass in Tibet in the north to northern Gangetic plains in the south. At long last, they collided with the British East India Company, ruling over India, resulting in Treaty of Sugauli in 1817. By which, within four decades after the death of great nation-builder Prithvi Narayan Shah, territorial limits of modern Nepal were fixed and Hindu kingdom of Nepal came to be recognized as semi-independent

Himalayan principality. Next three decades were the period in Nepalese history marked by court factionalism, intrigues, and murders of high functionaries and massacre of aristocrats and rule by the infant kings.

This was also the period (1816-1839), which was termed as the 'silent years' and the years of 'the silent cry' on the part of the Nepalese peoples. For Ludwig Stiller, not only was the legal dialogue of the period building up a record of legally sanctioned differences in custom and practice, it was also building up a record of differences in treatment meted out to citizens of different ethnic or caste backgrounds. The dialogues, besides preparing the way for a unified code of law was also preparing the way for a code of law that would fail to recognize that all citizens were equal before law (Stiller S.J.L.: 1976: 182). All these resulted in mass massacre of the functionaries in the royal court and emergence of Rana Jung Bahadur in 1846 as the effective power wielder in Nepal leading to an autocratic system of Ranacracy. Among many features of Rana regime, two may be noted as the most significant: complete internal autonomy and consistent friendship with the British colonial rulers in India. What resulted on the social scene of Nepal because of these developments was marked by extensive migration of the impoverished masses to India as job seekers in the form of soldiers, herdsmen, wage earners, porters, lumbers, labourers and sundry handy boys. The British did consider the Nepalese (the famous Gurkhas) as the reliable soldiers for their armed forces and constabulary and an inexpensive labour force for economic development of eastern Himalayan marches. And that is how Nepalese were encouraged to settle down in Sikkim in spite of the local opposition.

In words of historians, "Ever since king Prithvi Narayan Shah's reign in the 18th century, Nepali speaking Hindu high castes dominated the remainder of the population. In order to maintain their social position, the high caste groups had used two powerful tools — the Nepali language and the Hindu religion. The ruling elite successfully incorporated all the ethnic groups in Nepal into the caste system and those groups came to accept a subordinate position in Nepalese society as a direct result of this policy" (Hoftun *et al.*: 1999: 320). Rana Jung Bahadur promulgated the famous '*Mulki Ain*' ('national' or 'civil code') in 1854, which confirmed location of every community of Nepal in a hierarchy of social order. Among its salient features are the following: twice born supremacy (*tagadharis*), clean castes waiting to be incorporated among the twice born castes on certain conditions (*Matwali* clean castes), intoxicant communities divided into enslaveable and slaveable (*Matwalis*) ones and untouchable castes remain at the bottom of the social ladder. It attempted to arrange all the different groups in a countrywide hierarchy. John Whelpton presents a simplified form of the classical Nepalese social structure in a table adopted from Hofer's study of the 'code' and noted that the structure broadly corresponds to the present reality (Whelpton, J.: 2005: 9-10). The caste (ethnic?) hierarchy as per the *Mulki Ain* was the following:

1. *Tagadharis*: caste groups of "wearers of the holy cord" :
   Uppadhyayas
   Rajputs (Thakuris) — warriors
   Jaisis
   Chetris (Ksatri) — warriors
   Dew Bhaju (Newar Brahman)E
   Indian Brahman
   Ascetic sects (Sanyasi, etc.)
   "Lower" Jaisi
   Various Newar Castes E*
2. *Namasinya Matwalis*: Non-Enslavable Alcohol drinkers:
   Magar E
   Gurung E
   Sonuwar E
   Some other Newar castes E
3. *Mansinya Matwalis:* Enslavable Alcoholic drinkers:
   Bhote E (Tibetan and some Tibetanoids)
   Chepang E
   Kumal (potters)
   Hayu E

Tharu E
Ghart (descendants of freed slaves)

4. *Pani na chanya choi chito halmuna paranya*: Impure, but touchable :
Kasai (Newar butchers) E
Kusle (Newar musicians) E
Hindu Dhobi (Newar washermen) E
Kulu (Newar Tanners) E
Musalman *
Mlecch *
5. *Pani nachalnya choi chito halnuparnya*: untouchable castes:
Kami (blacksmith)
Sarki (shoemaker-tanner)
Kadara (Stemming from union of Kami and Sarki)
Damai (tailors and musicians)
Gaine (ministrels)
Badi (musicians)
Pore (Newar skinners and fishermen) E
Chyme (Newar scavengers) E

* = The position (status) of the caste within the group is not precisely determined.
E = Ethnic Groups

The points needs to be noted are that the Indo-Nepalese caste system had brought the Magars and the Gurungs within the caste framework by granting them position below the twice-born Khas, but above their impure castes. *Secondly*, Kiratis were placed in the same general category as the Magars and the Gurungs, — pure but not with the twice born. *Thirdly*, unlike the tribes in the western parts of Nepal, the Kiratis were not intimately associated with the Nepal State and possibly negotiated their internal autonomy and communal land ownership (*kipat* system) as the price for submission to the Gorkha rule. It is another matter that Newars and Kiratis were not admitted into the army in pre-Rana Gorkha State.

The significant point for us is that about 20 per cent population of Nepal known as 'other hill or mountain ethnic groups (tribes)' were termed as the clean castes, but were not entitled to wear sacred thread, a mark of ritual superiority among the Hindus. The communities counted among them were (Whelpton, J.: 1997:53): Magar (7.2%), Tamang (5.5%), Rai (2.8%), Gurung (2.4%), Limbu (1.6%), Sherpa (0.6%), Chepang (0.2%), Sunawar (0.2%), Bhotiya (0.1%), Thakali (0.1%), and Thami (0. 1%). While all ethnic groups could be enslaved in the first half of the nineteenth century, this could no longer be done to higher castes Hindus. It was in the course of the second half of the nineteenth century that first the Magars and Gurungs and then other ethnic groups were freed from liability to the penalty of enslavement (Pfaff-Czarnecka, J.: 1997:430). Various social groups were engaged in upward mobility by adopting traits of Brahminical style of life. Moreover, the *model of sanskritization* was available to ethnic groups to raise their status in the caste hierarchy of the country. By this way, they did invite the Brahmins to officiate as the priests on various rituals, ceremonials and on the eve of the rite-de passage among most of the communities and, at the same time, they continued to practice their local level ethnic customs and traditions. The communities began to adopt markedly Hindu festivals such as Dasai, Dewali, Sankranti, Holi and so on. They began to hire the Brahmins to solemnize their marriages, use vermilion and strings made of green small beads as marks of the Nepalese Hindu married women's symbols and even cremate their dead. All through Rana period in Nepalese history, the social scene of the country was governed by the above civil code. In spite of the democratic experiment in 1950s, the *Mulki Ain* continued till king Mahendra abrogated it in 1963, but ethnic situation remained frozen on the model of the past practices. Things began to change in 1980s, when we learn the formation of *MAGURALI* (MAGAR-GURUNG-RAI-LIMBU), as an informal hill ethnic federation. Stirrings were on till 1990, when Nepal was declared as a multi-ethnic and multi-lingual State despite calling itself a 'Hindu Kingdom'. So far the State is concerned, Nepal did not declare the ethnic groups as the 'scheduled tribes' and their 'untouchable castes' as the 'scheduled castes' as done under 1950 Constitution of Indian Union with serious political and socio-economic consequences.

Nepal Janajati Mahasangh: Nepal Federation of the Nationalities (NEFEN)

Very soon *Nepal Janajati Mahasangh (Nepal Federation of the Nationalities, NEFEN)* was established (in 1990) to bring in all the ethnic bodies under one umbrella. To begin with, NEFEN was founded as a federation of seven different organizations: four represented Newars, Tamangs, Magars and Gurungs, the other three were Kiranti bodies, one representing Limbus, and two Rais. By 1995 it was agreed among the members that there could be only one representative body per ethnic group and thus, the federation in 1995 accepted only 21 such groups as the members (Gellner, D.A.: 1997:20). On the pattern of neighbouring democratic India, the 'tribes' demanded political, economic and social shares 'reserved' for them in the political system of Nepal.The federation claims to speak on behalf of its members on ethnic matters to the 'State' as such. Nineteen federating units are listed in its pamphlet brought out in 1993. In spite of its claim to be a non-political body; its 17-point demands submitted to the government are unmistakably political. NEFEN maintained an anti-Brahmin attitude in its dealings with various communities. Its members were supposed to be avowedly anti-Hindu. So much so that when the associations of the Chhetris and the Dalits tried to join NEFEN, they were advised to shun Hindu practices before they could be welcomed in the 'club' and naturally their request was turned down (Gellner, D.N.: 1997:22). Thus, now there is a trend among the ethnic groups in Nepal at large to distance themselves from the Hindu caste system, Brahminical practices and what came to be termed as the Hindu great traditions. The ethnic groups are now engaged in emphasizing their distinctive markings away from the caste Hindus.

Further more, NEFEN responded on U.N. resolution of December 1993 calling for a *decade of Indigenous Peoples* on March 1994 by defining "Indigenous People" of Nepal as those communities:

"1. which possess their own distinct and original lingual and cultural traditions and whose religious faith is based on ancient animism (worshipers of ancestors, land, season, nature), or who do not claim "the Hinduism" enforced by the State, as their traditional and original religion;

2. those existing descendants of the peoples whose ancestors had established themselves as the first settlers or principal inhabitants in any part of the land falling within the territory of modern state (Nepal), or/and who inhabit the present territory of Nepal at the time when the persons of different cultures and ethnic origin arrived there and who have their own history (written or oral) and historical continuity;
3. which have been displaced from their own land for the last four centuries, particularly during the expansion and establishment of modern Hindu nation State and have been deprived of their traditional rights to own the natural resources (Kipat — communal land, cultivable land, water, minerals, trading points etc.);
4. who have been subjugated in the State's political power setup (decision-making process), whose ancient culture, language and religion are non-dominant and social values (are) neglected and humiliated;
5. whose society traditionally erected on the principle of egalitarianism — rather than hierarchy of the Indo-Aryan caste system and gender equality (or rather women enjoying more advantageous positions) — rather than social, economic and religious subordination of women, but whose social norms and values have been slighted by the State;
6. which formally or informally, admit or claim to be "the indigenous peoples of Nepal" on the basis of the aforementioned characteristics"(Indigenous: 1994:23).

Tribe, Caste and Community: the British Understanding

Coming to the Indian situation, it was Alfred C. Lyall, who initiated a debate on the nature of the Indian society in post-1857 period (Owen, R.: 1973: 223-243). And it was agreed as a policy to show India as a divided entity between castes, tribes, races, regions, religions, languages, food habits, dresses and what not and it was made loud and clear that India was just a geographical entity held together by the British might. Moreover, it was presumed that it was in the colonial interest to show India divided in various ways enumerated above. The census operations, district gazetteers, 'Peoples of India' series of publications and tribal monographs were used to show the variety within India with ethnographic support and purposefully collated write-ups were touted as the scientific treatises. Then came the British administrative policy to the distant areas inhabited by the turbulent tribes in the form of special dispensation to the frontier tracts. These tracts were turned into '*backward areas*' in the Government of India Act, 1919, which came to be known as the "*Excluded and Partially Excluded Areas*' as per the Government of India Act, 1935. Colonial administrators and some of the Christian missionaries were conspiring to carve out a *Crown Colony in North-East India and Upper Burma* in the second quarter of the twentieth century on the eve of the Indian independence. With a view to forestalling such divisive moves, the *Constituent Assembly of India* came out with provisions of the '*Sixth Schedule for the Tribes*' of North-East India in the Indian Constitution, applicable since 1950.

All through eighteenth and first half of the nineteenth century, British scholars did not distinguish between 'tribes' and 'castes' in Indian social situation. So much so that while what came to be known as the tribe were invariably termed as *savage, barbarian, primitive, wild* etc. and there were references such as the *Brahmin Tribes, Rajput Tribes, Jat Tribes, Muslim Tribes*, etc. indicating that there was hardly any difference between castes and the tribes in those days. Events of 1857 led to a racial polarization, in which the British went all the way to establish whiteman's racial superiority. Incidentally, this also marked the beginning of ethnological investigation allover the world. Charles Darwin's *Origin of Species* was published in 1858 followed by his *Origin of Man* and Louis Henry Morgan's *Ancient Society* in 1871. The age of geographical discoveries, scientific explorations, and a number of technological inventions preceded this. Australia, Latin America, Africa, and bulk of Asia were already divided among the European

Imperial powers. Science was the key word of the age; 'progress' was the *mantra* of the period; and whiteman of Anglo-Saxon extraction was taken to represent the apex of human civilization. Though African and Asians were considered as 'the Whiteman's burden, who were deemed *"half devil and half child"* (Kipling, R.: 1977). "That was also the heyday of the museums. Science teaching was focused around show cases exhibiting specimens classified by types — fossils, rocks, insects, stuffed birds, caged animals in zoo — fixed entities, changeless, everlasting" (Hugh-Jones, S. and J. Ludlow: 2000: 84). There was also a new movement to lay down Botanical Gardens all over the world, which did not only have scientific motives, but also commercial ones. Morgan's evolutionary formulations with its three-fold sub-divisions: savagery, barbarism and civilization was taken to be as if the final truth.

Human beings were 'objectified'; they were to be scientifically measured and photographed as specimens representing a type; their indices were to be established so that generalizations (principles) could be made. Edward Tuit Dalton reports in his *Descriptive Ethnography of Bengal* how a grand design of ethnographic mapping of India for the sake of scientific understanding was proposed in 1868. It was proposed that two specimens of every Indian community (as their nominated representatives) were to be sent to Jubbolpore, at the centre of India, to be measured and photographed with a view to developing an understanding of the Indian peoples. Unfortunately for the sake of the British science, the Chief Commissioner of Assam spoiled the game. He informed his superiors in Calcutta that he would not risk a rebellion on hand, as his specimens might die on way to or from Jubbolpore because of the hot climatic conditions between his domain and the place of proposed *ethnographic fair* in Central India. The Imperial government could not dare to risk such an adventure and the ethnographic fair could not be held on time. However, E.T. Dalton was asked to complete the *Descriptive Ethnography* on the basis of his own data, reports from administrators, missionaries, explorers, travellers and, in fact, anybody, who could volunteer to report and photograph the subjects. And that is how Dalton's famous Descriptive ethnography was compiled, which became a model for the future Peoples of India volumes (Dalton, E.T.: 1872).

The first population census of India was conducted in 1872, for which British ethnographers' help was sought in formulating the questions to be asked to the respondents. Since then, India is one of the few countries of the world, which has regularly conducted census operations every ten years. From the beginning, anthropologists were associated with its operations. Herbert H. Risley was the Census Commissioner for 1901, who in course of time, published *Castes and Tribes of Bengal* and *Peoples of India*. John H. Hutton was the Census Commissioner of 1931operation and his data on castes and communities are still considered as the most authentic such figures used by the Governments and the political activists. It was J.H. Hutton, who used the term, 'scheduled castes' for the communities known as such today and identified seven attributes for a caste to be so listed. The volumes on different 'provinces' were written for British administrators in a rounded manner; locations from where the data were collected not mentioned; differences in practice were ignored within a community and efforts were made to show the distinctions between the communities. Administrators, missionaries, explorers, adventurers and petty government officials provided the data for these volumes. It is interesting to note that data on origin, food habits, religious beliefs, social practices such as marriage, dress, ornaments, industry, tools and implements and even hair-do of the communities were described to show them different from 'others'. Similarly, the photographs of the community specimens were taken from front and sides, besides sex-wise indices.

In the year 1873, an *Inner Line Act* was passed, by which tribes residing in the hills were prohibited from crossing an imaginary line to the plains in Assam. Similarly, any non-tribal missionary, explorer, traveller, businessman, wood-cutter, hunter, and honey collector was to seek written permission from competent authorities to enter such designated areas. The British intention was to safeguard the tea plantations in the plains from tribal raids. Similarly, they intended to provide security to the non-tribal entrants to the hills from the tribes and tried to see that they did not exploit the 'simple' hill communities. The Governor of the province was to administer such areas at his discretion. Present day Arunachal Pradesh, Nagaland and Mizoram came under such dispensation. The Government of India Act, 1919, declared these areas as the '*Backward Tracts*' and kept them away under the special power of the Governor separate from the legislative perview of the provinces. In the year 1935, these backward tracts of Lakhimpur, Sadiya, and Balipara frontier tracts, Naga Hills District, and Lushai Hills District were termed as the '*Excluded Areas*' and the Garo Hills District and Darjeeling were clubbed among the '*partially excluded areas*'. It may not be out of place to inform the readers that the Government of India appointed J.P. Mills, ICS, a bureaucrat trained in anthropology, as the *first Tribal Adviser to the Governor of Assam* in 1940s, followed by another bureaucrat, Nari K. Rustomji. And for the last ten years, 1953-1964, it was Verrier Elwin, a self-taught ethnographer, who advised the Governor of Assam on tribal affairs. Once the Constituent Assembly met for drafting the future Constitution of India, it made the provision for listing such excluded and partially excluded areas under the 'Sixth Schedule' with special dispensations.

Tribal Policy in the Indian Union

Tribal communities attracted attention of Indian social reformers, political activists and the Hindu ascetics from western India. On the basis of their faith, customs, institutions and living in the contiguous hilly tracts, especially in the western peninsular India, these good-doers termed the tribes as the '*backward Hindus*'. On the other hand, the British administrators, missionaries, and anthropologists found the tribes a different world all together and they were to be treated separately. While the formers charged the latter to entertain the tribes as museum specimen, the latter found the formers swallowing the tribes under the discriminative caste ridden Hindu system. In this context, the acrimonious debate between assimilative Bombay sociologist, G.S. Ghurye and missionary turned ethnographer, Verrier Elwin (1943) is relevant. Ghurye charged Elwin to follow a policy towards the tribes, which he termed *'isolationist'* and *maintaining them as museum species for study of the anthropologists* (Ghurye, G.S.: 1943), a charge, which the latter vehemently denied and 'pleaded for a slow pace of development for the tribes; so that they could absorb the shock of change smoothly'. It is to the credit of the independent India that two great humanists, Jawaharlal Nehru and Verrier Elwin, evolved a rational, human and scientific tribal policy for the integration of the tribes within the larger Indian society, while maintaining their innate ethos. In course of time, this policy came to be known as the "*Tribal Panchsheel*", five co-related aspects of tribal development and administration (Elwin, V. : 1964).

Tribes were accorded special treatment along with *the Dalits* in the Constitution of India by providing special measures for their representation in the policy-making bodies, creating avenues for their socio-economic advancement and taking care of their over-all welfare. They were listed for such a treatment initially for a period of ten years, which was later extended indefinitely. As the resources were limited in early 1950s, welfare measures were also modest. Now, the measures for the tribal welfare have been increased in quantity and quality and, consequently, the quality of their life must have improved, though one must hasten to add that tribes continue to remain one of the least developed segments of the Indian population. Now there is an academic and also a common sense problem: Who are the tribes? What makes them distinct from that of the other population? Are the 'scheduled tribes' the same what anthropologists consider as the 'tribes'? Anthropologists, who claim to have specialized on studying the tribes, have advanced many definitions, which create problems in evolving a universally acceptable definition of the phenomena (Beteille, A.: 1974: 61-74). Beteille examines some of the definitions provided by the leading anthropologists and shows that most of the definitions are either contextual to the 'tribe' under study or they refer to a list of the characteristics found in the 'tribe' studied by the particular author. So much so that even the most standard and obvious source of definition of the phenomenon gives about half a dozen meaning of the term 'tribe'.

Anthropological Approach to the 'Tribes'

Oxford English Dictionary provides a definition of 'Tribe', which may lead to the following: (i) Tribe has varied meanings; synonymous with family, lineage, or even community with defined Territory. (ii) Tribe means 'an organization of peoples along ethnic lines'. (iii) Tribe is 'an administrative category as in Solon's Athens'. (iv) Tribe is 'a political division of people as in ancient Rome'. (v) Tribe is 'merely a geographical or a territorial category as in the Bermudas'. (vi) Tribe is 'a community of peoples claiming common descent and generally practicing endogamy. (vii) Tribe is 'a simple society guided by a headman or a chief' (Beteille, A.: 1974). However, this inability of the scholars to provide a comprehensive and, if not universal, near universal definition of 'tribe' does not necessarily display their academic inadequacy. It is also pertinent to understand that the extent, spread, variety, stage of technology, and sophistication of culture are as well responsibility for defining them in an acceptable way. Look at the scenario; from vanishing Red Indians to Arrant, Onge, Birhor, Santal, Agnate, Khasi, Monpa, Bhil, and etecetra: how to describe all of them in to a single definition? Thus, we are forced with accepting a working formula by identifying the salient features of the tribe. *Thus, we assume a tribe to be more or less homogeneous society having a common government, a common language/dialect, and a common culture.*

For the policy framers, above anthropological predicament of defining the tribe was of no help, as various pressure groups were in no mood to wait for an ideal definition of the tribe. They acted on the second best option they had. The Indian policy-makers were aware of the 'tribal tracts', excluded and partially excluded areas. Then there were hill districts. All these regions were known to be abodes of the tribes. Then there were census reports, in which communities were enumerated by castes and tribes. It became obvious that by the time of 1931 census, the distinction between tribes and castes had become an issue of some importance. Tribes came to be viewed more and more in religious and not just in ecological terms. " If a group could be shown clearly 'Hindu' in its religious beliefs and practices, it was a caste; if it was (an) 'Animist', it had to be treated as a 'tribe' (Beteille, A.: 1974: 63). Indian society in 1940s presented a confusing array of the variety in terms of hierarchy, economy, religiosity and ecological expanse. Demand on the political economy of the time was so pressing that special provisions had to be made. It is instructive to know that prior to terming the 'tribes' as the "scheduled tribes" in the Indian Constitution on the pattern of the 'scheduled castes' these communities were variously termed by the British administrators as the 'primitive tribes', 'aboriginal tribes', and 'backward tribes'. However, "before promulgating the list of the Scheduled Tribes in 1950, the State Governments were requested to suggest tests for determining as to which of the tribes should be treated as Scheduled Tribes. The criteria suggested by 14 State Governments were mentioned in Appendix IV of the First Report of the Commissioner for Scheduled Castes & Scheduled Tribes (1951). They offered conflicting views. However, the following appeared to be the features common to the tribes in various States: (i) tribal origin, (ii) primitive way of life and habitation in remote and less easily accessible areas, and (iii) general backwardness in all respects" (Tripathi, C.B.: undated). Thus, what construed, as the political management in the form of '*Scheduled Tribes*' has to be seen in relation to then existing politico-economic scenario of the country. Thus, it is difficult to identify a single way of satisfactory classification of 427 tribes originally listed as the 'Scheduled Tribes' in 1950. The writer of these lines is not aware of if any community has been de-listed from the above, but the current list of such communities has 698 entries.

The list of the Scheduled Tribes has a notional image of being economically backward, but it does not mean that all of them are equally and similarly backward. There are communities, which are extremely vulnerable from economic point of view such as Birhar of Chhotanagpur. Then, there are tribes like Nocte Nagas, who are Vaishnawite Hindus; others are similarly, Hindus, Buddhists, Christians, nature worshipers and even Muslims. They are spread from extreme north of the country, Ladakh to the south, Andaman Islands and east in Manipur to west in Rajasthan. Some of the tribes are located in only one small corner of the country, while there are some, which are spread in many states. There are tribes in the schedule, who number in double digit demographically and others, whose size run into hundreds of thousands. From cultural point of view, some of them have a tradition of very rich heritage and others have a simpler form. Way back in 1950s, Anthropological Survey of India (ASI) conducted '*cultural traits survey of India*' (Bose, N.K.: 1961). Some three decades later, the ASI similarly mapped out the country from cultural and social points view through its massive project of '*Peoples of India*' and published a series of volumes on various states. From political points of view, the Scheduled Tribes were organized in 'states,' principalities, chieftain ships, elders' councils, village panchayats and some other forms of administration. Sum total of the entire arguments is the conclusion that except being listed as socially and economically the most backward communities in the country, the Scheduled Tribes among themselves have very little in common. And that explains partly the absence of an all India forum for the Scheduled Tribes.

Most of the Scheduled Tribes of North-East Region are demographically small in size. And that's why none of the three largest Scheduled Tribes, Bhil, Gond and Santhal, are from North East India and their problem are also basically different, as these large tribes live side by with the hierarchical Hindu society. Commenting in a different context, a perceptive scholar has following to record: "The tribes of Central and Western India are completely different from tribal communities in North-East, where there is better education and other facilities and indeed, where tribal political elite have been in power for 50 years, as in the case of the Khasi, Jaintia and Garo Hills, which became Meghalaya in 1972. One could remark that so-called primitiveness of the tribes is more in the Fifth Schedule States (outside the North-East Region), where education, political awareness and empowerment as well health facilities are extremely poor and income levels at the bottom. The mainstreaming of these groups, where their lands have been taken over by plain settlers and others, has not really helped them very much. Indeed, it has devastated their culture, their environment and their social standing as well as their economic status" (Hazarika, S.: 2004).

Ethnic Scenario in Sikkim since 1950

On December 5, 1950 the Maharaja of Sikkim, Sir Tashi Namgyal, signed the Treaty between India and Sikkim. By then India had already sent J.S. Lall, ICS as the Dewan (chief administrator) of the State. The political parties were agitating for people's participation in the administrative affairs of the State. In this background, the Mahrajkumar (the crown prince, Palden Thondup Namgyal) made the representatives of the political parties agree to an '*ethnic parity*' formula in May 1951, by which Lepcha-Bhutia communities were equated with the Nepalese communities for political representation in the future. In January 1952, the ruler issued a Proclamation envisaging an elected State Council. The Proclamation envisaged that while the Nepalese candidates were to be elected by the entire electorate of the constituency in question, the Lepcha-Bhutia candidates were first to be elected by the Lepcha-Bhutia voters only of the constituency concerned and thereafter to be voted again by the whole electorate of the constituency (Basnet, L.B., 1974). The Maharaja issued a Constitutional Proclamation on March 23, 1953 laying down the rules for the formation of State Council, Executive Council, their powers and their functions. The State Council was to consist of six Lepcha-Bhutia, six Nepalese and six 'nominated' members. The plea was that the Lepcha-Bhutia were considered original settlers of the land and the Nepalese were seen as the recent migrants from Nepal. On the eve of the third General Election in 1967, one seat each for the 'Scheduled Castes' (Damai, Kami, and Sarki from among the Nepalese 'untouchables') and Tshongs (a section of the Limbus, who were alleged to be Buddhists) were added to the Council on the ethnic consideration (Sinha, A.C.: 1975).

Once the Tripartite Agreement was signed between ruler of

Sikkim, representative of the Government of India and leaders of the political parties in Sikkim, a thirty-two member State Council was envisaged. The Agreement envisaged a State Council in which there were to be 15 seats each for the Lepcha-Bhutia and Nepalese of Sikkim and one seat for the Scheduled Castes and another for the Buddhist monasteries. And 1974 election was fought on that basis and once the State was merged with India in 1975 the State Council was termed as the State Assembly. The Bill No. 79 (for re-arranging the seats in the State Assembly in Sikkim) was introduced in the Lok Sabha on May 18, 1979, which became an act in 1981.This parliamentary provision stipulated 12 seats reserved for the minority Lepcha-Bhutia communities, two seats for the Scheduled Castes, one for the Monasteries and rest of 17 seats were declared as the 'General, on which, any Indian who is a *bona fide* voter in Sikkim, could be elected. Keeping in mind that the Lepcha-Bhutias have a distinct culture and tradition, which is different from that of the Nepalese, they have been treated as the Scheduled Tribes under Article 342 of the Constitution of India (Kazi, J.N.: 1994: 339).

Consolidation of Nepamul and Emergence of the OBC

Nar Bahadur Bhandari's third term as the Chief Minister of Sikkim from 1989 onwards marked the gradual integration of the State into the Indian political system. This was also the year, Indian National Congress (I) lost the power at the Centre and a rag-tag coalition of political parties in Delhi under the leadership of former Congress man, V.P. Singh came to power. With a view to garnering Hindu support base in its favour, Bharatiya Janata Party (BJP) launched a movement to construct a temple of Lord Rama at Ayodhya, a holy site in the State of Uttar Pradesh on a disputed plot of land, where an unused mosque stood for centuries. This emotive move of B.J.P polarized the Indian society into Hindus and Muslims. With a view to counteracting such a development, Prime Minister V.P. Singh removed the collected dust from the Report of the 'Backward Class Commission', filed by a backward caste activist, B.N. Mandal and decided to implement some of its recommendations. In view of the Mandal Commission, a bunch of intermediary castes (below the twice born and above the untouchable castes) were identified as 'Other Backward Classes' (OBC) and 27 per cent reservation for them on the basis of their population in 1931 was recommended in the jobs and educational institutions. The communities listed as the beneficiaries in the Report mounted an aggressive demand for the implementation of the recommendations of the Report. Naturally, Sikkim could not remain untouched from this development. Chief Minister Bhandari, hailing from a Chhetri caste, instead of responding positively to the demand of the OBC, was spearheading demand for recognition of Nepali language as one of the Indian national languages.

By then Bhandari had reached a plateau in his political career as a leader of a regional political party, Sikkim Sangram Parishad. He was turning impatient and arrogant with his people, as the members of his political party occupied all seats in State Assembly. One of his long time associates, Pawan Kumar Chamling, a Minister in the State cabinet, raised the issue of implementing the Report of the Mandal Commission in Sikkim in 1992 and for that he was expelled from the Sikkim Sangram Parishad Legislature Party. Thus, P.K. Chamling occupied the lone seat on the opposition bench in the State Assembly. However, a turning point came very soon, the State Assembly passed the resolution against the implementation of the Mandal Commission Report in 1994. Very soon, 19 out of 31 members of the SSP legislature party deserted the Chief Minister Bhandari and formed a parallel Sikkim Sangram Parishad (Sanchman). Bhandari was voted out of office on May 19, 1994 and Sanchman Limbu was appointed the new Chief Minister. The first move of the new Sanchman government was to recommend to the Union Government to include seven communities from among the Sikkimese of Nepali origin as 'socially and educationally backward Classes' (OBC). Consequently, Bhujel, Gurung, Limbu, Mangar, Rai, Sunawar and Tamang were declared as the OBC in Sikkim on June 2, 1994.

Claim for the Scheduled Tribal Status and Looking for the Evidence

Even this belated step did not satisfy the aspirations of some of the communities such as Limbus, whose reserved seat in the State

Council as the Tshongs was undone in 1974. They continued to press for recognition of their status as 'Scheduled Tribe'. Thus, in December 2002, Limbus and Tamangs were accorded the status of Scheduled Tribes in Sikkim and Darjeeling district of West Bengal. Furthermore, in partial modification of earlier orders by Notification No.2/WD of June 2, 1994 and Notification No. 236/SW/251(3)/WD dated June 15, 2000, the State Government of Sikkim declared (i) Bhujel, (ii) Dewan, (iii) Gurung, (iv) Jogi, (v) Kirat Rai, (vi) Mangar, (vii) Sunawar, (viii) Thami as the 'Most Backward Classes (MBC) and (i) Bahun, (ii) Chetri, (iii) Newar and (iv) Sanyasi as the 'Other Backward Classes' (OBC) in Sikkim (Sikkim Government Gazette: Extraordinary. No. 308 dated Gangtok, Friday 19th September, 2003). To add to the pitch further, the State Cabinet decided on January 29, 2005 that the Lepcha Scheduled Tribe would be accorded the status of 'Most Primitive Tribe' (MPT) in Sikkim, a status unknown to the Government of India. It appears that the Government of Sikkim is not aware of the implication of such a move at all India level.

It is known since 1979 that the Government of Sikkim and people of Nepalese origin in Sikkim have been demanding for the reservation of seats for the Nepalese in the State Assembly, as it was done for the community between 1953 to 1979 in the State Council. However, it has not been conceded till date, but Sikkim has joined North-Eastern Council (NEC) for the purpose of overall development. There are a number of States in North-East India within NEC, which are known as the 'tribal States', as they have more than their fifty per cent population recognized as the scheduled tribes. The Government of Sikkim approached the Government of India to accord the status of the Scheduled Tribes to the communities listed as the Most Backward Classes (MBC) by them.

Reading the Ethnographic Reports on the Communities: Out of eight communities claiming status of the Scheduled Tribes, six of them filed their 'ethnographic reports' before the appointed Committee looking into the issue: Bhujel, Dewan, Gurung, Magar, Rai and Sunuwar. Two of them, Jogi and Thami, did neither approach the Committee with their demands nor their spokesmen could be identified by the concerned functionaries of the State Government for filing their petition, if any. All the communities claimed to be the 'kirat'; emphasised uniqueness of their daily practices distinct from others; tried to prove that they were ancient communities with history, kingdoms, language and script; claimed different food items, artifacts, crafts, architects, even vocations. None of them referred to their unique myths of migration, genealogies, animist belief as a form of faith. All of them quoted the same historical sources of British army recruitment offices, whose speculative reports may not have much scientific validity. Similarly, G.P. Singh's speculative Kirat history, based on largely conjectural Indological evidence, was taken as the proven historical fact. These claims run counter to certain realities: extensive inter-marriage among the demographically small migrant communities, largely mixed settlements of the Nepamul migrants along with local tribesmen and extensive sanskritisation of their social world. Instead of emphasising their folk traditions of pre-literate stage, the thrust had been on script and language, which are invariably neither written nor spoken today. They are trying to be tribals and accordingly, they are acting as such: "We must learn how to be a tribe. This is difficult for us, but very, very important" — said 70 years old leader of Darjeeling's Mukhia/Sunuwar/Rai Ethno-Political organisation, Mr. Mukhia in his Hill Boarding School English (Shneiderman, S. and Mark Turin: 2006: 54).

The above anthropologists referred a comical case of their own work. Mark Turin had compiled a thin pocket size volume of Thami dictionary of endangered native lexicon. The dictionary did not serve the purpose in the expatriate ethnic groups in India, who found it too small to help their claims of Scheduled Tribal status. The same year, in fact, a more substantial Thami-English Dictionary was published by a member of the community, bolstered by a high number of Nepali loan words. This served the ethno-political agenda far better, more words that could be included, the heavier and, therefore, a more appropriate component of a tribal portfolio. Taking the point further, they informed us how the State Government has got 13 tribal languages listed as official language, in which *Sikkim*

Herald, the Government weekly news bulletin, is published. It is entirely another matter that many of these languages are neither spoken, nor read by their claimed patrons. Similarly, they noted a peculiar Sikkimese phenomena of scriptophilia. Most of the communities staking claim for tribal distinctiveness, are busy evolving their 'lost ancient' scripts largely borrowing from the Deonagri script of Nepali, which is the lingua franca of Sikkim (Shneiderman, S. and M. Turin: 2006).

Field Observation from the Tribal Sikkim: With a view to understanding the ground reality, we decided to visit certain villages of the various communities to see for ourselves how unique they are in their actual every day lives. A glimpse of the field report is recorded below:

Gurungs /Thami: They claim that traditional vocation had been sheep rearing. In fact, some of them still tend sheep, their traditional vocation; they cannot graze them on the barren or forestland, as it is against the laws relating to the forests. They do spin woollen threads and weave them into blankets, rugs, and other forms of daily necessities. There were households, which were settled in the village for the last 8 generations, say around 1800 AD or soon after. They eat basically millet products; forment millet beer at home and use milk products on occasions of celebration. Though they take help of their community elders as medicine men, priests, sorcerors and diviners, there are occassions, when rich among them hire Brahmins to solemnize the weddings. In case of the inter-tribal marriages, which are more common than before, the community formally adopts the girl in the 'tribe', and then follow their normal marriage rituals. There are some Jogis and Rais in the village.

Megitara is a Buddhist village near Rinchenpong bazaar; They do sheep breeding along with cultivation of the dry crops on the slops, as there are no rice fields in the village. They are building a Lamaist Gompha in the village with monetary help from the government here too; nobody speaks Gurung language. We visited near by *Sangadorji* village, where we found three traditional Gurung houses on age-old structure. They were crumbling in the absence of maintenance. The Government should help these houses to be maintained as heritage, may be with help of INTAK etc.

Besides the Gurung Taksari (copper miner and coin minters) family of Mr. B.B. Gurung, there were two families of Gurungs: Dhanu Thikadar and Param Thikadar, who had taken land on lease from the Estate department of the Namgyal rulers. This has to be seen in the light of the Namchi Kazi family in Western Bhutan, who were ruthless landlords on the Duar settlers. They held land lease for mining lime, sand, and stone; clearing the forest and settling the Paharias for the Dorji family, who held fiefdom over the Western Bhutan.The question to be reconciled is : How come the Gurungs, who are traditionally the denizen of the region north-west of Kathmandu valley and engaged in sheep grazing, travelled all the way to the slops of mount Kanchanjunga and Bhutan Duars and, though most of them remain marginal subsistence cultivators, some of them were assigned feudal privileges of landlords and minting the copper coins?

Rais or *Khambus* : *Meyong* village is close by Rinchengpong dakbungalow and has 188 households. They are bilingual, speaking Rai or Bantawa at home and Nepali outside. The village was reportedly settled some 6 generations back; say in around 1870s. It is believed that a British lady, possibly the Political Officer's wife, camping at Rinchingpong dakbungalow, visited the village and found the Rai villagers so servile that they could mew their voice like a cat. Since then the village came to be named 'Meyong after cat's mew'. Right from the hilltop to the bank of the river stream down below, the entire slop is inhabited by the Rais. There are many Rai villages in the locality. Many of the Rais are strict vegetarian, as they follow Prarthana Samaj and Kabirpanth. Of late, some other Hindu ascetic sects, from outside Sikkim or local, have emerged in the region with considerable following :

Magar: Saldung, is a Magyar village in Chakhung Constituency and has more than 200 households and it has the distinction of being the biggest Magar village with as much as 1,000 voters. They claimed that it was an old village with a small Hindu Kali temple at the bottom of the slop, which produced a copper plate dated sambat 1913 (1856 AD) as the date of its foundation. We saw it, but an authority did not issue it, though its antiquity may be questioned, but if it was a genuine one, then the temple suggests that the village was in existence in 1850s. Apparently, it is an old village, as right at the top of the village on a hilltop, there are relics of Magargarhi or Magardzong, a Magar fort. As Jarathan, the alleged settlement established by the Gorkha General Jawahar Singh Thapa prior to 1700s , this area is likely to be under the Gorkhas during 1770 to 1815. And thus, the village has its antiquity. However, none of the Magars could speak their tongue in the village. Magars, Gurungs, Jogis and Dewans inter-marry among themselves.

Jogis: They claim to be the followers of Yogi Gorakhnath, a *tantric* sage of medieval period. Gorkha rulers, the ancestors of the present king of Nepal, were said to be his followers and Jogis claim to be the royal priests. They are unlike the Brahmins, who go on reciting holy prayers and *mantras* in the night and blowing conch shell for the welfare of the community and visit the householders in the morning to collect uncooked food items from the respective benefactors. They do not officiate as the priests for religious occasions. They are a type of degraded Brahmins, who do not live in compact settlements in the villages. They worship Kali and Bhairav. They claim to have 108 *Gotras* (clans) such as Kashyap, Kasi, Kaushila, etc. As their number is small and they live scattered in various villages, they inter-marry with Magars, Sunawars and others. For the purpose of the appointed Committee, nobody appeared before it or made memoranda or filed a claim for acquainting others with their problems, if any. It appears that the community does not have even a social or cultural or a welfare body representing them unlike the cases of other communities in the State. They do not have their distinct language and speak Nepali.

At long last, we could locate a Jogi, Man Bahadur (50), son of late Ganga Prasad Jogi, in the Magar village of Saldung, who had married a Magar lady some 16 years back. As his in-laws provided land to him, he resides in this village cultivating it and does not follow his caste profession of reciting *mantras* in the night and blowing conch shells, rather he appeared to be apologetic about doing so in the past by his ancestors. Earlier he resided with his father and brothers (M.B. Jogi, Chaturman Jogi and Kaila Jogi) and first wife, who expired, at Sherpa Gaon, Upper Burmiok, West district. His brothers reside at Hathi Dhunga, West district. Two of his nephews, Til Bahadur Jogi and his brother, sons of Jogi Kaila, reside at Rinchingpong village working as school teacher and in the State Electricity Department respectively. There are Jogis found in the following villages: 7/8 houses at Sherpa Gaon, Upper Burmiok; 5 houses at Dorong in Kamling Block; approximately 10 houses at Ralang; 8/10 houses at Jerung; 15/20 houses at Nandu Gaon in Namchi Assembly constituency; 3 houses at Lingchom in Geyzing Constituency; 5/6 houses at Soreng village; One house of one Arun Jogi at Tatopani near Reshi. Goverdhan Jogi (78) and Purna Bahadur Jogi (67) residents of Upper Burmiok claim that their families were residing in the village for the last four generations.

Bhujels: Their traditional occupations have been making of beaten parched rice (chira) and *palanquin* bearing. They are also found scattered in the villages; there is hardly a Bhujel village in Sikkim. The informant, Hastaman Bhujel (about 65/70 years of age), resides at Tadong in his father-in-law's house, as his father had sold all his land in the village Sanga Dorji. There are Bhujel houses at Chakhung, Gyalzing Kyonsa (one house) and Sanga Dorji (one household).

Sunawars or Mukhias or Koincho: It is the community, who by tradition make bamboo crafts: doko, thumse, nanglo, dalo and a variety of baskets. They are proficient hunters. The literal meaning of 'Koincho' is the one, who looks down from a height, i.e. who are proficient in climbing trees. They were also reported to be settlers of high mountain slops. They claim to have 12 clans such as Lawkush, Rujiz. They claim to have their own language, which they have forgotten and are trying to revive. They have their own tradition of diviners, who secretly perform their rituals at night.

However, of late they have been calling Brahmins to officiate as the family priests on occasions. It is reported that there are about 50 houses of the Sunwars at Chakhung, Chumbung and Pokki Gaon, where some of the respondants informed that they had been there for the last 5 generations. Furthermore, Sunawars are found at Galling (3 or 4 houses), Dara Gaon, Mendo Gaon to Khola Ghari in Chakhung Constituency (about 35 houses).

Dewan or the Yakhas: Limbus, Khambus and Yakhas claim to be the 'Quirt', which claim to have their kipat land. Yakhas, who relate themselves to the classical 'Yakshas' in the Hindu myths, are said to be a small community along with the other two in the Eastern Nepal during 1750s. It is alleged that they could not be subjugated by Prithvi Narayan Shah and for that matter he deputed his brave nephew, Chandrabir. When Chandrabir failed to defeat the Yakhas in the battle, he invited the adult Yakha warriors to his place of residence, Chainpur, in a picnic, where all the able adult Yakhas were killed. The surviving elder village headmen accorded title of 'minister' — Dewan like the Limbu Subbas, Khambu Rais and since then like other two ethnic groups, Yakhas got another ethnic nomenclature, Dewan. For Chainpur, the Yakhas claim that original name was 'Chiyan Gaon', meaning 'grave yard'.

They constitute a small community of about around 20,000 in Nepal, about 1,000 in Darjeeling and 500 to 600 in Sikkim (some 67 to 100 houses). As their number is very small and they do not reside in compact villages of their own, they have been counted among the Rais in Sikkim. They inter-marry with the Rais and are not enumerated separately in the decenial Census operations. Of late, the community has begun to identify itself separately by emphasising distinct marriage and death rituals. They have as well begun identifying a distinct language different from the Bantawa, the dominant Rai tongue.

Ratan Kamal Dewan, owner of the Himalayan Nursery in the Development Area in Gangtok, is the president of the Yakha Association. His father worked for the Namgyal rulers in the forest department and had come to Sikkim from Darjeeling in 1918. Similarly, Mr. R.K. Dewan and his sons work for the Government of Sikkim. Their most populous village is reported to be Ghum, 3 kilometre away from Namchi town in South District, where at one time there used to be about 20 houses of Dewans, presently it is reduced to 7 only. There are 2 households of Dewans at Tadong in the East District.

Jogis, the medicants and holy beggars, Bhujels, the *chira* makers and planquin bearers, and Sunwars, the hunters and basket makers are similar to clean occupational castes in the Gangetic plains, who are counted among the OBC. Jogis are apparently located in the caste structure as a part of the Nepalese caste system to serve the Hindu population at large. And naturally, they do not have their distinct language other than Nepali and recite some folk legends in honour of Gorakhnath or Bhairav, or Lord Shiva. Bhujel and Sunawar may have their tongues similar to Rais and Limbus as they lived among them. In view of the possibility that they may be recognized separately as an ethnic group, they are busy discovering distinctive attributes for their communities. It is logical that a community with a sizeable population should have its dialect, not necessarily different from that of the its neighbours. With the exception of the Lepchas, Limbus and to an extent Bhutias, all the communities in Sikkim are migrants from Nepal during the last two hundred years or so. Some of them moved to Sikkim during the Gorkha invasion in 1770s and it is logical that some of them would continue to reside in Sikkim.Thus, none of them can claim to a distinct territory in Sikkim. As many of the communities live in the mixed villages, their claim to an exclusive social, religious and cultural life is similarly limited. Even dominant four ethnic groups, Limbus, Khambus, Gurungs and Magars inter-marry among themselves and with the minor communities, such as Jogis, Dewans, Sunawars, and Bhujels. The communities counted among the Kirat commonwealth, like Limbus, Khambus inclusive of Dewans, Sunwars (?) and Bhujels (?) appear to have a near clear case to the status of Scheduled Tribes. One is not sure whether Gurungs and Magars can be counted along with the Kirat. But the case of the Jogis, is clearly the case of OBC, and in no case it should be counted among the Scheduled Tribes. It should also be noted that in States of Punjab, Himanchal Pradesh, Uttar Pradesh, Gorkhas, a term inclusive of all the Nepamul residents, are counted as the OBC. In Assam, the individual communites such as Rai, Gurung, Magar, etc. are counted among the OBC. It should be kept in mind that in most parts of India, internal ethnic and caste divisions within the Nepamul community is simply ignored and all are collectively lumped together as Gorkha or Nepalis.

There is another problem: Sikkim is the only State in India, where seats in the State Assembly is reserved on the name of the communities, because of their being the 'significant sections of population' on eve of its merger to India. As it was the part of the 'tripartite agreement', 12 out of 32 seats in the State Assembly are reserved for the two Scheduled Tribes, the Lepcha and the Bhutias. This issue was taken up even to the Supreme Court, which opined that the seat reservation was integral part of the 'agreement', on which ground Sikkim joined Indian Union. However, the impression continues among the communities in Sikkim that once they are declared as the Scheduled Tribes, they will have separate seats reserved for them in the State Assembly. And thus, the series of demands are made for being declared as the Scheduled Tribes. Inspired by the *Janajati* movement in Nepal, a number of communities in Sikkim have staked their claims to be counted as the Scheduled Tribes, and for that, they have begun displaying social distance from Nepalese caste practices. Further more, Sikkim has joined North-Eastern Council in recent years, a forum in which four out of eight States have 'an image of being tribal States'. This impression has created a possibility for being counted as the majority scheduled tribal State by according MBCs the status of Scheduled Tribes.

REFERENCES

Basnet, Lal B.: 1974: *Sikkim: A Political History,* S. Chand & Co. New Delhi.

Beteille, A.: 1974: *Six Essays in Comparative Sociology*, Oxford University Press, and New Delhi.

Bista, Dor B.: 1970: 'Hindu Kingdom and its Social Aspect' in *NEPAL: A PROFILE* (Ed.), Nepal Council of Applied Economic Research, Kathmandu.

Bista, D.B. : 1972: *The People Nepal*, Kathmandu, 2nd edition.

Bose, N.K.: 1961: *Peasant Life in India*, Anthropological Survey of India, Kolkata.

Dalton, E.T.: 1872: *Descriptive Ethnography of Bengal*, Government Secretariat Press, Kolkata.

Elwin, V.: 1943: *The Aboriginal*, Oxford University Press, Bombay.

Elwin, V.: 1964: *A Philosophy for NEFA*, NEFA Secretariat Press, Shilloing, second reprint.

Gellner, David N. : 1997: 'Ethnicity and Nationalism in the World's Only Hindu State' in *Nationalism and Ethnicity in a Hindu Kingdom* (ed.) by Gellner, David N. *et al.*, Harwood Academic Publishers.

Ghurye, G.S.: 1943: *The Aboriginals — So-called and Their Future*, Gokhale Institute of Politics and Economics, Poona.

Haftun, Martin, William Raeper & John Whelpton: 1999: *People, Politics and Ideology: Democracy* and *Social Change in Nepal*, Mandal Books Point, Kathmandu.

Hazarika, Sanjay: 2004: Comments on Draft National Policy on Tribals, MSS.

Hugh-Jones, S. and James Laidlaw (ed.): 2000: *Essential Edmund Leach, Vol. 1: Anthropology and Society*, Yale University Press, New Haven and London

Indigenous: 1994: Indigenous Peoples of Nepal towards Self-identification and Re-establishment, Proceedings of the National Consultation on Indigenous Peoples of Nepal, Kathmandu: National Ad-Hoc Committee for International Decade for the World's Indigenous Pepoles, Nepal.

Kazi, Jigmie N .: 1994: *Inside Sikkim: Against All the Tide*, Hill Media Publication, Gangtok.

Kipling, R.: 1977: *Selected Verses*, London.

Macfarlane, Allan: 'Death, Disease and Curing in a Himalayan Village' in *Asian Highland Societies: In Anthropological Perspective* (ed.), Furor Haimendorf, Sterling Publishing Pvt. Ltd. New Delhi.

Morris, C.J.: 1993: *The Gurkhas: An Anthology*, Low Price Publications, Delhi. First published in 1933.

Oven, R.: 1973: 'Imperial Policy and Theory of Social Change: Sir Alfred Lyall in India' in *Anthropology and Colonial Encounter*, (ed.), Adam Kuper, Ithaca Press, London

Pfaff-Czarnecka, Joanna: 1997: 'Vestiges and Visions: Cultural Changes in the Process of Nation-Building in Nepal' in Gellner, D.N. *et al.*

Sharma, P. R.: 1997: 'Nation-Building, Multi-Ethnicity and the Hindu State' in Gellner, D.N. *et al.*

Shneiderman, S. and Mark Turin: 2006: 'Seeking the Tribe: Ethno-Politics in Darjeeling and Sikkim,' *Himal Southasia Vol.18,* No. 5. pp. 54-58.

Sinha, A. C.: 1975: *Politics of Sikkim: A Sociological Study*, Thompson Publications, Faridabad.

Sinha, A. C. and Subba, T. B.: 2003: *Nepalis in India: A Community in Search of Indian Identity*, Indus Publishing Company, New Delhi.

Stiller S. J., Ludwig: 1976: *The Silent Cry*: *The People of Nepal: 1816-1839*, Sahyogi Prakashan, Tripureshwar, Kathmandu.

Tripathi, C.B.: Verification of SC & ST Certificates. MSS.

Dhimala, Ranju R., C.D. Rai, M.S. Dutta, & Sanchita Ghatak: 1993: *SIKKIM, People of India*, Vol. XXXIX, Anthropological Survey of India & Seagull Books, Kolkata.

Vansittart, Eden: 1992: *Notes on Nepal*, Asian Educational Services, New Delhi. First published in 1896 by Govt. Printing Press, Kolkata.

Whelpton, John: 1997: "Political Identity in Nepal: State, Nation and Community' in Gellner, D.N. (ed.).

Whelpton, John: 2005: *A History of Nepal,* Cambridge University Press, Cambridge, U.K.

ANNEXURES

ANNEXURE -I

WHY THIS SEMINAR?

A Seminar on the "Problems of Ethnicity in the North-East India" was over due. The need for protecting one's identity became an abiding concern of various groups of citizens in the North-East after Independence.

During over hundred years of inter-face with the British colonial rule divisive trends among various groups on basis of territory religion, etc. were encouraged and sharpened. The elite driven ethnicity and identity formation got impetus after the creation of Nagaland due to the benefits flowing with it. It led to an obsession with one's ethnicity and connected demands for territorial and political protection and identifications. Result was recognition of such sentiments in formation of a number states, like Nagaland, Mizoram, Meghalaya, Manipur and a host of Autonomous District Councils.

However, the appetite for ethnicity related demands, even new formations, has not declined. Such demands are rooted in a sense of security related to one's land and people. It has, however, led to conflicting demands, overlapping claims and even resort to passage of arms to reinforce one's claims. A stage has reached where neighbours do not communicate with each other and have hostile relations resulting in mutual suspicious and even bloodshed.

Another trend is the total dependence on the Central Government and the State Government's to intervene to resolve these demands in their favour. It is felt that a time has come to take a stock of the ethnicity related problems as it has become a major factor of destabilisation in the region. From Bodos, tea estate tribes, Karbis, Dimasas, Kukis, Paites, Nagas, tribes in Tripura, and now the Garos have their own perceptions, and often conflicting ethnic demands. In the absence of any mutual communications with neighbours and others affected, resolution becomes a problem. What is worse is that due to threats and fear of gun, the civil society leaders with positive agenda are being coerced into silence. Suppression of dissent by fear of arms is a reality in Nagaland, Manipur and Tripura.

It is surprising, because in the past several hundred years these various groups and entities have co-existed without any adverse fall out on each other. There is no history of any ethnic group having lost its identity, though regimes and rulers kept on changing as a natural historical phenomenon. Therefore, there is no reason why Bodos cannot attempt to reconcile with those living amidst them; why Nagas cannot talk to people living in Manipur, Assam and Arunachal Pradesh; why Karbi and Dimasas, who have shared the land for centuries, cannot reconcile there differences; why Meiteis, Nagas, Kukis and others in Manipur, who have a shared history of over thousand years, not work out once again harmonious existences or the tribes and plain's people in Tripura shed their prejudices and share a future of mutual benefit as neither can push the other out. It is difficult but benefits to the people and region demand a new approach and shedding of the negative baggage of the past.

It is felt that patience, mutual dialogue and understanding are the key factors to resolve disputes and problems. Prevailing realities cannot be wished away. Threats and actual use of force to reinforce one's claims are not only destructive but are becoming increasingly counter-productive and only result in misery and deepen the crisis. Besides, any effort to hurry the process by force of arms is no longer acceptable. Every protagonist, it is felt, must weigh his or her options and explore possibilities of dialogue and conciliation, To depend on the Central Government and the State Governments alone to resolve issues is becoming increasingly impractical. Given the restraint and wisdom, and local level initiative, with passage of time solutions can be found. The seminar endeavours to explore these possibilities in overall interest of the region.

There will be deliberation in all aspects of ethnicity related problems of the North-Eastern region of the country in the seminar. It will include, genesis and growth of ethnicity, ethnic identity formation, identity claims, growth of insurgency, factors strengthening ethnicity and insurgency, clash of ethnic and territorial claims, conflict resolution initiatives, etc. Eminent scholars, Members of the Parliament, former Vice-Chancellors and administers, journalists, eminent columnists, educationists and social activists shall deliberate in the seminar.

ANNEXURE-II

Statement of the Seminar

In the two days seminar on the "Problems of Ethnicity in the North-East India" held in the India International Centre on July 6-7, organized by Astha Bharati, a total number of 14 papers were presented on a wide range of ethnic identity issues relating to North-East India. The seminar was successful in bringing together a variegated group of experts ranging from academics, policy-makers, economist, retired Governors, social activists, media people and retired Government civil and military officers who had served in the region in various capacities. The deliberation of the seminar was mainly on two issues — *First,* why are ethnic identities proliferating in North-East India — and what are the challenges they pose to the stability and development of the region? *Second,* what viable actions or vision plan can be taken up to mitigate the problems?

The seminar deliberated on the genesis and growth of ethnicity in the region, administrative and legal segregation of the hills and the plains by the British, their design to form a crown colony by separating hills (Coupland Plan); the colonial myths of race, isolation, core-fringe conflict, hegemony, exploitation, etc., thus creating separatist mindset and weak participation in freedom struggle due to isolation. Creation of Nagaland waiving economic and viability criteria, and the benefits flowing to the Nagas, tempted others in the region. Nagaland was replicated throughout the region, which has spillover effect even in North Bengal.

Land security, needing utmost Government attention, is a vital issue for the growth of separate ethnic identity in the North-East region. As a result of variety of factors such as nature of modernization and development, encroachments and occupation by the illegal immigrants, the tribal people are gradually getting alienated from their ancestral land. The issue of absentee land ownership is becoming very vital in states like Meghalaya where the tribal land has been transferred to big multi-nationals by various fraudulent means.

Democratisation of the District Councils and the traditional institutions and their positive role in development process, people's participation in the development process, their involvement in decision-making through effective Panchyati Raj system is necessary. It needs mention that the District Councils under the Sixth Schedule of the Constitution has not been able to make palpable impact in the region.

It was also deliberated upon that bad governance is a vital factor for such proliferation of ethnic violent identity in the region. Due to rampant corruption and inefficiency in the service delivery system, the major chunk of the development money is being eaten up by the ruling elite. The governance is adversely affected due to the tendency of All India Service officers managing to remain away from the region, and thus acquiring the name of "suitcase officers".

It was more or less agreed by all the presenters that the challenges of ethnic proliferation in the region could not be neglected. If these issues are not handled properly, ethnicity will become one of the greatest sources of instability in the region. Identity politics that polarize people and groups, is creating fault lines between "us" and "them". Growing distrust and hatred threaten peace, jeopardize co-existence, development and human freedom.

In the light of such challenges that ethnic identity proliferation pose in *North-East India, a wide range of observations and recommen-dations* were made:

1. Ethnicity-related problems need multi-dimensional/multi-stage tackling, including that on intellectual and human rights fronts.
2. There is need to learn from the past mistakes. When negotiations are intended, it should be with all the factions of that particular society, e.g., Naga, and should finally be approved by the people with the consensus building amongst the civil society.

3. It should be ensured that the voice of the Civil Society in Assam, Nagaland and elsewhere finds expression in solving the ethnic problems. After all ULFA and NSCN-IM, which are negotiating with strength of arms, are in minority and continue to throttle the popular voice emanating through media and public fora. Here, it needs mention that the Civil Society in Assam and Nagaland has started voicing their concern against violence. Assamese self-critiquing has blunted the edge of the chauvinism and opportunism of Ulfa based on the personal agenda of its leaders.
4. The issue of common bond among the people of North-East, through a process of dialogue, was also highlighted. The Civil Society can play a cementing role in this regard. In order to accommodate the burgeoning demands of the ethnic groups, it was suggested that a State Social or Ethnic Council could be constituted by the initiative of the Civil Society, which can look into the distinct socio-cultural issues and address the common concerns. It will be a dialogue forum where groups can raise their issues of concern. The inter-and intra-ethnic conflicts have led to social and cultural distancing and, at times, overt conflict and violence. This trend needs to be arrested by encouraging local mutual dialogue and discourse, rather than running to the Central and State Governments to resolve the issues. In this context, it was felt that the urgent need to "recover the old sense of mutuality" which preexisted present fragmentation, mostly encouraged by the colonial rule to divide the people.
5. *While peace efforts should be allowed and facilitated with utmost sincerity, the Governments — Central and the State — should ensure* that the terms of cease-fire agreements are strictly adhered to and none falls prey to insurgents' bullets.
6. It was felt that the Naga demand for sovereignty and Nagalim is unrealizable. Even if the NSCN (IM) accepts autonomy within the Constitution, it would keep the "Nagalim" issue alive to retain support among people. It

was felt that the terms of Naga settlement would also influence the content and course of other ethnic demands.

7. It was also felt that though the Indian state has made mistakes in the past in dealing with the ethnic identity related problem, yet the Constitution of India has, by and large, been resilient and inclusive of urges and aspirations of various groups. The inclusive policy and approach and respect for the multicultural identity and diversity of North-East should continue to form basic thrust of Central Government's approach on governance and economic development issues.
8. The participants felt that demands for demarcating inter-state boundaries in the north-east and for redrawing the India-Myanmar border would lead to the opening of a Pandora's box. It is suggested that every State Government should respect the constitutional boundaries and should be more sensitive to the urges of the territorial minority groups. Territorial and devise forums where these concerns could be articulated.
9. It was felt that the Central Government should (i) formulate proper policy regarding the ethnicity and insurgency related problems; (ii) learn to say 'no' to the impossible demands of the insurgents, e.g., the demands of inclusion of parts of Assam where not even two percent Nagas reside; (iii) ensure proper utilization of the funds flowing to the States; and (iv) initiate positive changes in the system of education with the help of the State Governments, UGC and the Central Universities of the region.
10. The State Governments should ensure (i) the stoppage of extortions and pilferage of the public funds; (ii) gradual assumption of their duty of mobilization of local resources and sharing the financial burden more and more.
11. It is essential to answer every myth and lie, counter every wrong signal emanating even from the governments' wrong actions, counter every propaganda of the insurgents and the media supporting them. It needs intellectual activism

and active involvement of the conscientious citizens and the media.

12. The inter- and intra-ethnic conflicts have led to social and cultural distancing and, at times, overt conflict and violence. This trend needs to be arrested by encouraging local mutual dialogue and discourse, rather than running to the Central and State Governments to resolve the issues. In this context, it was felt that the urgent need to "recover the old sense of mutuality" which pre-existed present fragmentation, mostly encouraged by the colonial rule to divide the people. Government should not be hustled into agreement on contention issues like Nagalim, sovereignty, etc., which require patience and consensus building that are time consuming.
13. The political parties and the civil society in the North-East should ensure that (i) the State governments properly deliver; (ii) blame game - blaming Delhi for every local failure; as for example, the failure of the State governments to pay salaries of their oversized workforce on the name of Centre's 'lack of concern' – stops; (iii) local and intra-regional conflicts, as far as possible, are resolved peacefully and democratically with local/regional initiative, (iv) ethnic cleansing is stopped; (v) inter-tribal and inter-communal hatred is discouraged.
14. The combined strength of the police force of the States of the region is large. They should play greater and effective role in controlling insurgency and violence so that need for and dependence on Army and paramilitary forces is reduced to the minimum. It was also urged that the Government of India abandon some of its exclusive military principles and coming out of its bureaucracy-centric policies. It should involve people from North-East and elsewhere, who know and can deal with the situation better than those who are deciding the future of North-East.
15. Growth of infrastructure in the region was considered the most important factor for speedy economic growth of the region.

INDEX